Affiliate Marketing And Amazon FBA

(2-Books-In-1)

Learn

Affiliate Marketing And

Amazon FBA Business In 5 Days

And Learn It Well

By

Michael Ezeanaka

www.MichaelEzeanaka.com

Copyright ©2021

All rights reserved. Except as permitted under the U.S. Copyright Act of 1976, the scanning, uploading and distribution of this book via the Internet or via any other means without the express permission of the author is illegal and punishable by law. Please purchase only authorized electronic editions, and do not participate in or encourage electronic piracy of copyrighted material.

Disclaimer

This publication is designed to provide competent and reliable information regarding the subject matter covered. However, it is sold with the understanding that the author is not engaged in rendering investment or other professional advice. Laws and practices often vary from state to state and country to country and if investment or other expert assistance is required, the services of a professional should be sought. The author specifically disclaims any liability that is incurred from the use or application of the contents of this book.

Table of Contents
BOOK 1 – AFFILIATE MARKETING

INTRODUCTION 6

CHAPTER 1 7
    What Is Affiliate Marketing? 7

CHAPTER 2 14
    Low Ticket vs. High Ticket Affiliate Marketing 14

CHAPTER 3 18
    How To Become An Affiliate Marketer 18

CHAPTER 4 24
    The Top 20 Affiliate Marketing Programs 24

CHAPTER 5 31
    How To Choose An Affiliate Marketing Program 31

CHAPTER 6 35
    Writing Content For Affiliate Marketing 35

CHAPTER 7 42
    Using Social Media Platforms For Affiliate Marketing 42

CHAPTER 8 49
    Common Affiliate Marketing Mistakes 49

CHAPTER 9 55
    Choosing the Right Niche 55

CHAPTER 10 59
    Building your Email List 59

CHAPTER 11 69
    Affiliate Marketing Strategies 69

CHAPTER 12 77
    Tips to Become a Successful Affiliate Marketer 77

CHAPTER 13 84
    Proven Ways to Improve Website Traffic 84

CHAPTER 14 100

Analysis Of Ten Traffic Sources 100

CHAPTER 15 153

7 Ways To Track And Optimize Your Traffic Sources 153

CONCLUSION 176

BOOK 2 – AMAZON FBA MASTERY

INTRODUCTION 178

CHAPTER 1 179

Amazon FBA Business Model Explained 179

CHAPTER 2 191

Getting Started 191

CHAPTER 3 201

Product Research 201

CHAPTER 4 206

Sourcing the Product 206

CHAPTER 5 213

Shipping the Products 213

CHAPTER 6 218

Preparing the Product for Sale by Branding 218

CHAPTER 7 222

Product Launch 222

CHAPTER 8 230

What Comes Next? 230

CHAPTER 9 235

Scaling $10,000 a Month and Beyond 235

CONCLUSION 239

THE END 239

Affiliate Marketing Made Easy In 2020

Simple

Effective And Beginner-Friendly

Strategies For Earning A Six-Figure Income

With Affiliate Marketing

By

Michael Ezeanaka

www.MichaelEzeanaka.com

Introduction

Are you looking for an online business that you can start today? If so, affiliate marketing is for you. This method of earning money through the Internet has been around for more than two decades and people are still using the same model today as 20 years ago.

This book will teach you everything you need to know about affiliate marketing. It discusses how it all started and evolved to the multi-billion dollar industry that it is today.

In this book, we will discuss how you can get your slice of the affiliate marketing pie. You will learn how you can start with this business and build your affiliate marketing assets from scratch. You will also learn how to develop content and drive massive amounts of traffic to them through organic (free) and paid methods.

Lastly, we talk about the different strategies on how you can become successful as an Internet marketer and how you can **earn a lot of money** with Affiliate Marketing. With the help of this book, you will be on your way to earn a *six-figure* monthly income.

Start building your affiliate marketing empire today!

Inspiration #1

"There are no secrets to success. It is the result of preparation, hard work, and learning from failure."

Colin Powell

Chapter 1

What Is Affiliate Marketing?

Affiliate marketing refers to programs that aim to sell more products for a company through partnerships with third party online sales people called affiliates or publishers. Unlike traditional Contextual Advertising, affiliate marketing programs allow content publishers to connect directly with advertisers.

A successful affiliate marketing campaign can lead to a higher income to publishers compared to publishing contextual ads from services like Google AdSense. From an advertiser's standpoint, affiliate marketing is an efficient way of promoting one's products because the reward system is based on the publisher's productivity. The advertiser only needs to pay if the publisher successfully facilitates a sale.

History of Affiliate marketing

The affiliate marketing business model is not new. It has been around shortly after the first few businesses started offering products and services in the web. The affiliate marketing commission system was likely inspired by the commission payment system of offline sales people. In the sales world outside the internet, sales people have been paid via commission or a percentage of the payment amount for the longest time. In particular, it is a common sales model in the cosmetic, homeware, car and pharmaceutical industries.

The first recorded transition of this business model to the online world happened in 1994. It was a flower selling business called PC Flowers and Gifts. Its founder, William J. Tobin, designed and patented the use of revenue sharing and tracking of visitor's activities. The first affiliate network was the Prodigy Network, an IBM owned subscription service that offered online services like access to news, games, polls and many more. Subscribers of the network were given the opportunity to earn commission for facilitating a PC Flowers and Gifts sale to other members of the network.

In 1996, Amazon launched what we now call Amazon associates. At the time, Amazon focused on selling tangible books. A website owner can post a banner ad or a link that leads directly to the product page of a specific book. Commission is paid if a visitor who used the link purchases the book.

In the years that followed, many other affiliate marketing schemes were launched but Amazon Associates became the most popular among them. Since then, the popularity of affiliate marketing as a website monetization method has increased. In 2006 for instance, sales generated by affiliate marketing in the UK, amounted to $2.92 billion.

The popularity of affiliate marketing increased even more when more and more people took part in online content creation. In the early 2000s, Web 2.0 types of content became increasingly popular online. People turned to blogs and forums for answers when they face problems. Some of these blogs and forums monetized their online properties using affiliate marketing programs. By positioning affiliate products as a solution to people's problems, they were able to earn from the content they post on their websites.

Around 2011, Google cleaned up its search engine results pages with what is commonly called the Panda update. This update in the search algorithm penalized websites with poor content. This was largely due to the fact that many website owners gamed the process of ranking in Google's search result pages. This process is called Search Engine Optimization or SEO.

By doing practices frowned upon by Google, webmasters with websites that hardly have any useful content in them managed to reach the top spot of search result pages. Practices like stuffing a webpage with keywords or creating thousands of fake links that point to a websites allowed these webmasters to raise their spam webpages in the rankings. Most of these spam webpages were monetized by affiliate links and banners. With Google cracking down on webpages like these, the black hat days of most affiliate marketers came to an end.

After the Google Panda updates, websites that provided useful and engaging content rose to fill the top positions of the search result pages. Because of this, websites with excellent content managed to get the affiliate marketing sales.
In the following years, affiliate marketers saw the emergence of social media websites. Together with this, smartphones and other mobile devices replaced personal computers as the primary tools used for accessing the internet. With these changes in the internet marketing world, affiliate marketing strategies also evolved. The internet became a truly multimedia experience. Text content no longer ruled the internet. Instead, videos and images dominated the screens of internet users.

This gave way to a new breed of affiliate marketers. Some of them do not even own a website. They only use their Facebook pages, YouTube Channels and Instagram accounts to generate affiliate sales. These days, people no longer spend countless hours surfing the web. Instead, they stick to one or two apps, fully engaged in the content in these apps. This is the current state of affiliate marketing. The old ways of succeeding in this business still has some value. You could still earn by posting useful content in your website. However, if you want your affiliate marketing game to improve, you need to master the social media-marketing world as well.

The Affiliate marketing business model

As we discussed above, affiliate marketing is a revenue sharing business model designed to increase the sales of a particular product or service. Before we talk about how you can take part in this business model, let us first discuss the different players in this type of business:

The Advertiser

To understand affiliate marketing, one needs to understand the three parties involved in this type of marketing program. The first one, is the advertiser or the business that wants to promote its products or services. They set up their own affiliate marketing program or they sign up with an affiliate network to manage the marketing program for them. The advertiser's goal is simply to sell more products and to reach new markets through the internet. Most of the time, they set up this kind of program because they want to reach online markets that they normally cannot reach by traditional online advertising.

Affiliate marketing also has other benefits for the advertiser's online presence. By setting up this program, more content creators will be talking about their products. Some of these content creators have thousands of fans. Each one of these followers will be exposed to their products. Even if these followers do not purchase a product now, they will still become familiar with the promoted product. They may choose to look for the product in the future, without passing through the affiliate marketing channel.

The advertisers should provide the tools needed by the publishers. For instance, they could provide marketing materials that the affiliate publishers will use to promote their products. They should also provide the platform to make it easier for the publisher to participate in the program. Most affiliate programs come with an account to the affiliate marketing website. This website serves as source of all the tools provided by the advertiser. It also comes with a dashboard where the publisher can tract their performance.

The consumers

The next party in the affiliate marketing business model is the consumers. The consumers refer to the people who buy the products of the advertiser. The advertisers want the right types of consumers to see their marketing materials. If they like the advertiser's product or service, they can click on the link provided with the marketing material and start the purchasing process.

The internet is filled with people who can become consumers. However, the best types of consumers are those that are willing and able to buy the advertiser's products. A willing consumer is interested in the product or service. He or she has a personal reason for wanting or needing the product. A consumer is able to buy the product if he or she can complete the purchasing process. First, the consumer needs to have the technical knowhow on completing an online purchase. He or she should also have enough funds to pay for the product or service offered.

The Publisher

The last party is the publishers. Publishers are the people who post the marketing materials of the advertisers so that the consumers can view them. Affiliate programs usually require their publishers to have an online asset that they can use to attract the attention of consumers. Most affiliate programs require that you have a website where you will promote their products or services. While a website is usually required when signing up, the publisher is not limited to promoting the advertiser's marketing materials in there. Depending on the affiliate program guidelines, the publisher can use contextual advertising, social media marketing, and other means to bring attention to the affiliate offer.

If you want to earn money in affiliate marketing, the best way is to become a publisher. It will be your role to generate leads towards the websites of your affiliate advertisers. This means that you need to attract people who are likely to buy the products of the advertisers and encourage them to go to the advertiser website and make a purchase.

This part however, is easier said than done. Though billions of people use the internet every day, you will not be able to reach the majority of them. A big chunk of the online population does not speak English. Among the English speakers, only a small percentage is interested in the topics you are discussing in your blog, your videos or your podcasts. Even among people who are interested in the topic you are discussing, only a small percentage have intentions of buying online. The majority of people still prefer to buy things through brick-and-mortar stores if they are available. Many of those who habitually buy things online have their preferred online stores. Many of them just buy from the popular sources like Amazon.

The most successful publishers earn through affiliate marketing consistently by establishing themselves as authorities in their chosen fields. You may also follow this path. Most of these people are already experts in their fields and they only use online marketing as a source of extra income. If you want to create content related to your job for example, you can brand yourself as an expert. A trainer in a gym for example, can create a website where he puts contents that gym goers can do when they cannot go to his classes. In the process, he can promote fitness related products that the visitors of his website can make use of. Because the gym trainer is an expert in his field, the visitors in his website are likely to follow his advice.

You can also take the same approach by starting an affiliate business based on what you do for a living or on a hobby you like to do. By doing so, you can establish yourself as an expert in that field. It will also be easier for you to find your first website followers. You can encourage the people you meet in your job to visit your website. In there, you can provide free advice to keep the visitors coming back to your website. In the process, you can monetize the website by suggesting products and services that you use yourself. You could then use affiliate links to direct your visitors to these products and services.

A carpenter for example, could provide free carpentry lessons in his website and his social media accounts. Together with his content, he could provide Amazon Associate links to the product pages of the tools and other products that he uses in his carpentry lessons.

To establish yourself as an expert, you will need to provide evidence to the visitors of your website. For instance, you can create an about page where you put your credentials and your achievements in the field. You could also provide photos where in you are working to show people that you are who you say you are.

While it is easier to convince people to buy the affiliate products if you are an expert, there are other approaches to become a trusted source in the affiliate marketing business. For instance, you can also become a successful publisher even if you are just a beginner at your chosen topic. Instead of providing advice based on your personal experience, you can also give them as you learn a new topic. A beginner carpenter for example could show people his journey in learning to become an expert. In the process, he could share the lessons he learned together with the tools he uses to learn.

Many people who go to the internet are beginners who want to learn something. It is rare to see a free website that will teach you everything you need to know to learn a skill. Most websites that teach specific skills tend to be paid and often demand a high price. You can give the audience a free version of these websites. Instead of charging the people for the information, you can earn through the affiliate marketing income instead.

Chapter 1 Quiz
Please refer to Appendix A for the answers to this quiz

1. What do you call productivity-based programs that partner with online sellers to encourage the sale of products and services?

    A) Contextual marketing
    B) Affiliate Marketing
    C) Cost Per Click Marketing
    D) Search Marketing

2. What do you call the third-party sellers that promote affiliate products to consumers?

    A) Advertisers
    B) Online Sellers
    C) Affiliates
    D) Programmers

3. Where did the commissions payment system used in affiliate marketing originate?

    A) Real-world sales industry
    B) Online contextual advertising industry
    C) Email marketing
    D) The bakeshop business

4. When was the first affiliate marketing program started?

    A) 1994
    B) 1996
    C) 1991
    D) 1998

5. When was Amazon Associates launched?

    A) 1994
    B) 1996
    C) 1991
    D) 1998

6. What are businesses that set up affiliate programs called?

    A) Affiliates
    B) Advertisers
    C) Business Partners

D) Consumers

7. What do you call the percentage of the purchase price paid to the affiliate?

    A) Success Rate
    B) Commission Rate
    C) Conversion Rate
    D) Payment Method

8. Who are the general target audience of affiliate programs?

    A) Children
    B) Business owners
    C) Advertisers
    D) Consumer

9. What are the two requirements of an ideal product consumer?

    A) Willingness and capacity to buy
    B) Social media and search engine usage
    C) Facebook account and credit card
    D) Computer and twitter account

10. How are affiliate marketers paid?

    A) Commission System
    B) An agreed upon fixed amount
    C) Based on the cost per click rate
    D) Based on the number of impressions

Inspiration #2

"If you really want to do something, you'll find a way. If you don't, you'll find an excuse."

Jim Rohn

Chapter 2

Low Ticket vs. High Ticket Affiliate Marketing

If you want to become an affiliate marketer, there are many products and services you can choose from. Veteran affiliate marketers classify these products based on their prices. The price of the promoted product is important to the affiliate marketer because the commissions they earn are usually a percentage of the product's selling price. With this in mind, affiliate marketers classify low cost products as low-ticket affiliate products and those that are more expensive to be high-ticket affiliate products.

As you start in the affiliate marketing business, you need to decide whether you want to promote cheap or expensive items. Most affiliate marketers choose to promote low-ticket affiliate products because they think that it is easier to convince people to buy cheap items. However, this also means that you need to sell **A LOT** more items to reach your income goals.

Let's say you have a website that promotes small bedroom items. The average price of the products you promote is $5 and you earn a 10% commission for each sale you promote. That means that for each $5-item you sell, you make only $0.50. If the minimum payout amount is $100, you will need to sell 200 $5-items to reach your goal. You will need a *massive* amount of traffic to make this number of sales in a month.

High-ticket items on the other hand are those that sell for $100 and up. These items are harder to sell because they require a bigger financial commitment from the consumer. However, you only need a few sales of these items to reach your income goals. If you are selling a $100-item on your website for example, and your commission rate is also 10%, you only need to sell 10 items to earn the minimum payout amount of $100.

It is not wise to make the decision of going for high ticket or low-ticket affiliate programs right now. You will need to consider many factors when making this decision. First, you will need to consider the industry or niche market that you wish to take part in. After that, you will need to consider the types of content that you enjoy creating.

You cannot expect to be successful promoting gadgets and tech-related stuff if your content is all about sports. The product you choose should fit seamlessly with the content you create. They should be aligned with the needs of the visitors of your website. The types of people who visit your website will depend on the content that you have in there and the marketing efforts you put in.

The types of offers available in the market will also limit your options for affiliate products. If you are promoting tangible products, you will always have the option of selling Amazon products through the Amazon Associates program. The majority of products in Amazon are low-ticket. In addition, the commission rate for almost all categories start at 4%. This rate is low in the affiliate marketing industry.

Most people who stick with Amazon however, do so because of the company's reputation and reliability. Most people who go to your website already know what Amazon is and you no longer need to upsell the retailer. On the other hand, if you are selling a product from an unpopular source, you will first need to introduce the retailer, talk about their track record and why your readers should buy from them.

Chapter 2 Quiz
Please refer to Appendix B for the answers to this quiz

1. What do you call inexpensive affiliate products?

    A) Low-Ticket Items
    B) Cheap Affiliates
    C) Clickbait
    D) Affiliate bargain

2. What is one advantage of selling an inexpensive affiliate product?

    A) It has a high commission
    B) It always comes with a high commission rate
    C) It is easy to sell
    D) It requires higher financial commitment for the consumer

3. What is one disadvantage of selling an inexpensive affiliate product?

    A) It does not come with a warranty
    B) It is too easy to sell
    C) You need to pay a lot in advertising fees to promote it
    D) You need to make a lot of sales to reach the payment threshold

4. How do you earn big with this kind of products?

    A) You need to have high quantity of sales
    B) You only need to sell two or three items every week
    C) You need to pay more on advertising
    D) You need to focus your efforts in search marketing

5. What do you call expensive affiliate products?

    A) High-ticket Items
    B) Low-Ticket Items
    C) High rollers
    D) Golden affiliate products

6. What is one advantage of selling an expensive affiliate product?

    A) It comes with a lot of freebies
    B) It can come with a one-year warranty
    C) It is easy to sell
    D) You only need to make a few sales to reach the pay out

7. What is one disadvantage of selling an expensive affiliate product?

    A) It is easy to sell
    B) It is faster to sell
    C) It comes with a lot of disclaimers
    D) None of the above

8. Why is it harder to sell this type of item?

    A) It requires higher financial commitment for the consumer
    B) It is difficult to ship
    C) It comes with a high shipping fee
    D) It does not look appealing to the buyer

9. What factor should you consider when choosing between inexpensive and expensive affiliate products?

    A) The need of the consumers
    B) The price of the competitor's products
    C) The reach of your marketing efforts
    D) The state of the world economy

10. What example of low-ticket market was mentioned in the chapter?

    A) Amazon
    B) ClickBank
    C) Shopify
    D) eBay

Inspiration #3

"Don't let the fear of losing be greater than the excitement of winning."

Robert Kiyosaki

Chapter 3

How To Become An Affiliate Marketer

To become an affiliate marketer, you only need to become a member of a good affiliate marketing program and start spreading the affiliate link. To make money consistently however, you need to be smart in your approach in the business.

Here are the things you will need to start with this business:

A website

As stated in the previous chapters, most affiliate programs require that you have a website before you will be accepted. Advertisers check the website to see what types of content you have. Some advertisers are extremely picky when choosing affiliates. They only accept those whose websites can bring in huge amounts of traffic. Don't worry though, because there are also beginner level affiliate marketing programs that will accept even publishers with new websites.

A profitable niche

You cannot just create any type of website if you want to become a successful affiliate marketer. In particular, you need to be careful in choosing the niche market. We will discuss how you can choose the right niche market in future chapters. For now, just remember that the types of affiliate marketing products that you can sell will depend on the niche market you choose to participate in. If you want to sell only high ticket items for instance, you need to make sure that the niche market you've chosen have high-ticket affiliate marketing programs.

An organic source of traffic

In the world of internet marketing, there are two ways for you to get traffic, organic and paid. While some affiliate marketers do use paid methods to earn through affiliate marketing, these methods exposes you to a higher financial risk. Those who use these methods have developed their skill over years of trial and error.

For now, you should focus on building assets that will help you gather organic visitors. This includes social media accounts and pages, forum memberships, accounts in niche specific online communities, offline traffic sources and other similar assets. You will need to think about where you will get your traffic for your website if you want to be successful from day one.

A membership to an affiliate marketing program

There are tons of affiliate marketing programs in the web. However, not all of them will be suitable to offer to the type of traffic that you can get. You will need to choose an affiliate program that fits the needs of the audience. We will discuss how to choose the best affiliate marketing programs for your audience in the following chapters.

The four factors above are the minimum requirements for becoming a successful affiliate marketer. After choosing an affiliate marketing program, you can apply directly from the web. Most of the application processes just require you to fill up a form with your personal details. In addition, the application form may also ask how you plan to generate traffic for your affiliate offers and what types of products you wish to promote. The form may also ask you how much traffic your own website gets a day and what other monetization methods you use in the said website.

In addition, you may be asked to fill up a tax form. This part will depend on the requirements of the country of origin of the affiliate program. When signing up for Amazon Associates for Amazon.com for instance, US citizens will be asked to fill up a US tax form. A different form will be required if you are applying for Amazon.ca (Canada) Associates program.

How hard is the application process?

For some affiliate programs, getting in is easy. Some may even automatically approve your application. There are more specialized programs though, that will ask for more requirements after you apply. The most demanding programs will have their employees scan your website for the quality of the content. If they are not satisfied with the design or the quality of the content of your website, they may reject your application.

These extremely selective programs usually do this for different reasons. The majority of them do it because they want to protect their brand. Big brands only want to be associated with websites that have good quality content. Some of them will only accept websites that have been around for a long time with hundreds of archived content. Some brands will also reject your application if they see that your website or your contents are not aligned with their target consumers. If your website is in English for example and you apply with an affiliate program for Spanish people, you are likely to be rejected.

My application has been approved, what now?

It is after the application process that the real work begins. Now that you have a product or service to promote, you can now start gathering traffic and funneling them towards your affiliate links. There are multiple methods on how you can do this.

First, you can use paid methods as a source of traffic. You can use advertising platforms that allow affiliate links and pay for the clicks or the views that your ad gets. With this method, you are spending money to make money. You will need a bankroll of hundreds, if not thousands of dollars to make this strategy work. You will also need to make sure that you follow the guidelines set by the affiliate advertisers.

Most of them will restrict you from using certain keywords in the advertising targeting. If you are selling Nike rubber shoes for example, the affiliate program contract may restrict you from using the keywords like Nike. They do this to prevent affiliate marketers from competing with the mother company in the advertising bidding.

The second method of sending traffic is to spread the link around the web. In the past, people used to do sleazy techniques to get clicks on their affiliate links. Some of them for instance, put their affiliate links in the signature part of their forum accounts. This way, when people see their forum comments, they also see the affiliate links. Many forums learned about this technique and now ban the use of links in the signature.

Some affiliate programs also allow the use of redirects and pop-ups to gather traffic. An affiliate marketer using redirect for example, may set up a page that will automatically redirect to the affiliate website. When the visitor visits that page, they are automatically transferred to the affiliate program's landing page. The problem with this strategy is that most people who go through the automatic redirect are sent to the affiliate program's website unwillingly. The majority of them will bounce (i.e. leave rather than continuing to see other pages on the website). This excess traffic of non-buyers will eventually take its toll in the advertiser's website. This is the reason why many affiliate programs ban the use of redirects.

Some people also use link pop-ups to send people through the affiliate link. They may set the pop-up to appear after a certain link in the website is clicked. Upon clicking the said link, another window or tab will open. This works both for desktop and for mobile browsers. When the pop-up opens, the affiliate link is triggered and the affiliate landing page starts to load.

This process of sending traffic to affiliate programs is also problematic. Aside from being prohibited by most affiliate programs, browsers also tend to have pop-up blocking technology. This prevents most of the pop-ups from opening even when the right link is clicked.

The recommended way of gathering traffic for your affiliate programs is through the use of content marketing. Simply put, content marketing is the process of gathering internet user's attention by using different types of content media. One has the option of using text, audio, images, videos or a combination of all these to invite people to go to your website.

News websites are a classic example of websites that use content marketing. They create news articles and accompany them with videos and relevant images. After creating them, they post their content in their social media properties. They spread their news articles through Facebook, Twitter, and other social media marketing platforms. When a person interested in the news sees the article, the headline and the accompanying image should compel them to click on the link of the article. This will lead them to the news website.

After reading the article, they may press the up-vote button for the content. Some may even share a link of the content to their friends. By doing this, they are spreading the news and increasing the reach of the news article. Other people interested in the news may also click on the article. Afterwards they may also share the content with their own social media followers, continuing to spread the news.

Some people who may be looking to read that specific news article may also go to Google and do a search. Because of proper search engine optimization practices, the article landed in the top spot of the search result page with its relevant keywords or key phrases. Because of this, more people from Google manage to read the content. Some of the readers who are interested in the content of the article may also choose to share it with their friends.

While this may seem like a simplistic illustration of how content marketing works, this is how it happens for most content on the web. Content creators simple make the content and share them in the relevant online hotspots. They develop their skill in getting people's attention over thousands of hours of practice.

You could also do the same with your affiliate marketing business. You could lure internet users to go to your website by creating and sharing content that are relevant to their interests and needs. In the process of viewing your content, they should also see the affiliate ads that you share in your website. A percentage of them will click on these marketing materials and make a purchase. You will receive a percentage of the sale amount that your referred customers spend.

Chapter 3 Quiz
Please refer to Appendix C for the answers to this quiz

1. What is the primary marketing asset of the affiliate marketer?

    A) Website
    B) Money
    C) Affiliate program
    D) Friends

2. What do you call a topic that the affiliate website is focusing on?

    A) Preferred topic of interest
    B) Featured Topic
    C) Favorites
    D) Niche Topic

3. Why does a website need marketing?

    A) To send massive amounts of traffic to the advertiser's landing page
    B) To help the website become popular
    C) To increase the chances of winning affiliate promotions
    D) To prevent spammers from infiltrating the affiliate networks

4. How do demanding affiliate programs judge your application?

    A) They ask you to sell them a pen
    B) They email your referrals to check if you are a real person
    C) They use bots to look up your information online
    D) They check your website manually

5. Why are some affiliate programs strict in accepting affiliates?

    A) They are protecting their brands from Spamming marketers
    B) They do not want to accept low-ticket marketers
    C) They do not have enough slots for more marketers
    D) They reserve their slots only for high-ticket marketers

6. What are the two general ways of sending traffic to your affiliate website?

    A) Paid and Free
    B) Social and Search
    C) Email and Search
    D) Ads and Search traffic

7. What do you call the strategy of using content to attract traffic to a website?

   A) Search Marketing
   B) Content Marketing
   C) Social Media Marketing
   D) Banner Marketing

8. Where is content marketing most effective?

   A) Social networks
   B) Email Marketing
   C) Offline Marketing
   D) Banner Marketing

9. What do you call the process of making your content rank well in search engine result pages?

   A) Social Engine Marketing
   B) Search Engine Optimization
   C) Search Media Optimization
   D) Traffic Source

10. What is an example of a type website that uses content marketing routinely?

    A) Software support website
    B) Purely Ecommerce website
    C) Membership website
    D) News Website

Inspiration #4

"If you can dream it, you can do it."

Walt Disney

Chapter 4

The Top 20 Affiliate Marketing Programs

There are hundreds of affiliate marketing programs to choose from. However, to become successful, you need to find the one with the best potential for earning. You need to consider many factors such as the stability of the company running the network. You should also consider what types of advertisers and products they have in their network. In this chapter we will discuss some of the biggest affiliate programs right now.

1. Amazon Associates

Amazon is probably the most commonly used program by beginners. It allows you to earn from any type of item sold in Amazon, aside from digital kindle products. The program though, covers all tangible products. The commission rate varies for each product, depending on the type of product your associates account sells. Most items start out at 4% for the first six sales of the month. The rate for the seventh until the 30th item on the other hand is 6%. The rate increases as the number of products you sell also increases. In this affiliate program, affiliates are rewarded for selling a high quantity of items. The more items you sell in a month, the higher your commission rate will be.

Unlike most affiliate marketing programs, Amazon does not have a fixed landing page for their products. They allow the affiliate marketer to choose a product and use the product page as the landing page.

The best part about selling through Amazon Associates is that the affiliate marketer will be credited for any item bought by a person that clicked their link. The person you referred to Amazon does not need to buy the product you suggested. As long as they clicked your link, you will receive commission for everything that they buy in the website.

A person who clicks your regular Amazon Associates link has 24 hours to make a purchase for it to be credited to your account. If they do not make a purchase after 24 hours, the cookie will expire. Any purchase they make after the cookie expires will no longer be credited to you.

A special type of link that you can generate in your Amazon Associates account automatically leads to the clicker's cart page after they log in to their Amazon account. If you use this kind of affiliate link, the affiliate cookie extends to 90 days. As long as the item is kept in their cart in the 90-day period, you will be credited for the sale. In addition, if the person buys other things from Amazon in addition to the item in their cart, the sale of these items will also be credited to you.

Apart from the lower commission rates based on the industry standards, the only downside with selling through Amazon is that it will not redirect the Amazon links for you based on the visitor's location.

2. CJ.com

CJ or Commission Junction is one of the longest running affiliate network in the world. CJ is an affiliate network that connects affiliate marketers with advertisers. After signing up to CJ.com, you will be able to apply to the different advertisers they have in the website. Some of the advertisers allow immediate approval of applications. Others however, will manually check the application and may reject it depending on their acceptance standards.

CJ.com provides the tools that you will need for setting up the affiliate links in your website. They will also provide you with a dashboard where you can check how many clicks your affiliate marketing efforts get. This is also the place where you will see the amount you earn from the clicks you get.

The links that you will get from your CJ.com console will go straight to the advertiser's landing page. It is important that you choose the landing pages that you use. Choose a landing page, that you think will have a high chance of converting visits into sales.

The commission rates for affiliate programs in CJ vary per advertiser. This rate is usually written in the description of the program. While Amazon Associates rates are capped at 7.5%, it is normal for some advertisers in CJ.com to offer 10%. If you prove that you can send a good quantity of high quality leads, you may even request the advertiser for a higher commission rate.

3. Clickbank

Clickbank is also popular among affiliate marketers, mainly for its high commission rates. They sell a variety of products and services, from arts and entertainment to travel and leisure. Just go to their website at clickbank.com and go to the Affiliate Marketplace. In this page, you will see the different categories of affiliate offers that they have. Upon clicking on one of these categories, you will see a list of products and services. After choose a product or service that you would like to promote, you will need to sign up to the program by clicking the "Promote" button.

Most of clickbank's affiliate advertisers sell digital product and online services. Because of this, they can offer extremely high commission rates. Some of them offer up to 70% of the price of the purchase. These types of rate are only possible with online products and services. Because of the high commission rates, affiliate marketers prefer to promote clickbank content.

4. Rakuten Linkshare

Rakuten Linkshare is also one of the most popular affiliate programs. The sign up process for this program is fairly simple. You only need to fill up the usual information fields as well as complete the tax form. After which, your account will be registered and you will be allowed to sign up.

Once logged in, you will be able to select a category of products. The number of products available in Rakuten Linkshare is significantly fewer compared to the other affiliate networks discussed above.

However, Linkshare has the reputation of being reliable for fast payments for both US and non-US based affiliates.

5. JVZoo

JVZoo is new to the market but it is one of the fastest growing affiliate program in the industry. It offers features that are not commonly found in other affiliate programs. For instance, they are the only program that commits to timely payment delivery. This is a common issue among many programs. It usually takes them time to validate sales reports to make sure there are no sales frauds in the records. Some of the longest running programs like CJ.com and ClickBank still take weeks and even months to deliver payments for members with large volumes of sales.

6. Avantlink

Avantlink is less popular than the first few programs we've discussed above. However, its wide range of advertiser categories and its beginner-friendly user interface also makes it a great affiliate network.

7. eBay

EBay tends to be forgotten in the affiliate marketing world because of its strict approval process. Because eBay does not sell its own products and does not take responsibility in the quality of their products, affiliates tend to avoid promoting products from there. It's brand however, makes the network an easy sell to the average shopper. The shop is particularly popular among bargain hunters. If your website attracts of bargain hunters, eBay affiliate may work for you.

8. Shareasale

Shareasale's competitive edge is the size of its network. It offers more than 4,000 advertisers in various categories. Its user interface is also easy to use and it collects some types of analytics data not available in other networks. It is also one of those networks that pay on a monthly basis.

9. Avangate

Avangate exclusively offers affiliate offers from software. They offer the best brands in software downloads and online services. As with other technology-based affiliate programs, Avantgate advertisers tend to offer higher commission rates.

10. Affibank

Affibank.com is also a newer player in the market but they are making a name for themselves among affiliate marketers because of their high commission rates. Many of the offers in the Affibank give out commission rates of 75%. This means that a big chunk of the money you refer goes back to you. The offers in this marketplace are similar to those found in ClickBank. The only downside is that they are currently offering few offers and most of them are in the Health, Beauty and Fitness Categories.

There are hundreds of other affiliate marketing programs available for you to explore. Here are ten more that you can look into if you cannot find a program you like in the marketplaces listed above.

11. Maxbounty

12. RevenueWire

13. ReviMedia

14. Flexoffers

15. Commission Factory

16. PeerFly

17. ClickFunnels

18. Tradedoubler

19. AffiliateWindow

20. BankAffiliates

While these marketplaces are the best places to start, you can also look into in-house affiliate programs in specific companies. Some online companies maintain their own affiliate marketing programs. If you have a company whose products you wish to promote, you can search their company with the key phrase "affiliate program" added to it.

If they do have an affiliate program, there is no doubt that it will show up in the search result pages. Think of the products and services that you have been using in the past and check online if they do have an affiliate marketing program set up. One example is Shopify. You can promote it to people who want to start an online store and earn while doing it.

Chapter 4 Quiz
Please refer to Appendix D for the answers to this quiz

1. What types of products can you sell with Amazon Associates

    A) All tangible products sold in Amazon.com
    B) All products in Amazon.com and eBay.com
    C) Products in Amazon.com, Amazon.au and Shopify
    D) All digital products in Amazon.com

2. What affiliate program consistently offers high commission rates

    A) CJ.com
    B) Affibank
    C) Amazon Associates
    D) eBay

3. Why is Shareasale a strong network?

    A) It has lots of advertisers and offers
    B) It has a strong social media following
    C) It is recommended by celebrities
    D) It offers a high commission rates

4. What is JVZoo's defining feature?

    A) High number of offers
    B) Fast payment processing
    C) Longest running affiliate network
    D) Multinational reach

5. What type of products does a Avantgate offer?

    A) Sports equipment
    B) Software
    C) Computer Hardware
    D) Cars

6. What is eBay's best feature?

    A) Brand recognition
    B) Product quality
    C) Business process
    D) Superior customer service

7. What is Amazon Associate's best feature?

    A) High commission rate
    E) High volume of products
    F) Superior customer service
    G) Fast payment processing

8. What is CJ.com's best feature?

    A) High commission rate
    B) High number of advertisers
    C) Superior customer service
    D) Fast payment processing

9. What is an example of a company that offers in-house affiliate program

    A) Shopify
    B) Nike
    C) Under Armour
    D) ESPN

10. What do you call a company that hosts its own affiliate program without passing through a network?

    A) Affiliate network guru
    B) Business process outsourcing
    C) Virtual Assistants
    D) In-house affiliate program

Inspiration #5

"Many of life's failures are people who did not realize how close they were to success when they gave up."

Thomas Edison

Chapter 5

How To Choose An Affiliate Marketing Program

Choosing an affiliate marketing program is an important factor in becoming a successful affiliate marketer. If you choose the wrong program, you may end up not making any money from all your efforts. You need to align the content you created with the right types of products in the affiliate marketing program. You also need to make sure that the commission rate in the program you've chosen is big enough. Lastly, you need to make sure that the company behind the program provides excellent customer support and fast payment processing.

Check the advertisers

The advertisers should be the primary reason why you should join an affiliate program. If you find an advertiser you like in an affiliate network, you should join that network. Not all advertisers you would like to partner with will all be in one program. To be able to sell all the products and services that you personally like, you may need to work with multiple advertisers. This means that you will need to work with multiple affiliate accounts.

Find the programs with the best commission rate

Aside from the types of advertisers they have, you should also join programs based on their commission rates. The commission rate of a program varies depending on the type of product sold. Usually, the commission rate goes up when the product is digital (such as in the case of software) or when the product is hard to sell. Companies that are having a hard time selling their product tend to add a high commission rate to their product to increase the motivation of online marketers to sell them.

You should also watch out for the types of products that also offer residual payments. In affiliate marketing, residual payments happen when the people you refer to the program renew their membership in a merchant. This type of payment usually applies towards services that require customers to become members. Many web hosting affiliate programs for example, offer this kind of deal to people. With this type of commission payment, you will continue to make money from people that you referred even years ago.

Based on the quality of backend services

Lastly, you need to consider the quality of service of the affiliate program. Most affiliate programs tend to offer a do-it-yourself approach to marketing. However, they do offer one-on-one support when the affiliates need help with technical parts of the website. Choosing a company that has good customer support is important so that there will be someone to help you in the future when problems in your account arise. Whenever you find a new program that looks promising, look into the reputation of its customer service online.

If the company has a poor customer service, you will hear about it in the forums and blog posts. Check other people's experiences about how fast the company responds to queries and reports. More importantly, you should also research on how fast the company delivers payments and what types of payment methods they use.

Chapter 5 Quiz
Please refer to Appendix E for the answers to this quiz

1. What should be the primary reason for joining an affiliate program?

    A) The advertiser
    B) The competition
    C) The email marketing service
    D) None of the above

2. What determines the amount paid to the advertiser?

    A) Success rate
    B) Commission rate
    C) Popularity of the product
    D) Customer service

3. What do you do if the advertisers you want are in different affiliate networks?

    A) Apply in both networks
    B) Abandon one network over the other
    C) Find an alternative advertiser in your preferred network
    D) Create to websites to promote different products

4. What is a common problem among affiliate programs?

    A) High bounce rates
    B) Slow internet connection
    C) Slow payment processing
    D) Spam marketing content

5. What usually determines the commission rate of the program?

    A) The popularity of product
    B) The type of product sold
    C) The number of annual sales
    D) The popularity of the website

6. What do you do when you encounter a technical issue with your affiliate program?

    A) Transfer to another affiliate program
    B) Replace all your affiliate links with working ones
    C) Contact the affiliate program support group
    D) Wait for the problem to be solved on its own

7. What makes a good affiliate program support team?

    A) Making excuses for not solving problems
    E) Presence of email support
    F) Fast and accurate responses from the team
    G) Great reviews from online bloggers

8. How do you check if the affiliate program support group is any good?

    A) If they are available in multiple communication channels
    B) If they are good at upselling products from the affiliate program
    C) If they are available during business hours only
    D) If do not respond through emails

9. How do you make sure that an affiliate program pays?

    A) Find program reviews in YouTube and in personal blogs
    B) Wait until you reach the payment threshold
    C) You cannot have any guarantees
    D) Buy the affiliate products yourself to reach the payment threshold

10. From a payment standpoint, what should you check before you apply with an affiliate program of network?

    A) The past earnings of other people
    B) The total revenue of the affiliate advertiser
    C) The methods of payment offered by the program or network
    D) The cost of contacting the affiliate support team

Inspiration #6

"The secret of success is to do the common thing uncommonly well."

John D. Rockefeller Jr.

Chapter 6

Writing Content For Affiliate Marketing

To start your content marketing campaign, you should begin with the product or products that you wish to promote to your visitors.

Promote products you've used in the past

Ideally, you should share products that you have used in the past, so that you can share your firsthand experience in using them. This will make your content authentic. Online authorities usually use this kind of approach. A welding teacher for example, uses his website together with YouTube to create a multimedia content experience. In his articles and videos, he shows people how to do welding techniques and projects. In the process, he shows them the tools that he is using. By showing the people that he is using the tools, he is more likely to convince them to buy from his affiliate marketing sources.

If you choose to present yourself and your website as an authority in the subject you are using, you can also use this strategy. When thinking about the topic that you are going to discuss, also research on the possible products that you may promote to your online visitors. It's better if you already have some of these products so that you no longer need to buy them.

Presenting products you haven't used

Some affiliate marketers in the market also suggest the use of products they have never used in the past. This type of affiliate marketing suggestion usually works for generic products that people will still buy regardless of the price or the brand you present. Weight plates for dumbbells are an example of this type of product. Even if you do not show that you are using weight plates, you can talk about them, show photos of them and present an affiliate link for them.

Because they are common products, your readers are familiar with what these products are. They will also be willing to buy them even if you do not show yourself using them. If you post a link to an Amazon product page with an acceptable price range, some of your uses will make the purchase.

When presenting products that you haven't used yet, you should do all the research you can about it. The web today is rich in information, you can do your research about any product out there. If the product can be found in Amazon, you can even use the review section as your source for doing product research. The people posting these reviews mostly have firsthand experience in using them.

Beginners make the common mistake of being too positive about the products they present. This makes them sound as if they are doing a sales pitch; you do not want people to see you this way when you are talking about your content. Instead, people want hard facts about the products you are presenting. Show them both the pros and cons of using the product.

What type of content should I create?

When choosing the type of content you will create, choose the ones where in you can actively and naturally suggest the products you use. Listicles (list articles), tutorial articles and tips articles are some of the types of contents where in you can naturally plug a product in. Ideally, you should create three types of content. An article in your website for people who prefer to read, a video in YouTube and an audio version of the video for iTunes. You can embed the video and audio files in your article page to make all your content come together.

In addition, you can also create additional content such as behind-the-scenes videos and photos. You can then post these photos in your social media accounts or your website blog. By doing so, you will be able to keep your accounts active. Some of the people who see your social media content will also be interested in what you are up to. If you show a photo doing a project for example, your followers may become interested in knowing what project you are working on.

By posting these behind-the-scenes footage and content, you will be able to build excitement in your audience base. This increases the potential views of your different contents from the different platforms you use.

All these pieces of content have one important purpose, to redirect the attention of the visitor towards the affiliate links and buttons. Your target market will be minding their own business, using social media or doing a Google search. In the process, they may stumble upon your content and spend some time to watch, read or listen to it. This is what you are fighting for when doing content marketing, your potential visitors' time and attention. You want to keep them tuned in to your content long enough so that they will see or hear your product pitches.

Putting the Tips into Action

Now that you know how the basic content marketing process works, let's consider an example of a successful content marketing campaign for an affiliate marketing program.

Mary is a stay at home mom and she wants to start doing affiliate marketing to supplement the household income. In her free time, Mary likes to work on her garden and she has had some success in growing both flowering and fruit-bearing plants. Because she enjoys gardening and she has the experience to teach people how to do it, she decided that this will be her niche topic.

Mary begins by researching about the types of information that are already in the market. As she expected, there are already a lot of content about general gardening. Because of this, she decided to make her niche narrower. She looked into creating content only for specific aspects of gardening such as organic gardening, composting, and similar contents. She found that while there are already a lot of content in this area, she has some article ideas that no other website have discussed with depth.

With her niche market set, Mary begins to craft her content marketing strategy. In the beginning of the website, there will not be a lot of traffic because people will not be aware yet that the website exists.

This gives Mary the opportunity to create and refine her content. She starts by creating a series of posts focused on planting lettuce in her backyard. She did her research and outlined her content so that everything will be organized and easy to follow.

While researching, she also followed the tip of listing down all the tools she will need for her series of articles. In her list, she included both generic garden tools and some brands that she personally uses. After creating the list, she looks for these products in Amazon and uses her Amazon Associates account to generate links for each one of them.

Now that the information for the content is ready, Mary starts to create. To create her content, she works on her garden and uses her smartphone camera to take photos and to record videos. She plans to edit these videos and share them in YouTube. She also takes photos and short videos and shares them in Instagram, Pinterest, Twitter and Facebook. In the process, some of her friends start interacting with her content, asking her what she is up to. She lets them know that she is working on her garden and creating an article about it. With her initial social media content, starts to pique the interest of her natural audience.

After her gardening project, she managed to create 5 articles about plating lettuce, one video about how to plant them from seeds and multiple social media posts about it. These become her first contents for her website and her YouTube Channel. In both her articles and her YouTube video, she actively discusses the tools and planting products she uses. She then tells her content viewers that they can also get the same products through the link she provides. In her articles, she posts the link directly after mentioning them. In her YouTube video, she puts all her affiliate links in the description of the video. She also includes a link towards her articles so that people from YouTube will be able to go to her website easily.

Now that her first set of contents are ready, Mary begins the second part of her content marketing effort. She now starts to spread her content around the web. She continues to post in her social media platforms about the progress of the growth of her plants. In Instagram she posts photos of the sprouts coming out of the ground, she also posts about the different plants in her garden.

She also shares the same content in her Twitter account. In there, she also talks with other Twitter users about gardening. Every now and then, she mentions her articles and her videos. In Facebook, Mary posts her articles and uploads a copy of her video. In the beginning, only her friends and family talked about it. Mary entertained her audience in the comments. With people engaged in her articles and her video, the reach of her content increases. Because of this, other people outside of Mary's social circles start seeing her contents. They press the up-vote button while some leave a comment and share the content.

Aside from social media marketing, Mary also optimizes her content so that it ranks high in search engine result pages. She uses her target keywords in the title of her content as well as in different paragraphs in the article. In her YouTube video, she also created a long description with the relevant keywords included to make it easier to find for people looking for videos.

All these marketing efforts increased the views of Mary's articles and video. Out of the thousands that viewed her content, some clicked on the Amazon links she provided. The purchases of these referred visitors allowed Mary to earn some cash from Amazon Associates.

In this example, our protagonist did all things right to make money through Amazon. Here are some of the content marketing best practices she did right:

Pick a topic you enjoy working on

You are stuck with the topic you pick until you see success or until you give up on your affiliate marketing business. To make sure you do not get fed up making content on the same topics, you should pick one that you love doing, in our example, Mary chose to work on gardening, one of her natural interests. If you have a long-term interest or hobby, you can also pick that topic for your content marketing.

Create specific types of content based on your marketing platform

Right now, the Google and Facebook are the two biggest sources of website visitors. They are so influential that they are rumored to be used for important political events like elections. While they are both excellent places to share content, not all types of content will work in both of them. For Google, it's best to use keyword-rich instructional contents. People go to Google when they have problems or when they are looking for specific information.

For Facebook on the other hand, the best types of content are those that provoke certain emotions on the readers. They do not need to be necessarily useful. In fact, many of the contents in Facebook are purely for entertainment purposes. Content in Facebook become popular if people engage with it. Engagement in social media marketing is defined as any positive action done by the user towards the content. In Facebook, reactions such as "Likes" are examples of engagement. Comments and Shares are even more powerful forms of engagement. The Facebook content management algorithm will show your content to more people if it received a lot of these positive reactions in the first hour of posting.

Encourage followers to engage with your content

In our example, Mary knew that engagement is important in her content marketing game. Because of this, she entertained the comments of people in the content she shared. The more comments and reactions the content gets, the higher the number of people that gets to see it.

You should also do the same when doing content marketing is social networks. Make your content rise in the newsfeeds of your friends and family by entertaining comments. Also encourage people to share the content by directly asking them to do it in the content description.

State a clear call-to-action to go to the affiliate website

People will not just click on your affiliate link just because you added it to your content. They will only click on it if you directly invite them to do so. In our example, Mary directly invites her viewers and website visitors to click on the affiliate links she provides. Even better, she shows people that she is using the affiliate products she invites them to buy. Affiliate marketing is more than just a selling business. It's about helping your community solve their own problems. You can only earn if you convince people that your way of solving the problem is better.

Do not be afraid to over use your call-to-action statements and buttons. The business is all about directing the attention of your audience towards your links. If you are shy with making people click on that affiliate link, you will fail in achieving your goal. If you believe that the product you are selling will solve the problems of the people viewing your content, you should not be afraid of sounding to salesy.

Chapter 6 Quiz
Please refer to Appendix F for the answers to this quiz

1. Ideally, which type of product should you promote?

    A) Products that other bloggers are promoting
    B) Products with high ratings on Amazon
    C) Products you have used in the past
    D) Products that look great

2. Why should you promote products you've used in the past?

    A) To increase your credibility as a reviewer and product ambassador
    B) So that it is easy to find out what qualities to upsell
    C) To make it easier to fool consumers
    D) To sell more products

3. What makes a good content in promoting products and services?

    A) Showing people that you use the product
    B) Showing stock photos of the product
    C) Writing only positive qualities of the product
    D) Showing that the product is on sale

4. How do you present yourself and your website as a content authority?

    A) Make up information about your achievements
    B) Show content on how to use a product
    C) Talk about how good you are in your niche topic
    D) Build a visually appealing website about the topic

5. What is the best way to find information about products you've never used before?

    A) Copy content of other affiliate marketers about it
    B) Make things up about the product
    C) Buy the product yourself to test it
    D) Use the information written in the marketing flyers of the product

6. Which of the following is a good source of user information about the product?

    A) It's website
    B) Other blogs
    C) Amazon's review section
    D) Magazines

7. What type of content would probably do well in Facebook?

    A) A link post to your latest content
    B) An emotional video related to your content
    C) An image of your website's front page
    D) A rant about your competitors

8. How do you make sure that your content does well in social media?

    A) Post your content in other people's pages
    B) Buy social media up-votes
    C) Create a specific type of content for your chosen social media platform
    D) Post your content in as many groups as possible

9. How do you encourage users to engage with your content?

    A) Put more videos in your content
    B) Entertain people's comments in the website
    C) Talk about how good your content is
    D) Make a pop up that forces people to make a comment

10. How do you convince people to click on your affiliate link?

    A) Fool the user to thinking that he is going to a different website by clicking the link
    B) Fill your webpage with affiliate links
    C) Rant about how bad other products in the market are
    D) State a clear call-to-action to click on the link

Inspiration #7

"The only place where success comes before work is in the dictionary."
Vidal Sassoon

Chapter 7

Using Social Media Platforms For Affiliate Marketing

As mentioned above, social media is one of the best sources of traffic right now. Next to Google search, social media apps will probably become your best source of traffic. Learning how to funnel traffic from these sources can lead to a significant increase in your earnings. To learn how to make use of the different apps in the market, use the following steps:

1. Find the social media website or app where most of your target audience spend their time

There are hundreds of social media apps out there. However, you do not have to participate in all of them. Instead, you only need to find the online communities where most of your target audience hangs out. If you are targeting adults between the ages of 25 and 40, Facebook, Pinterest, Twitter and LinkedIn may be the best options for you. For young adults between 20 and 25, Instagram and Snapchat are the more popular options.

There are more social media options available depending on your target country and the interests of your audience. If you can clearly define what demographics your target audience belongs to, you will be able to choose the right network.

2. Identify what content to share in each network

Each social network favors different types of content. You want to know what type of content each social network requires before you start your social media marketing campaigns.

Facebook is a truly multimedia social networking platform, in that you can post any type of content in there. However, since the time video content was allowed, it has dominated all other types of contents in terms of engagement and reach. You will still need to mix it up though by posting images, text content and links from time to time to add variety to your page.

Instagram on the other hand is focused on hosting images and short videos. Pinterest is used as a tool to collect images from around the web. If you have a project for example, you can use your Pinterest account as a vision board of inspirations.

LinkedIn is just like Facebook. However, the users in this network prefer content that are related to careers, professional networking, finance and personal growth. If you post so-called viral content in LinkedIn, most users will unfollow you. They just do not want their feeds to be filled with distractions.

Twitter is ruled by short text content. You will also find some pictures and videos in there but text conversations dominate this network. You can post your opinions and your thoughts in twitter as long as you make your message fit in the character number limit of the network. You can also react to other people's tweets by pressing or tapping on the heart icon under each tweet. The retweet option however, is the primary sharing feature for tweets. The most popular tweets in the worlds are retweeted millions of times.

Businesses are fond of twitter because they can use it to communicate directly with their fans. It works both as a customer service and a marketing platform.

3. Find out how content is spread in the network

Each social network has a unique way of spreading content. Most social networks use a system where in users can follow other users. When a user follows you, they will see every public post you share in your account. This system is used in almost all the popular social networks today such as Facebook, Twitter, Instagram and Snapchat.

A user with millions of follower is considered an influencer or authority. They hold a lot of power in the social network because any of their posts can be seen by millions of people. As an affiliate marketer, you want your social network accounts to reach this kind of status. You can do this by sharing excellent quality posts.

Aside from increasing the number of followers, you can also share your content by encouraging engagement. This is a second feature common to all social networks. They allow users to engage with content. In Facebook for example, the network allows the users to select a reaction for the content shares. The thumbs-up icon is called the like button.

This is a form of an up-vote towards the content. In recent years, Facebook also added other reactions to convey the user's emotion towards the content. A person who finds the content funny for example, can choose a laughing emoji. If the content is sad, the user also has the option to use the sad emoji. All these reactions however, count as a form of engagement. The more reactions a content gets, the higher the likelihood will be that the content will spread.

Aside from reactions, Facebook can also leave a comment below the content. Facebook comments are powerful engagement signals because sometimes, they encourage other users to also engage in the discussion. The tagging feature of Facebook also helps content spread wider through the comment feature.

In Facebook, the newsfeed is the primary sharing feature among users. When a user shares something on Facebook, that user's followers will see the shared content in their newsfeeds. As an affiliate marketer, you want your shared content to show in the newsfeeds of your target audience. Driving the engagement up in your contents will help you achieve this. More people will discover your content if other users are engaged with the content.

Instagram also has an up-vote feature in the form of a heart. By double tapping an image in Instagram, you are able to up-vote a content. Just like Facebook, Instagram also allows users to comment and to tag other users. While Instagram also has feeds that shows the shared content of the users you follow, this is not how other people will discover your Instagram account.

Most of the content discovery happens in the search screen of the app. When the user taps on the magnifying glass icon in the bottom of the app, the search screen will show. In this part of the app, the user can search for accounts, hashtags, and places. In the same part of the app, they will also see suggested images and video content. The suggestions in this part of the app are based on the perceived interests of the said user. This perceived interest is based on many factors like the accounts followed by the user, the types of images and videos they clicked on or up-voted in the past and past searches made by the user.

For your content to be shown to the right people on Instagram, you should establish your accounts identity. You can do this by controlling the types of content your share. If your Instagram account is about gardening, you should post mostly images and videos about your garden. You can also post about significant events, but you should still increase the frequency of posting content related to your affiliate marketing topic.

You could also establish what your content is about by putting a detailed description of your account in the account Bio. This is the part just below you profile picture and your name when you are looking at your profile page. To make your content spread, you should also add descriptions below your content that are relevant to your affiliate marketing topic. Your content will also reach many other users if you include the right hashtags to it.

Twitter also uses many of the social networking features discussed above. Users in this network can follow one another to subscribe to each other's tweets. However, one does not need to be a follower to participate in the public conversations of other people. Just like with Instagram, people use the search feature to find content here. They can also find related tweets by clicking on hashtags.

Twitter is well known for its high click-through rate. Users in this network are more open to clicking on links. If many of your target audience are twitter users, you may have the opportunity to earn big.

4. Completely create your account and start sharing

If you do not know where to start in using social media, start by choosing a platform where most of your users are found and create an account there. To be successful, you will need to complete all the details of your account. In most cases, you will be required to add a profile image and a larger cover photo in the case of Facebook, Twitter and LinkedIn.

You will also be asked to write a description about yourself or your page. Just fill in whatever form the account creation process gives you.

After creating the account, you should plan how and where you will get your content. It is possible to grow your social media accounts by using other people's images and videos. However, you will find more success if you have an option to create your own content.

5. Facebook and LinkedIn groups

One of the best ways of using social media to keep your audience tuned into the content you create is by using the group feature of social networks. Networks like Facebook and LinkedIn have features that allow you to create groups where network users can join. These groups are effective in keeping your audience engaged with the content you are promoting.

A gardening blog owner from Canada for example, can create a group in Facebook about the topic for his home town. He could then ask his friends and relatives who are interested in gardening to join the group. In the group, he could create conversation topics regularly. An active group can have hundreds to thousands of new content per day. What matters most however, is not the actual number of posts but the amount of engagement of the group members in those posts. Among the different ways to engage in post, comments are probably the biggest newsfeed ranking indicator. The more comments your content gets, the greater its reach will be.

There are two steps to social media group marketing. The first step is the process of growing the group. You can start building the group by talking adding the people you actually know to the group. If you know for sure that a person you know is interested in your affiliate marketing niche, talk to them about it and ask them if they want to join your group.

After tapping your natural circles, you can start using your other marketing tools to promote your group. You can begin by talking about it in every other post in your website. You could then leave a link to your group. You could also promote your group in your different social media accounts. If you have a Facebook page, you should link it to your group.

The easiest way to increase the number of member of your group is by introducing it to the people you meet every day who are also interested in the niche topic. If you meet a coworker for example who also likes your content, you could tell them about your group. This group is an effective way for you to create a place for all your followers to meet each other. Your follower can be from different social networks and some may even find you on Facebook. By having a group in Facebook or LinkedIn, you will have a place where they can all meet and have a conversation amongst themselves.

If you are not familiar with how social media groups work, you could begin by joining one first. Ideally, you should join one that is related to your chosen affiliate marketing niche. Observe how the manager or administrators of the group keep the users engaged. Take note of the types of content that he or she is posting in the group. The purpose of these groups is for people to have meaningful conversations about the common topic that they are interested in. However, it could also be for other purposes. Sometimes, people use these groups to build relationships. Others do it to solve problems. They do this by posting a question in the group, hoping that group members will be able to answer it.

While you are in the group, start participating in the conversation. If you see a question that you know the answer to, answer it for the person asking. Also, while you are there, observe how different types of content rise up in the groups newsfeeds. Just like in any other type of social media newsfeeds, the content in social media groups are usually shown based on the amount of engagement they get. In short, contents with a lot of comments and reactions tend to be shown to more viewers.

Also, take note of how the members interact and how they react to posts. In places like Facebook, you are more likely to see people talking in a casual manner, sometimes even using informal writing to communicate. In LinkedIn, people tend to communicate in a more respectful and politically correct way. You will need to set the tone with how people communicate in your own group in the future.

The group will only continue to grow beyond the people you add if the community becomes active. To do this, you could make the group come alive by keeping the conversations going. You could do this by sharing content to it. You may also appoint some of the most active members of the group to become your co-administrators. These people will help you police the group and to make it a pleasant place for the members. They can also help in keeping the community members active. You should not worry if the progress of growing your group seems slow. As long as you keep adding content and keep participating in your own group, it will continue to grow.

The content that you share in the group does not have to be always your own. You could put content from other sources as well, as long as they fit the purpose of the group. Every time you post a new content in your website however, be sure to post it in the group.

If the group grows, you can even use it as a way to drive some affiliate sales. The members of a group about professional networking for instance, will be interested in new books about the topic. If the group owner sees an interesting book, he could make a post about it in his book. He could then use Amazon Associate links to promote the book in the group. If some of the group members buy from Amazon after using the link, you may earn commission from it.

Chapter 7 Quiz

Please refer to Appendix G for the answers to this quiz

1. Which of the following statements is true?

    A) You should create accounts in all social networking websites and apps
    B) You only need to learn how to use Facebook
    C) Instagram is the best app to use right now
    D) The choice for the best social media platform to use depends on your target audience

2. From a marketing standpoint, what is the most important aspect of a social networking app or website?

    A) The visually appealing content
    B) The underlying technology
    C) The community of likeminded individuals
    D) The ease of entry to the app

3. What is the best way to communicate your website to social media users

    A) Communicate with the social media users in a natural but charismatic way
    B) Flood your account with promotional content
    C) Pay other users to do the marketing for you
    D) Attack the beliefs of others users to gain attention from the rest of the community

4. Which social network should you use if you have a great video content to share?

    A) Instagram
    B) Twitter
    C) LinkedIn
    D) It depends on the topic of the video

5. Which social network is great for promoting products for professionals?

    A) Instagram
    B) Twitter
    C) Pinterest
    D) LinkedIn

6. How does content spread in Facebook?

    A) People share them
    B) They naturally spread through newsfeed algorithm
    C) They only spread through ads

D) Only private contents are allowed in Facebook

7. Which of the following has a high impact in the spread of content in Social Media?

   A) Mention of brand names and celebrities
   B) Time of posting
   C) Hashtags
   D) Engagement with the content

8. What feature of Facebook allows people of the same interest to meet?

   A) Facebook Live
   B) Facebook groups
   C) Newsfeeds
   D) Messenger

9. What feature in groups will have the biggest impact in helping the spread of content?

   A) Likes
   B) Comments
   C) Spam
   D) Pinning of content

10. What is the best part of having a successful social media group?

    A) Being liked by the members of the group
    B) Being popular in the social network
    C) Instant likes in your posts
    D) Access to a homogenous audience

Inspiration #8

"Success is not final; failure is not fatal: It is the courage to continue that counts."

Winston S. Churchill

Chapter 8

Common Affiliate Marketing Mistakes

Many people who try to build an affiliate marketing business fail because they make common mistakes that end up ruining their business. In this section, we will discuss the most important mistakes so that you will be able to avoid them when you do start your own affiliate marketing career.

1. Thinking that a website is the only way to sell affiliate products

Many affiliate marketers make the mistake of focusing too much on their website and not finding other opportunities outside to promote their affiliate products. Every now and then, your followers will forgive you if you promote to them through Facebook, Twitter or even Instagram.

When guest posting in your friends' website, you can also post affiliate links relevant to your topic. Make sure that you get the permission of the website owner first. Few will actually allow you to do so. However, if it is possible, you should take the opportunity.

2. Not building a community from day one

The biggest affiliate marketers in the industry can demand certain discounts, freebies and other promotions. They can do this because tens to hundreds of thousands of people follow their content. This is your goal and it makes sense to start building this goal for day one.

From your first article or video, you should already start considering your audience as a part of that community. If you have this kind of mindset, you will be able to avoid making some of the basic mistakes in this list. With a community building mindset, you will put your community member's interest first. You will not focus on factors like commission rates of your products or conversion rates of your marketing tools. Instead, you will be able to focus on helping the members of your community. You can do this by providing useful content to your audience (community members) and opening them to exclusive offers that only you can give them.

In the beginning though, try to help your community members by providing them with the information they need. As your community grows, you will be repaid by the love they show your content. They will talk about it, not only in the comment areas of your website but also in other places online.

3. Becoming too salesy by claiming exaggerated results

Many affiliate marketers think that selling is all about highlighting the positive parts of the products they promote. This is far from what is actually happening in reality. The population of internet users is becoming smarter each year. They are becoming more mindful of false information. This is especially true with internet buyers. With thousands of products available online, the average consumer have options on where to get their products.

If you make exaggerated claims regarding the features and benefits of the product you are promoting, most people will call you out for it. People are more vigilant now with these types of schemes. If they think that you are fooling people with your claims, they may make a post about it in social media. It is common nowadays for regular people to attack business by posting negative things about them online.

When posting about your products in any of your content, you should make it a habit only to talk about the facts. When using a product for instance, you should only talk about how you like to personally use it. Talk about the pros and cons of the product based on your experience. If you set an extremely high expectation, your audience will be disappointed when the product actually arrives in the mail. Because you have a website, they will be able to go back to your claims and leave negative comments. They may even call your entire business a scam. You do not want this to happen to you.

4. Not working with a partner

An affiliate marketing business is easy to start. You can definitely fund it and work on it on your own. However, it is also the ease of entry that makes it easy to let go. Many of people who fail at affiliate marketing give up on the task before they even start making money. When they fail to see results in the first few weeks of creating content, they start to doubt the process and consider quitting. Many of them give up on their project before the sixth month period.

One way to avoid this is by working with others who believe in your vision. I am not talking about hiring an employee. Instead, I am talking about working with a partner. A business partner motivates you to work on the business even when you do not want to. It also has the same effect on your partner. They will also be forced to work on the business because you are holding them accountable.

A partner not only increases the amount of work hours put on a business but also gives it a longer financial runway. In startups, the runway refers to amount of time that the capital fund of a business can fund its operations. If all business partners chip in to fund the affiliate business, the financial risk will be divided.

In the beginning, the first few people you will convince to use your affiliate links are your family and friends. Your friends and family members will be the first group of people who will see the content and marketing materials you share in your social networking accounts.

With a partner, the reach of your organic marketing will significantly increase. You will be able to double the amount of people who sees your marketing materials if both partners share the content with their personal social media accounts.

5. Shiny Object Syndrome

Another reason why most affiliate marketers fail is because of what is known in the industry as the "shiny object syndrome". This phenomenon is common among entrepreneurs. The minds of entrepreneurs are so active in looking for business opportunities that it continues even when they are already working on a business. Many of the entrepreneurs who lack discipline jump from one business opportunity to another. In the middle of working on an affiliate marketing project, they decide to abandon it and start doing another type of business. This usually happens when the first idea takes too long to start showing progress.

You can avoid this common mistake by plotting the steps that you need to take to reach your goal and holding yourself accountable for reaching these goals. Consider that if you start with another project while you are in the middle of another one, you will go back to square one. Instead, you should just take note of your business ideas for you to start later on. For now, put all your focus, energy and effort on the current project you are working on. The more time and resources you put on this project, the better its chances will be of becoming successful.

6. Not delegating tasks

Affiliate marketing is a business. All businesspeople need to use the power of delegating to be successful. Creating a successful community for your affiliate marketing offers will require a lot of work. You will need to write hundreds of thousands of words of content. You will also need to create hundreds of hours' worth of video and audio content.

Creating content is more than just writing or recording. You also need to do a lot of research before writing, proofread your articles, edit your videos, create featured images for your blog posts, and create thumbnail images for YouTube.

The point is that your success depends on thousands of hours of work. To become successful, you will need help. This is where a VA can help you. VA stands for virtual assistant. To hire a real assistant, you will need to consider many factors like his or her pay, benefits, tools for working and other things. A VA on the other hand, is hired by a third-party company. You only pay the company a fraction of what you would normally pay a full time personal assistant. In turn, they will provide you with an assistant that has the skills that you need for your business.

Today's Virtual Assistants come in different forms. Some of them are jack-of-all-trades. They can do pretty much everything from writing your content to editing your YouTube videos. There are also some types of VA with specialized skills. Some can act as a personal assistant, answering emails and scheduling appointments for you so that you no longer have to deal with these kinds of tasks. Some specialize in specific industries, like real estate, accounting, finance and many more.

You can also use VAs to get some of your tasks off your plate. If you do not have the skills for editing your own videos for example, you can look for a VA with this kind of skillset. You can agree on a price and start on a per-project basis. If they deliver in terms of the quality of work and deadlines, you could hire them again for future projects. If their quality of work or work ethic is problematic, you have the choice to give them another chance or to let them go.

Finding a good employee is just as complicated online as it is offline. It may take you a few tries before you find one that works well for your business process.

7. Failing to track results

After building your affiliate marketing assets, you cannot just sit back and wait for the business to make you money. You need to continue observing the system you've developed and examine how it could be improved. Examine each step that your customers take before they end up making a purchase and find ways to improve their success rate. In some cases, you may need to improve your activities in gathering traffic. There may also be some improvements needed in converting your traffic into paying customers.

You can only learn what improvements are needed if your track the important data in your website. Luckily, you can do this free with tools like Google Analytics, Google Webmaster Tools, Twitter Analytics, Facebook Pixels and other forms of website activity tracking technology. They are easy to set up but the insights they provide can be the different between success and failure.

Chapter 8 Quiz
Please refer to Appendix H for the answers to this quiz

1. Which statement is true?

   A) You can only promote affiliate links in your website
   B) You can only promote affiliate links in your blog posts
   C) You can only promote affiliate links by spamming social media
   D) You can promote affiliate links in many places online

2. What do you call a person who trusts your vision enough to invest in your business and work with you to make it succeed?

   A) Virtual Assistant
   B) Business Partner
   C) Angel Investor
   D) Affiliate

3. What is an advantage of having a partner?

   A) Bigger operational capital
   B) Easier working process
   C) Larger affiliate sales numbers
   D) Faster spread of content in search engines

4. How do you track your sales numbers?

   A) Through the affiliate dashboard stats area
   B) Through the commission you receive
   C) Through Google Analytics
   D) Through Social Media Insights

5. What do people hate when they are looking for good content about a product?

   A) Engaging videos
   B) Images of the product in use
   C) Exaggerated claims
   D) Formal grammar

6. What is an example of an exaggerated claim?

   A) This laptop has 4GB of RAM
   E) This phone can be submerged until six inches of water
   F) The casing is made from aluminum

G) This chair is the best computer chair I've ever seen in my entire life

7. How does the "Shiny Object Syndrome" affect your success?

    A) It allows you to accomplish more tasks in lesser time
    B) It doubles you productivity at night
    C) It prevents you from finishing projects
    D) It prevents you from selling affiliate products

8. What do you call workers who can do specific tasks for you over the internet?

    A) Virtual assistants
    B) Drones
    C) Crowdsourcing
    D) Ghostwriters

9. Which of the following statements is true?

    A) Virtual assistants are good only for menial tasks
    B) Virtual assistants will steal your ideas
    C) Some virtual assistants have specialized skills
    D) Virtual assistants are too expensive for the affiliate marketing business

10. Which of the following statements is true?

    A) You can succeed only by delegating all your tasks to virtual assistants
    B) You can succeed by doing everything things on your own
    C) You can start delegating tasks to lessen the workload on yourself
    D) Virtual assistants cannot be trusted

Inspiration #9

"Don't be afraid to give up the good to go for the great."
John D. Rockefeller

Chapter 9

Choosing the Right Niche

Choosing the right niche is just as important as choosing the right affiliate program to join. Many beginners start out just making affiliate marketing websites for the first topic that enters their minds. Three months into the project, they are no longer motivated to work on the topic. This is one of the primary reasons why beginner affiliate marketers quit on their project. In this section, we will discuss how you can choose the best niche for you:

Make a list of your hobbies, interests and passions

First, you will need to make a list of the hobbies, interests and passions you have in life. Consider the things that you spend the most of your time in. You could also include a topic about your occupation if you enjoy talking about it. Also, think about the topics that you would like to learn. Choose at least 15 topics and list them down.

Arrange the topics you've chosen according to how much you enjoy talking about them

Next, you should arrange the topics based on how much you enjoy it. Right off the bat, you will notice that there are some topics that you enjoy more than others. Look into these topics first when you are deciding on an affiliate marketing niche.

Survey other people's interest about the subject

Starting with the first topic on your list, you should start researching the interest of other people in the topic. You want to start working on a topic that people are interested in. You can start by surveying the content in your big traffic sources (Google Search, Facebook, Twitter, and Instagram). You could do a quick Google search about the topic and take note of the content that comes out. You could also look into the content marketing accounts in social networks that deal with this type of content. You can guess the popularity of a topic based on the number of engagement they get in social media.

Survey the competition

If you are satisfied with the amount of interest that that a topic gets, you should check the competition in the market about it next. You probably already encountered some of your content marketing competition when you were doing the previous step. Any website that is doing some sort of content marketing is one of your competition because they are trying to take your target audience's attention away. The more competition you have, the harder it will be for you to stand out in the content market place.

Ideally, you should pick a topic with the least amount of competition. However, at times, you can succeed in a high-competition niche by narrowing your content's focus only on the more profitable topics. With the topic recreational running for example, you could choose to focus only on the topic of running gear. You could share content about the latest and best running shoes, clothing and gadgets in the market.

Find the most commonly searched problems about this niche

Now that you have a niche in mind, start planning the types of content that you will create. You should start writing about the content before you even set up your affiliate marketing website. This way, you will be able to start promoting the moment the website is live.

To find topics to talk about, you should start with the problems that people interested in the niche face. If you are just learning about the topic yourself, you should look into the problems that beginners tend to run into. This way, you will also be writing with a beginner's point of view.

Find affiliate products that can solve the problems in these niches

After choosing the niche based on its popularity and the amount of competition in the market, you should look into the available affiliate products you can sell in that niche. You could start by looking for products that will solve the problems established in the previous step.

The easiest way to start is to look for products and brands in Amazon. Amazon sells pretty much everything. If you cannot find the product that you would like to promote in other companies, there is a good chance that it will be available in Amazon.

Amazon though has a low commission rate. To get better commission rates, you should check if the product you want to promote can be found in other affiliate networks discussed previously.

Chapter 9 Quiz
Please refer to Appendix H for the answers to this quiz

1. What do you call a small segment of a larger market where certain products can focus their marketing efforts?

    A) Finance market
    B) Business to Business Market
    C) Niche Market
    D) Open Market

2. How does focusing on a niche market help your website?

    A) It attracts a group of people with specialized needs
    B) It allows the website to attract a bigger number of visitors
    C) It gives the websites opportunities for special promotions
    D) It increases the number of possible content

3. How do you start finding the right niche for you?

    A) Ask the people around me for the best niches
    B) Explore my own hobbies and interests
    C) Look for products online
    D) Build the website and see which content ranks well

4. How do you check if other people are interested about the niche topic?

    A) Visit popular news websites regularly
    B) Ask your friends and family if they will be interested about it
    C) Check related content in social media and the amount of engagement they get
    D) Do an initial ad campaign about the topic

5. Which topic should you take?

    A) Topic with the most competition
    B) Topic with no competition
    C) Topic that has more products associated with it
    D) Topics that has one expensive product associated with it

6. How do you differentiate your website from the strong competitors in the niche market?

    A) Copy the content of the competitors
    B) Pick a specialized niche topic that few people have talked about
    C) Post 5 or more contents every day

D) Use a catchy domain name

7. How do you look for content on your chosen niche topic?

    A) Make things up
    B) Research on the common problems that people encounter when researching about the topic
    C) Research on the ways on how you can promote products to visitors
    D) Buy products in your niche and review them

8. If you are writing how-to contents about the niche topic, who are likely to come to your website?

    A) Random people
    B) Experts in the topic
    C) Beginners in the topic
    D) People who need to solve the how-to problem

9. If you are writing news content about the niche topic where will your content be most effective?

    A) Search engines
    B) Social Media
    C) Forums
    D) Question and Answer websites

10. If you've chosen the basketball sneakers niche, which type of content should you create and share?

    A) Articles about the latest sneakers in the market
    B) Articles about girlfriend of basketball stars
    C) Videos about basketball highlights
    D) Videos about rumors and gossips in basketball

Inspiration #10

"Successful people do what unsuccessful people are not willing to do. Don't wish it were easier; wish you were better."

Jim Rohn

Chapter 10

Building your Email List

Many of the people who go to your website will not necessarily click on the affiliate link. Most of them will just leave without taking any action that helps your business. You can use an email marketing campaign to keep a percentage of these people coming back to your website. Email marketing is effective because it makes you part of one of the most common habits among professionals, checking emails.

People treat emails with a higher level of priority compared to other forms of communication because it is usually used for work. Checking one's emails is one of the first things that most people do when they get to work. By setting up an affiliate marketing campaign, you will be able to put your affiliate marketing business in the screens of people who do have the power and the willingness to buy the products you promote.

To implement an effective email marketing campaign, you will need to learn the steps on how to make people sign up and how to use email newsletters to keep them coming back to your website. The basic steps of an affiliate marketing campaign come in three basic steps:

- ❖ Capturing emails
- ❖ Automated response
- ❖ Sending out newsletters and email-exclusive promotions

Experts say that it takes at least seven interactions with your brand before the average new customer decides to buy. If you want new visitors to come to your shop and buy using your affiliate links, you will need to make them keep coming back to your website, constantly. An email campaign is an effective way to do this. First though, you will need to convince your visitors to give up their email addresses.

You can do this through your content marketing campaign. In your website, you could set up an email capturing tool that appears together with the content. The placement of these email capturing forms is important. Here are the places where you should be placing them:

Before your content

An email form before the content will ensure that the visitors see it. In this position, more people will see it and a higher number of visitors may sign up. Make sure though that it occupies only a small part of the screen and it can be dismissed.

In-content

Most online readers have developed a habit to skip everything above the fold and go straight to the content. Their eyes go from the title of the article straight to the first paragraph. For visitors with this kind of habit, you can put your email capturing tool inside the article. This strategy works because you can use the text in the content or the other types of media to bring attention to the email subscription form.

In pop-ups

Pop ups can be good or bad depending on how you use it. If you use it to promote unwanted ads, then people will hate your website. In the case of email subscription popups on the other hand, you are actually offering something that people may like.

The best part about popups is that you can choose an action that will trigger it. For instance, some popups are triggered after you have spent a considerable amount of time in the website. Some of them are also triggered by activities like clicks or pressing the close button to leave the page. With these triggers, you can capture the emails of visitors based on their intended activity in the website. You can have it triggered for example by a call-to-action button. Or, you can also capture it when the person is about to leave.

In the Sidebar

In the past, bloggers and content marketers mostly put their email subscription forms in the sidebar. This makes the form easily visible, especially if it is placed above the fold. Unfortunately, because of the use of the sidebar for placing ads, internet users have generally developed the habit of avoiding looking at the sidebars. Because of this, the effectiveness of forms placed in this section has decreases.

The increase in the use of mobile devices to view websites has also made sidebars less effective. In a mobile-responsive theme, the sidebars are placed under the content. This means that your forms at the sidebar will only be viewed after the visitor read the content. Unfortunately, between 40-60% of readers never get to the bottom of articles. If you post mostly long articles, expect that the sidebar forms will be ignored. If you post short posts on the other hand, a large part of your traffic may reach the bottom of your content and more people will see your forms.

AMP Pages and Facebook Instant Articles

Facebook and Google are both promoting the use of stripped down pages for mobile devices to increase the speed of webpage loading. Google calls this type of webpage AMP or accelerated mobile pages. Facebook has its own version of this and they call it Facebook Instant Articles.

Both of these traffic sources have guidelines on how to create these types of pages. For Google, you only need to create a special part of your website dedicated to AMP. This type of page is stripped down its usual features. Any extra code is removed and only the essentials are left.

For Facebook Instant Articles, you will need to create alternate versions of your content inside of Facebook. The Instant Articles will be hosted by Facebook themselves and you will need to pass an application process to be able to use this feature.

These types of pages are effective in collecting emails because they are fast loading and they tend to have higher capturing rates compared to the average webpage. The lack of distractions in the AMP and the Facebook Instant Articles makes it easier for people to see the email form you set up. In the case of Facebook instant articles, the email address of the Facebook user is already typed in the form. A user only needs to click the subscribe button to sign up to your email newsletter.

Other social networks

You can also get more email newsletters from the other social media assets you have. If you have an Instagram page for instance, make use of it by mentioning your email newsletters in your post descriptions. You could then add the link to your email subscription form in the bio. This is a much better approach than just to drive Instagram users to your latest content. It will consistently create a call to action that can lead to returning visitors.

Aside from Instagram, you could also mention your email newsletters in your personal and business twitter page. Together with your regular marketing posts, you could include a call-to-action link leading to your subscription form pages. It will be challenging for you to craft a good copy in twitter because of the limit in the number of characters that you can use. You can use other types of media though, like images and videos, to capture the attention of your audience better.

Above, we talked about Facebook Instant Articles. This is not the only way though to collect emails from Facebook. You can also put your email subscription link in the description of your Facebook content. While Instant Articles can also be effective in spreading the news about your website, contents like videos and viral images will have an even greater reach to your audiences in Facebook.

To start, you should pick one piece of content that you will use as your carrier. Ideally, you should choose the type of content that has no other call-to-action feature. For example, you can use a how-to video in your niche. You could also use an image that you think your target market can relate to. If you are satisfied with the content, you could then post it in your Facebook page.

In the description section of your content, you could then add a paragraph for promoting your email subscription form. In this section you could state some of the benefits that they can get for signing up. Together with the text marketing copy, you can then add a link to your sign up form.

Creating a Lead Capture/Squeeze page

A lead capture page is a type of landing page designed to capture opt-in email addresses from potential subscribers. The goal of a squeeze page is to convince, cajole, or otherwise "squeeze" a visitor into providing one of their most sought-after and coveted pieces of personal data: the email address. An example squeeze page is shown below:

To be successful collecting leads, your capture pages need to have the right balance of "ask" and "reward." The "ask" are the form fields you use, and the "reward" is the offer you're promoting.

A lead capture page that asks visitors for irrelevant information to the offer is abandoned because a poorly-optimized lead capture form is one of the leading causes of landing page friction. Ideally, your form should not ask for more than basic contact information on the user's first interaction with your company.

A number of companies provide softwares that help you design these capture pages. One of the good ones out there is clickfunnels. Below are the reasons why:

- Clickfunnels provides you with a LOT of pre-built funnel templates. For those who have never designed a funnel before this will be perfect for you!
- Great visual drag and drop editor which is very beginner friendly
- Huge selection of page elements (name field, telephone number, countdown timer etc.)
- The ability to share your funnels with your friends and clients!
- Amazing onboarding process - Wrapping your head around all that ClickFunnels can do may seem daunting at first. But this is helped by a fun on-boarding process. When you first sign up, you're presented with the 7-day challenge. It consists of 4 different games with each one having a number of steps to complete. Every step features a task and a short video clip of Russell explaining what you need to do to finish it.
- If you're interested in getting a 14 days free trial, go to the clickfunnels website or my website at www.MichaelEzeanaka.com (disclaimer – I am an affiliate)

Limit the number of times you ask for visitors' emails

People do not like it if you keep pestering them with intrusive call-to-action features. You do not want people to leave because your marketing campaign is too aggressive. With this in mind, you should limit your popups to just one per session. You can even program popup plugins in WordPress to stop showing to repeat visitors. This will ensure that your visitors will not get the wrong impression from your aggressive ways of capturing emails.

Ask for emails in a natural way

The language you use when asking for email addresses affects the effectiveness of your tools. Ideally, you should talk in the language of your average visitor. If you are talking to professionals for instance, you can use formal English to talk to them so that they are more likely to engage. If you are talking to young adults for instance, try to use modern colloquialism that young adults use. Your familiarity of your target audience plays a big role in your ability to create your call-to-action statements.

State your email campaign's unique value proposition in your email subscription forms

People will not just automatically sign up to your email newsletter service just because you have your forms set up. You still need to convince them to sign up by promising them the right things. We call this part your unique value proposition. This is a paragraph or a statement that comes with you subscription form where you state the benefits of signing up. You could tell them what they will get for signing up to your website.

Think of different ways for you to get the attention of your viewers towards your signup forms. Some affiliate marketers for instance, give out free digital products like a free eBook or a free trial to a service, to encourage people to sign up to the email campaign. You can also do the same. One way to do this is to create an awesome eBook that fits the interest of your niche market. You could then sell the eBook to Amazon and other eBook selling platforms. Doing this will allow you to establish the value of your books. After setting it up in these websites, offer a free version of your book in your website, telling them that they will be able to read the book for free if they sign up to your email service.

In the process, you could also explain the other things that they can get for signing up to your email newsletters. You could state what types of content you send out and how often you send them out. For instance, you could tell them that you have a video tutorial series that are available only to email newsletter subscribers.

Creating many types of lists

As your website grows, you will eventually find that you have multiple categories of content. This can lead to attracting audience that has different interests and goals for coming to your website. If you are attracting a heterogeneous traffic, you may need to create multiple types of email lists, categorized according to the interests and goals of your market. If the person first arrived in an article about planting green leafy vegetables for instance, you could have him sign up in a newsletter that promises content about planting green leafy vegetables. You also notice that great deal of your visitors is attracted towards your articles and videos about composting. You can create a different type of list exclusively for these people.

It goes without saying that you will need to craft very different autoresponder messages for these two lists. The welcome message and future messages should be related to the interests of your subscriber. You could also create a different list based on the buying stage of the subscriber. You could create an email list for beginners for instance. You could create another one for those who are interested in advanced level contents. Beginners for a topic will need a different set of content and affiliate offers compared to those who are already in the advanced or expert levels.

You could then create a sales funnel. In a sales funnel, you try to convert passive readers of your email newsletters into buyers of your offers. You can do this by adjusting the content that you send to your subscribers, from entertaining and informational to contents that suggest buying products and services.

Engaging with the customer

You should capitalize on the hype that the visitors get when they sign up with your email campaign. The energy and enthusiasm of subscribers are highest at this point. When they sign up, they are eager to see what types of content you have to offer in your email marketing campaign.

Creating your autoresponders

The signup process for email newsletters is pretty straightforward. After signing up with your email subscription form, your subscribers will expect a welcome email. You can set this up with your autoresponder service.

Create your content with your chosen email marketing management service. The email should read in a warm manner, making your new subscribers feel welcome. If you made any promises in the sign up process, you can start fulfilling them in the welcome email. If you promised a free eBook for instance, you should have the link to your eBook in the welcome email of your newsletter.

In addition to the welcome email, you should create more content related to your unique value proposition in the email subscription process. If you promised unique types of content in your email, you could craft them ahead of time and have them sent out daily through your autoresponders. Let's say that your website is about home keeping. You could begin by creating list article where in you talk about 5 ways to keep the home organized. Instead of showing the entire article to your audience however, you could have the content drip in the email newsletter auto responder. You could then have them scheduled to be sent out twice a week so that people will anticipate them.

Make sure that the content in your welcome emails and in the succeeding auto-response to be substantial so that people will find them valuable. If your email subscribers do not view these emailed content valuable, they may end up ignoring your emails or they may choose to unsubscribe.

To automate the process of sending out these autoresponders, you could use email campaign management services like Aweber. With this tool, you can create prepared emails with the names of the future subscriber in the content. You can also set up the emails to send every week. As at the time of writing, they do an initial 30-day free trial. Alternatively, feel free to check it out at my website (disclaimer – I am an affiliate).

Choose your email marketing approach

There is more than one way to craft your autoresponders and email newsletters. In this section, we will discuss the different approaches and email layouts you can use to create your emails.

The personal approach

If you website is heavily reliant on your personality, you may need to use the personal approach in creating your emails. With this method, you are communicating towards your subscribers as if you are writing a letter to them. The goal of any content you add is to create a personal relationship with the subscriber.

This method requires that you show your face throughout the email marketing process. It begins with the sign up process. In your sign up form, you could enhance the effectiveness of your opt-in tools by putting your own smiling face beside it. People love to join email marketing campaigns wherein they know who is behind it. By putting your own image with the marketing materials, you are establishing the trust between you and the subscriber. Remember that you are asking them to give up their email address at this point. For most people, giving up an email address is a sign that they are giving you're their trust. The best part about this is that you will significantly increase the success rate of your opt-in tools. People are more likely to signup if they see a familiar face.

The personal touch continues with the rest of the content that you send to the subscriber's emails. It begins with the welcome email. Together with your picture, you could also write a letter that sounds welcoming and personal. The idea is to thank your news subscribers by personally welcoming them into the program.

To continue this approach, you should aim to write personalized letters to your subscribers as a way to introduce your email content. The more interactions you have with these people, the better your relationship with them will be. With this kind of relationship in place, they are more likely to follow your suggestions and your recommendations. This will lead to higher sales numbers.

The brand approach

If you do not like putting your face in all your marketing tools, you may also choose to use the brand approach. In this approach, your aim is to have your subscribers trust your website, rather than your real persona. While many big businesses use this approach, it may take time for you to develop a brand name and to have people trust that brand.

With this approach however, you will be able to distance yourself from the business. With the personal approach, you need to be present to continue creating email content for your subscribers. They expect personal treatment from you.

With the brand approach on the other hand, the trust is with the brand that you have developed. Because of this, it will be easier for you to delegate task to the people around you. You can send out an email to your list with a less personal note and no one will notice because they trust the brand rather than your persona.

To start with this approach, you need to create uniform way of presenting your brand. To start with, you should decide on a brand name, a tag line and a logo. The brand name will be the name that your visitors will use when talking about your website. The tagline is a short phrase that tells new audiences about what your brand is about. The brand name and tagline should be easy to understand and say. They should roll off the tongue easily. You will also need to design a logo that represents what you stand for. Make your logo characteristics match the overall theme of your brand. If your website is about gardening for instance, your logo could be green and it could have images related to gardening. You can have such a logo professionally created for $5 in Fiverr.com.

To develop your website's brand, you need to show people that your website is a reliable source of information. To do this, you need to make sure that the website is already complete by the time you launch it. There should be no lacking aspect of your website. This will show that the website is backed by competent professionals. Next, you will need to add content to your website in a consistent manner. The content in both your website and your social media marketing assets should be professionally done. Ideally, they should be unique and not copied from other website.

Now that you have established that you run a professional website, the next step is to make this reflect in your email marketing campaign. While people using the personal approach can get away with sloppy newsletters, brands cannot. It is easy to forgive a person for common mistakes but it is significantly harder to forgive brands.

Chapter 10 Quiz

Please refer to Appendix I for the answers to this quiz

1. What is the primary purpose of an email marketing campaign?

    A) Increase affiliate sales
    B) Keep people coming back to your website
    C) To send people unwanted messages
    D) To reach strangers who have never been to your website before

2. What do you call the emails that are automatically sent after a person signs up?

    A) Autosender
    B) Autorepeater
    C) Autoresponder
    D) Autoblogger

3. What is an example of an email campaign management service?

    A) GoDaddy
    B) Aweber
    C) Facebook Pixels
    D) Google AdWords

4. What do you call the faster, stripped down version of webpages used by Google for displaying content in mobile devices

    A) AMP
    B) CBS
    C) BBD
    D) Instant Articles

5. How do you share your email subscription form in Instagram?

    A) Put a link of it in your bio and mention the link in your posts
    B) Put a link in your bio and the description of your posts
    C) Use private messaging to reach random people
    D) Comment the link in the images and videos of celebrities

6. In which placement position is an email form most likely to be engaged with?

A) In the sidebar
B) In-content
C) In the footer
D) In a new window pop-up

7. This is the part of the email subscription call-to-action that states the offer that only you can give the audience. You offer this feature to them in exchange for giving up their email addresses in the form...

   A) Free products
   B) Instant promotion
   C) Email newsletters
   D) Unique value proposition

8. Which practice should you avoid when showing your email subscription form?

   A) Put the form in the body of the article
   B) Show the form in 3 pop-ups for each visitor
   C) Put the form in your social media accounts
   D) Talk about the unique value proposition in the sign up

9. What is a good example of a freebie that you can give people to encourage them to sign up?

   A) Free eBook
   B) Membership to an exclusive websites
   C) Free coffee beans
   D) Discount with one of your promoted affiliate programs

10. What are the two approaches for talking with your audience through email?

    A) Brand and Personal approaches
    B) Business and Social approaches
    C) Single and Married approaches
    D) High-ticket and low-ticket approaches

Chapter 11

Affiliate Marketing Strategies

An effective affiliate marketing strategy should be efficient. One way to ensure this is by keeping the number of clicks between the traffic source and the affiliate marketing landing page as few as possible. The fewer clicks it requires to reach the affiliate marketing website, the higher your conversion rate will be.

If you post your affiliate link directly to Facebook for example, there will be only one click between the source and the affiliate landing page. This is the shortest route between the traffic source (Facebook) and the landing page.

The model looks something like this:

Facebook > Affiliate Marketing Landing Page

In most cases however, this marketing model is not effective because most people are likely to avoid your content if it only contains an affiliate link. It may work to some degree in the beginning. Eventually though, your success rate will go down. Your audience will eventually catch on with what you are trying to do and they may avoid your post.

In addition, convincing people to move from a traffic source to the affiliate marketing landing page can be difficult. Most people do not want to move away from their social networks or their preferred websites. People only willingly click away from these websites or apps if they are motivated to do so. Most people would only move away from their Facebook or Twitter apps if there is an article they want to read or a video they want to watch.

The most successful content marketers use a different approach. They first send their traffic to their website content, where they can convince them to buy the product. They use the content marketing strategies, similar to the ones discussed in this book, to drive traffic from the traffic source to their websites. The model looks like this:

Facebook (Sample Traffic Source) > Website Content > Affiliate Marketing Landing Page

In this model, the process is still somewhat efficient because there are only two clicks between the traffic source and the affiliate marketing landing page. With this model, it will be easier for you to lure your target audience from the traffic source with the use of the right types of contents.

Track the movement of your users

When you are successfully sending traffic to your website through the various traffic sources, you need to set up your analytic tools to track how people move in your website. In the beginning, a big portion of your traffic will bounce. Bouncing refers to the act of leaving a website after viewing just one page. People usually bounce when the content in the website did not pique their interest. This is common with news websites where the average bounce rate is just above 80%. This means that 80% of the traffic leaves the website after reading just one news story.

As an affiliate marketer, you want your viewers to keep reading your content, transferring from one page to another. If this happens, it means that your contents are effective in keeping the attention of your website users. With this method, you will be able to track the movements of the users and identify the types of content that they are likely to click on.

You could also track the total number of clicks that your affiliate links get. The most accurate number will be posted in the statistics portion of your affiliate marketing account. In affiliate programs like Amazon Affiliates and ClickBank, these clicks are shown directly in your account dashboard. You can get the total success rate of your website in sending people to the affiliate landing pages by dividing the total number of clicks on your affiliate links by the total number of unique visitors to your website in a given period. You could then multiply the quotient by 100% to get the percentage value.

Let's say that you want to get your website's success rate for an entire week. You should take the total number of clicks on your affiliate links (found in your affiliate account) and the total number of unique visitors for the week (found in your website analytics) for the said period. You could then use this formula to get the effectiveness of your website in converting users:

Success rate = (number of clicks/total number of unique visitors) * 100%

Let' say that for that week 2,500 unique visitors went to your website. Of that number, 50 people clicked on your affiliate links. Using the formula above, we will get a success rate of 2%. With the success rate, you will be able to predict how well your website performs in sending people to an affiliate landing page in the future.

Judge each affiliate program based on their landing pages

The success rate metric alone however, is not enough to predict how much you will earn in the future. To get this prediction, you will need to get the average conversion rate of the landing page. The advertisers' landing pages are supposed to be designed to increase conversion. A 2-4% conversion rate is normal for a non-optimized affiliate landing page. These numbers can significantly increase to 10% and up if the advertisers test different pages and stick to the page layouts and designs that lead to the most conversions.

Online advertising professionals put a lot of time, working on increasing the conversion rates of their landing pages. However, some landing pages just work better than others. If all other factors are equal, you will earn more if you promote an affiliate program with an excellent landing page. Because of this, you want to stick only with advertisers whose landing page performs well. Unfortunately, you can only check how well a landing page performs by sending leads to it and measuring the results.

The conversion rate of a landing page is usually shown in the analytics section of your affiliate marketing account. If this is not the case however, you could calculate this yourself. To do this, you first need to find the total number of leads (unique visitors) you sent to a particular landing page. This should be reflected in the number of clicks that a particular affiliate link gets. You will also need the total number of sales generated for that particular link. You can usually get this number in the sales report section of your affiliate account.

You can then divide the number of sales by the number of leads you sent and multiple the result by 100%. A higher percentage means that the landing page is effective in converting leads into customers. Sometimes, different websites will have completely different conversion rates even if they are sending traffic to the same landing page. This happens because many factors affect the success of a landing page. We will discuss them in the following section. You can check these factors whenever you are inspecting a new landing page of an advertiser

Factors that affect landing page conversion rate:

The design and layout of the page

You can choose advertisers based on the design and layout of their landing page. If a landing page has no published conversion rate, you may need to base your decision to use it based on these two superficial factors.

Ideally, the design should focus on the purchasing features of the page. The landing page's sole purpose is to convince the people viewing it to make a purchase. If the page has too many distractions or if the purchase buttons are too small to be seen, this may lead to a low conversion rate.

An effective way of checking the design and layout of an affiliate landing page is by using the help of your loved ones. Before you use a landing page, let the people you know check it out first. You could have a questionnaire ready when they check these landing pages. You will need to ask them the following questions:

1. From a scale of 1-10, how likely are you to buy from this page?
2. Do you see a purchase button or link immediately?
3. How do you find the design?
   - Distracting or too cluttered
   - Helpful for buyers
   - Unattractive or outdated
   - Informative or educational
4. If you like the product being promoted, are you going from this page or are you going to find another source of the same product? Why?

By letting the people you know check the landing page and answer the questions above, you will be able to get an idea of how an average person with no marketing background views the page. You will be able to get multiple opinions on the quality of the page. If you just base your judgment on your own opinion, you may have personal biases that may prevent you from choosing the best landing page. Knowing what other people think about the page will help make your decision of choosing a landing page objective.

The quality of traffic that you send to it

At times, an affiliate marketer may get a lower conversion rate than the published rate of a landing page. The affiliate network metrics for example, may say that a landing page gets 7% conversion rate but it only converted 3% of the traffic you sent to it. This may happen when the quality of the traffic you send to the landing page is not at par with the industry standards.

Here are the qualities of the visitors that you should send to your affiliate marketing landing pages:

A. They should have a buying intent

Landing pages work best if you send people to it who are already in the verge of buying the product. This factor is most important to people who are buying something pricey. Low-ticket items are open to impulse buys. A person with no buying intent may buy a $5 shirt from an online retailer without thinking too much about it. Everything changes when more money is on the line. Consider your own personal process when buying something expensive. Do you research first or do you buy impulsively?

Before an average person buys a new laptop for example, they first look around for the newest models from different brands. They then, collect information on the features that are important for them. A person on a budget for example, may take note of the prices of the different models. A computer gaming enthusiast on the other hand, may not be as interested in the prices as he or she is in the performance specs of the laptop. Only after people have collected enough information are they likely to make a buying decision.

You can make sure that the people you refer to your affiliate links have buying intentions by adjusting the types of content in your website. If you already have a website with a lot of articles and other contents, check each of them. Assess your website contents and check whether they are important in the beginning, middle or end of the buying process. Plot the normal buying process for the products you promote. Then, you should create content that will capture more people who are towards the end of the process.

Let's say you are promoting action cameras in your website. You use a GoPro to record your activities like playing with your dog, playing sports, going on vacations, etc. With the content you share in social media, you are able to attract a lot of users from social networks.

The problem with this method of gaining traffic is that the people you attract do not necessarily have buying intentions. They are only there to view the photos and videos you took with your GoPro. Because they do not have a buying intent, they are less likely to click on your affiliate links. To convert these people from being passive audiences into buyers, you will need to create multiple contents (articles and videos) where you can naturally promote the action camera. For example, you can film your trip to a local vacation spot and make a how-to article and video about how to get there and what to do when you are there. In the process, you can write that their experience will be greatly enhanced if they bring an action camera with them. You could then include an affiliate link in your article. In the video you create, you can talk about the same thing and mention that you have link in the description of the video for the item you are recommending.

Aside from these types of contents, you can also create series of contents that are designed to highlight the product you are promoting. For example, you can write an article of record a vlog talking about your own buying decision when you bought the action camera. You can also make a comparison article or video, comparing the product you are promoting with competing brands. Lastly, you can talk about the prices of the product from different sources and the discount coupons they can use to save money when purchasing.

As a recap, here are the types of contents that you should create:

1. Articles and videos to a local tourist spot where you use the action camera
   - Target Audience: Beginners and Social Media Users
2. Article and video about your personal buying decision
   - Target Audience: Beginners and Social Media Users
3. Comparison article and video against competing brands
   - Target Audience: People with buying intent, Google Searchers
4. Article and video talking about the price and the best sources of the product
   - Target Audience: People with buying intent, Google Searchers

These are only some ideas on the types of content you can create for this particular product. You can create all these articles and videos in a matter of weeks. You should also consider not stopping with these four contents. You can create more articles and videos about going to the different tourist attractions in your area. Aside from the action camera itself, you can also make product reviews about its different accessories. Just keep creating content about it and how to use it and people will eventually buy it.

B. They should be capable of buying the product

There is no use promoting your website in places where the majority of people are not capable of buying your product. If you are promoting products from Amazon.com for example, you should make sure that you are promoting to people from the US. Make sure that the tips and recommendations you post on your articles and videos are significant to US consumers. The same goes for the coupons and other promotions you offer.

Aside from ensuring that you are promoting to people from the right location, you should also make sure that the people you are promoting to have the necessary tools for purchasing. This means that they should have access to a credit card or any other method of payment allowed by the retailer you are promoting.

Promoting affiliate products towards children for example, is not just against that law but also ineffective. Children do not have the financial freedom to purchase the product themselves.

C. Shopping seasons and the level of competition in the market

The conversion rate of a landing page will also be affected by the season. A landing page that has a high conversion rate in regular days may experience a dip in its effectiveness during the holidays when there are many other competing offers in the market. In the US for example, the time around thanksgiving and Christmas is usually considered shopping season. People love the promotions in these days. If the products in the landing page that you are using are still offered at their regular prices in these times of the year, your visitors may choose to buy the competing brands or from others sources of the item where there are discounts.

As a response, you should always keep track of the different competing offers in the market. Check the different source for the products that you are offering. If you see that the other sources of the products are offering discounts, you can talk to your affiliate marketing manager about it.

Chapter 11 Quiz
Please refer to Appendix J for the answers to this quiz

1. How do you keep your affiliate marketing strategy efficient?

    A) Keeping ads expenses low
    B) Using a cheap hosting package
    C) Keeping the number of clicks low between the traffic source and landing page
    D) Using hosted blog platforms like blogger

2. Why is posting affiliate links directly in public ineffective?

    A) It may be copied by other people
    B) People will go directly to the website without going through the link
    C) People will avoid clicking on it, thinking it's spam
    D) It is against the rules

3. What motivational trick can we use to make people click on shared content?

    A) Use great headlines and featured image
    B) Promise free gifts
    C) Offer them money for clicking
    D) Use bright colors in the post

4. What do we call the event wherein the person leaves the website after viewing just one page?

    A) Trounce
    B) Bounce
    C) Once
    D) Exit

5. How do you make an intelligent guess if an affiliate link has a high conversion rate before even making it live?

    A) Examine the landing page
    B) Buy the affiliate product yourself
    C) Ask your friends to clock on it
    D) Test it with children

6. What two factors affect the quality of the visitors you send to a landing page?

    A) Intent and capacity to buy
    B) Credit card brand and location of visitor
    C) Country of origin of the product and the visitor

D) Religious and political orientation of the visitor

7. How to you improve click-through rates in your landing pages?

    A) Gather the right type of traffic
    B) Build more websites
    C) Post more often in social media
    D) Buy ad placements in popular websites

8. Which type of visitor has the highest intention of making a purchase?

    A) Search engine users who arrived with a product related key phrase
    E) Facebook users who clicked on your content
    F) Instagram users who clicked the link in your bio
    G) A user that came to check images

9. How does the shopping season affect the performance of landing pages?

    A) People don't buy online during holidays
    B) Bargain hunters spam landing pages to make them unusable
    C) People like to shop during this time of the year therefore, increasing the price
    D) The level of competition increases during this season, making regular offers obsolete

10. What should you do to have a competitive landing page during high volume traffic seasons?

    A) Find landing pages for competitive offers and promotions
    B) Stop affiliate marketing during the holidays
    C) Use more ads during this time of the year
    D) Keep expectations low during this time

Inspiration #12

"The way to get started is to quit talking and begin doing."

Walt Disney

Chapter 12

Tips to Become a Successful Affiliate Marketer

Success in affiliate marketing can mean earning millions of dollars every month. The very best players in the market achieve this level of earnings on a regular basis. How do you reach this level of success? Check out these tips to start:

Sell things and services that you are knowledgeable about

It is easier to become an effective affiliate marketer if you know what you are talking about. If you create a website about a niche topic, experts in the industry will eventually check your websites and view your content. The experts in the industry will know if you are only posing as an expert. If an expert in the niche exposes you, you may end up losing credibility with your audience.

As we've discussed earlier in the book, it is easier to have people obey your suggestions if they see that you are an expert in the topic. Because of this, it is ideal if you start your affiliate marketing career in a niche topic that you are an expert on.

In the beginning, focus on providing good quality content and getting traffic. Many aspiring affiliate marketers focus too much on earning their first buck. If you have this mindset from the beginning, you will be disappointed when the income is slow as you are just starting out. Instead of focusing on the income, shift your focus on the process of creating high quality content first. After you've created your first few articles and videos, turn your attention to getting people to see them. This book provides you with the tools on how you can do this part of the process. All you need to do is avoid worrying about the first few bucks and shift your focus on catering to the needs of your audience.

Keep your online assets active

Aside from creating content and driving traffic to them, you should create a system for keeping your online assets active. You will need to work hard and work smart to achieve this. In the beginning, you will not have a lot of funds to work with. You will be using your personal funds to pay for the business. Because of this, you will need to do much of the work yourself in keeping your website and your other social media assets active.
As you start to earn money, you can reinvest part of it back to the business. Instead of spending all of it, you could use part of the income to hire a VA, as suggested in earlier chapters. Hire them to do simple projects like creating a series of related articles or for managing your social network posting schedule.

Hiring a VA is worth the money if he or she can take tasks that you hate doing. If you do not like communicating with other website owners and bloggers for guest posting, you could have a VA do the email tasks for you. All you have to do is to instruct him or her on what to do, state the steps for his or her work process and supervise everything he or she does every day. By letting your VA do some of the work, you will be able to shift your focus to getting more traffic and continuing to grow your business with high quality content.

Don't stop with one website

There is a limit to the potential of a niche topic. Let's say that your website is about scuba diving and your content is focused on diving related articles and videos. In the process, you use your content to promote scuba diving related gear and equipment. Even if you do get the top spot in Google and your social media pages and accounts become super popular, your success will be limited by the number of people who are interested in scuba diving. If something happens that makes people want to avoid scuba diving (like news about scuba diving accidents), your business may suffer.

To prevent these types of events from damaging your business, you should diversify and explore other niches when you are contented with your first website. This way, you will be able to earn from other niche markets.

You will need to make sure that your first website is earning and self-sustaining before you commit to working on another one. This way, you can leave the operations of that one to one of your VAs and only go back to it once or twice every week.

Learn to cross sell related products

In each of your affiliate marketing websites, you will have one bestselling item. Sometimes, the product that sells best is something that you are not promoting. A scuba diving website for instance may sell more Go Pro accessories than actual scuba gears and equipment. To maximize the growth of these websites, you need to learn about which products are most effective to promote. You also need to learn how to promote related products. When showing a video in your website for instance, you could mention the type of camera that you used to shoot that video and have an affiliate link pointing to that camera in Amazon.

Create a core team to grow your business

The most important part of growing your business is having people around you that you can trust to help you out. As you become more successful, you can hire people to do the work for you. Whether they are virtual assistants or real employees, you should try to keep them if they can do good work.

Each person in your group should play an important role in the group for increasing the income of the business. Keep a core team of great performers and compensate them well so that they will stay with you. You can even take in business partners if they are willing to chip in with the capital of building the business.

Reinvest profits to growing your business

With affiliate marketing, you are using your money to earn more money, especially if you start using paid methods of gaining traffic. In the beginning, the risk is high and there is good chance that some of your ad campaigns will lead to losses. Everything changes however, if you manage to match the right group of people to the right affiliate program. By following the tracking practices discussed in the previous sections, you will be able to make your ads target and reach the right kinds of people.

When you find success with your ad targeting and affiliate program, you should try to maximize profits by increasing the scale of your add campaign. To do this, you will need to reinvest the amount you earn from your affiliate marketing ad campaigns. Use it to fund more ad campaigns or to promote new products to the same audience. If you successfully promoted a camping tent to a group of audience for example, you could cross sell other camping equipment to them. You could then use part of the profits from past campaigns to fund this one.

Renegotiate the terms with the advertiser

If you experience success in promoting a specific product, you may be able to find some leverage to negotiate with the advertisers. You will not be able to do this with big online retailers like Amazon or eBay. However, you may be able to do it with some affiliate networks.

You will be able to contact the advertiser through the support team of the affiliate program. When negotiating, you can ask for special perks that are not available in the regular affiliate marketing program. For example, you can ask for higher commission rates to keep promoting their products. You will need to have a long relationship with the advertiser to be able to ask for something like this. You also should be bringing in a lot of sales for you to be able to demand a pay raise.

You could say for example, that a competing company has contacted you to promote their products and that they are offering a higher commission rate for products of the same price. You could then ask the advertiser if it is possible for them to match the offer.

You could also ask for other types of requests from your advertiser. For example, you could ask for a special promotional coupon that is specific to you website. When a person uses your coupon, the sale is automatically assigned to you. This is a common practice among affiliate marketers who create video content. For this type of affiliate marketers, links are ineffective because they cannot just put links on their videos. YouTube linking features for example, usually do not show in the same way when viewed from mobile phones.

Because of this, many video content creators miss some affiliate sales. Instead of using links to validate a sale, they use coupons because they can mention the coupon code in their videos. The viewers are also likely to use the coupon because it will give them a discount. If you show strong sale numbers, you may be able to ask for this kind of set up from your advertiser.

Don't just create websites, create brands

Your website just serves as the headquarters for an entire network of content marketing assets. The entirety of your online business spreads far beyond the webpages of your website. To make the most of your online assets and all the expenses you put into building and developing it, you should create a brand.

A brand is a business entity that is easily recognizable to the consumers. When your website becomes familiar to the average internet user, you no longer need to write your website name and your tagline for them to know what your website is about. Instead, you only need to show your logo and the visitors will understand what your brand is about. Together with being easily recognized, brands are also associated with certain qualities that are unique to their products, services and company culture.

In the same way, you can also build your website and all your other assets to represent your brand. While your primary method of earning is called affiliate marketing, your business is actually called a content marketing business. With this type of business, you are using your content to drive attention towards your online assets. In the process, you make suggestions in your content that lead to affiliate marketing sales.

A branded content marketing company is not new. All news websites and online magazines are considered content marketing companies. You can also transition your small affiliate marketing website to become a strong content marketing brand. To do this, your audience needs to see positive qualities that they will be able to associate with your brand. Start by making sure that your website and your social media assets are updated in a consistent manner.

You could include a blog in your websites for example, where you talk about tips regarding your affiliate marketing niche. The constant addition of new content will improve your SEO ranking in some keywords. It will also give you something to share organically in your social networking pages. If people expect your website to update regularly, they will remember to go back to it every now and then. While not all of these people will buy from your affiliate links, many of them will help in spreading your content, increasing the reach of each post in your website.

Aside from posting content consistently, you should also aim to continuously improve the quality of your content. If you post spam in your social networking pages, people will associate your brand to spamming. To prevent this from happening, you should only post high quality content in your website. You should not just create and post content for the sake of checking the task off your to-do list. Instead, you should focus on making content because it will be useful to the people who regularly visit your website.

To further establish your brand, you want to maintain a consistent image in all of your online marketing assets. Your logo, name and website tagline should be the same in all these assets including your website, your social media accounts and even your offline presence. The way you talk in these assets should also be the same. If you are using professional English in your website to attract professionals, you should also use the same way of talking in your social media communications. If you choose to make changes in your brand identity (like changing the logo), you should do it simultaneously in all your online assets.

Lastly, the most important quality of a brand is its staying power. Most of us do not actually know how profitable our favorite brands are. Because of this, most people judge whether a brand is successful or not based on its staying power. Brands that still exist are considered strong and those that are becoming less relevant, are considered weak. To establish that your content marketing brand is strong, you should maintain your consistency of posting and creating content. Every now and again, you could create promotions and special events for your readers.

With consistent content creation and marketing, people will look up to your brand as a reliable source of information. If they see your brand's domain name in the search result pages, they are more likely to click on it even if there are other search results entries above yours. They are more likely to trust your content when they see it in their social networking feeds, whether it is in Facebook, Twitter or LinkedIn. Every now and again, they will see your content in apps like Instagram or Pinterest. This may motivate them to give your website a visit. With continued exposure to your content, they will eventually click on your affiliate marketing links when they need the product or services that you are suggesting.

Chapter 12 Quiz

Please refer to Appendix K for the answers to this quiz

1. What can happen if you pose as an expert in a niche you have no experience in that may damage your business?

    A) You will get more sales
    B) People will see you as an expert
    C) Someone may call you out as a fraud
    D) Your brand will look stronger

2. What two activities should you focus on in the beginning of your affiliate marketing career?

    A) Social media marketing and making ads
    B) Gathering traffic and building high quality content
    C) Finding people to work with and passing the work to them
    D) Collecting and sending emails to strangers

3. What is the risk with depending on just one website?

    A) People will not trust your website
    B) You will not have enough domain names for promoting multiple products
    C) People will view your website as amateurish
    D) The business may suffer when the niche market has negative news

4. When negotiating with an affiliate, what should you use as leverage?

    A) Your excellent sales performance
    B) The size of your website
    C) The number of followers you have in Instagram
    D) The number of employees you have

5. What is one factor that makes up the brand identity?

    A) Social media ads
    E) Content length
    F) Website Logo
    G) Website color scheme

6. What make great brands unique from other generic companies?

    A) Unique, recognizable and positive company culture
    B) Low prices
    C) High product demand

D) Unique color schemes

7. What is an example of a positive quality that people can associate with a good content marketing brand?

   A) High quality content design
   B) Video content curation from YouTube
   C) Long articles
   D) Timely and consistent posting of content

8. What is an example of an activity that can hurt your brand?

   A) Creating contents with no videos
   B) Posting long articles
   C) Posting Spam
   D) Removing the comment section

9. Which of the following characteristics contributes to a strong brand image?

   A) Removing the comment section in posts
   B) Posting memes every day in your website
   C) The presence of employees
   D) Consistency in website and social media marketing

10. What is the most important brand quality?

    A) Staying Power
    B) Great Logo
    C) Long articles
    D) Funny videos

Inspiration #13

"The successful warrior is the average man, with laser-like focus."

Bruce Lee

Chapter 13

Proven Ways to Improve Website Traffic

Success in affiliate marketing can mean earning millions of dollars every month. The very best players in the market achieve this level of earnings on a regular basis. How do you reach this level of success? Check out these tips to start:

Gaining traffic is probably the most difficult part of affiliate marketing. You will need to attract massive numbers of the right types of people to your website. You want the types who are likely to be interested in the products you promote and the content your offer. Here are some of the tested and proven ways of gaining traffic:

Guest posting

This method of getting traffic is one of the most intimidating for most internet marketers. In this section, we will discuss how to do it properly so that you will be able to push through with it.

The first step of guest posting is always to create an excellent article. You want to write content on something that you are confident writing about. You want to write about something that is related to the topic of your affiliate website.

When creating the content that you will offer for guest posting, you will need to make sure that it is well researched and it is pleasant to read to the readers of the other website. The readers will judge you based on the quality of content that you will share. If they like your content, they may go to your website and check out your other articles. If they do not like your content, they may ignore you, or worse, talk about how bad your content is in the comments.

After creating the new content, it's time to look for a website where you will share it. To begin with, make a list of websites where some of your target audiences may regularly visit. Ideally, it should not be another affiliate marketing website. Instead, find websites that are considered as authorities in your niche industry.

One option is to approach real world publications and offer your services as a freelancer. You can find a write-for-us section in websites like the Huffington Post or Bleacher Report. These popular website get thousands of requests from aspiring writers every day. You do not want to go after these general publications. Instead, you should focus on the big publications or online magazines that cater to your niche.

Make a list of at least twenty of these online publications. After creating the list, you will need to contact these companies to ask if you can write in their website. To achieve this, you will need to email the administrators of the websites. Most of them have a contact-us page or a write-for-us page. Do not expect that you will be compensated in any way for your guest posting. You will need to do this service for free.

In your email, be courteous and go straight to the point. You could use the same emails for all your applications, changing only small details. In the email, you could provide a link back to your website so that they will be able to see samples of the articles you have written. This will allow them to inspect your content easily, giving them an idea of the type of content that you can share in their website.

If you have confidence that the content you created will stand out and increase the chance that your offer will be approved, you could also mention it in the email. You could talk about what the content is about and how it can be valuable to their website.

If you hear back from them, you may need to ask for the terms of the partnership. In exchange for writing for their website, you need to ask to have a link back to your own website. The link will help your own website in terms of search engine ranking. If the website you will be writing for has a strong marketing arm, you may even get some traffic from the link.

If you are accepted and you agree on the terms of the guest posting, you will be asked to submit a file of the article that you will post. In most cases, the administrators of the website will have suggestions on how you will change the content. The changes are not always significant. They will mostly be done to make your content fit the other types of content in their website.

After some editing, your content will be posted in their website and you may see some traffic come out of it. Make sure though that the terms that were agreed upon are followed. Your name should be mentioned as the author of the content and there should be a link going back to your affiliate website. If there is no traffic surge to your website, you will still get some SEO juice from the link in your content. Once your guest post is up, do not think too much about it. The content is there for everyone to see. If the website has a strong SEO presence, you may have your guest post rank well.

Now that you are done, you should shift your focus on working on a new guest post. You should do one of these guest posts a month. The overall goal is to increase the number of contents you have from other websites. With each guest post you set up, you will get a legitimate backlink to your own website and you may get some traffic.

Some of your contents will be more successful than others. If you see that one of your articles get a lot of attention in one website, you can ask the administrators if they would like you to do another one. You should do this for the websites where your guest posts get a lot of positive results like great search ranking and a high number of referred traffic.

Guesting on a Vlog

Guesting opportunities online do not only apply to online articles. They can also be applied in podcasts and in vlogs. You could follow the same strategy discussed above to book other promotional events. For instance, you could message a YouTube channel manager if you could talk in one of their shows or if they would like you to become a guest in their shows.

If you have a tech website for instance, you could ask to guest in tech shows and news websites. You could also look for podcasts about your topic. The best part about this type of guesting is that you get your name and your work out there without the need for excessive preparations. This allows you to reserve your writing talents to your own contents. Becoming a guest in internet shows can be fun and it does not take a lot of work.

You do not have to travel to the exact place of the vlogger either. You can set up your own working place so that it is suitable for internet videos. News agencies use skype all the time to talk to their guests in the show. You and the vlogger can also do this. This way, it will not cost you much to appear in the shows of other influencers in your circles.

To become a guest, you will need to meet in person or virtually with the vlogger and review what you will talk about in the show. Most vloggers will only invite you in their shows if you are already an established expert in your niche and your inputs in the show matches the needs of their audience.

Search Engine Optimization

The best way to get traffic to your website is through search engine optimization. Search engines are the primary tools used by internet users to get around online. Unlike social media, these tools are used not just for entertainment and communication. They are used to look for specific types of content in the searchable web. Search engines "crawl" and collect information all public websites online. They organize the websites based on the data they collect about it. Mostly, they are concerned with the information found in the website. However, they also collect information related to user experience such as website speed, server uptime and the presence of malware or other dangerous types of codes.

If your website is found to be safe, legal, and easy to use, it will be added to the search database. To match the information in your website the needs of internet users, Google and other search engines use keywords and phrases.

When the internet user enters a word or phrase in the search bar, the search algorithm uses this information and searches all the websites they've crawled for matching information. Because multiple websites have the same type of information, reaching the top spot of the list in the search result pages will require you to deal with intense competition, especially in the most popular topics.

If you do manage to outrank all the other pages in your niche topic, you will manage to attract the people in your niche market. This type of traffic is considered by most affiliate marketers to be superior in quality compared to the ones coming from social networks because they are using the internet to deal with a specific need. If you happen to have the solution to their needs, you can earn by suggesting affiliate products to them.

How to optimize content for search engines

Search engine marketing comes in many phases. The first phase starts in the building and development of your website. In this part of the process, you need to decide on the identity of your website. To establish your website's identity, the search engines will check factors like your domain name, your website tag line and the different internal links (links that lead to other pages inside the same website) you offer in your website's primary menu. Secondary to this, your website identity will be determined by the headlines of your posts.

Ideally, these headlines should have an H1 tag. Ideally, you should start adding the most important keywords in your niche at this part of the process. If possible, you can include your keyword and phrase in the domain name. You should also use related keywords and phrases in the relevant links in your website, especially the ones in your menus. This makes up the basic parts of your site-level optimization.

The second phase of search engine marketing involves page-level optimization. This is the more crucial part of the two because it will be your pages that will be individually ranked in the search result pages. It all starts with the keywords you use in the title of your article. Ideally, the keywords or phrases should be placed in the beginning of the headline. Also make sure that the title includes 50-60 characters only. Google displays this range of characters in the search results.

Next to the title, you should also consider what to write in the meta description of the page. The meta description is the paragraph that will be used below the SEO title. This part should help establish the information in the page to the internet user. You do not have to overthink this part. Just tell the reader, in a conversational manner, what information is included in the page. Ideally, you should make this paragraph be around 320 characters long. You should also include the relevant keywords or phrase in this paragraph.

Next, you will need to create the body of your content. From an SEO standpoint, the body should be at least 350 words long for short content types like news, blog posts and updates. For posts that require instructions and steps, the word count should be north of 750 words to be competitive. The text components of the body should include paragraphs (with a <p> tag) and headings (h2, h3...). You should mention the keyword or phrase multiple times in the paragraphs. It should also be included in at least two paragraph headings.

If the content is intended to show a process, like how-to contents, you will need to use the list tags (<ol> or <ul>). This will tell the search engines that you are presenting a list to the intended audience. Aside from using the list content as your paragraph headings, you should also include multiple types of media to make the content easier for the eyes.

The first type of media that you should add is the text. The text portion of the content is easy to optimize for the search engine because you can simply write the keywords and phrases as they are needed in the paragraphs.

Ideally, the keywords and phrases should comprise 1-2% of your text content. The first one should be included within the first two sentences of the first paragraph. If you have a 1,000-word long article, you should use your keyword or phrase ten to twenty times. You should not allow the content however, to contain more that 4% of the keyword or phrase. More than that, Google may flag you for keyword stuffing. This may have your content penalized for gaming the search engine algorithm.

Next to text, the second most important type of content is the image. The presence of images in the page indicates a break in the wall of text content. By breaking the content into chunks with the use of images, you will make your content easier for the eyes of the user. To make the images help in your SEO efforts, you should include the keyword or phrase in the alt-attribute of the image. In most website content management systems, the option to change the alt-attribute is present when the image is uploaded or edited. Adding a caption also helps to establish the nature of the image.

Lastly, you will need to add a video whenever there is a need for it. The video should complement the content of the website. Of the three types of content discussed in this section, you should be least worried with optimizing the video content. Focus your SEO on the other two types of content.

With these three types of contents, you will be able to establish what the page is about. The next step is to use links to establish how it relates to the other contents in the web. Links come in two types, inbound links and outbound links. You could use your outbound links to link to other pages that may be useful the user. You should do this when the linked page has information that is not included in your own page. The links in your page are either internal (going to other pages in the same website) or external (going to pages of other websites). Feel free to use internal links as you see fit.

However, you should be more careful when linking externally. Make sure that the third party website that you are linking to is safe to use and hosts legal contents. Ideally, the page you are linking to should be related to the topic that you are talking about in the page. Linking to other websites is supposed to supplement the knowledge of the user about the topic. The search engine crawlers (robots that check your website) will use the content that you are using to guess what type of content your website has.

Linking externally should be done naturally. If you mentioned a technical term that a few people may not understand for example, you can add a link to a page with the definition of the said word. Adding the right links is important in affiliate marketing. By making your readers become accustomed to the use of links, you may increase the chances of clicks to the affiliate text links you add to your content.

Now, let's talk about the SEO functions of inbound links. Inbound links are used by the search engine algorithm as a metric for how popular and useful a website is. Inbound links refer to the links from other websites that lead to the webpages in your website. You can use tools like the Google Search Console (sometimes also called Google Webmaster Tools) to check which websites are linking to your pages.

Each link that points to your webpages has a different value. The search engine ranking algorithm considers factors like the age of the domain, its Page Rank and many other different metrics to decide whether a link adds value to the webpage it is pointing to. Many online marketers for instance, believe that links from difficult to obtain domains like the ones with a .gov or .edu extensions are more valuable than those from .com domains.

There are multiple legal ways for you to get inbound links to your webpage. The first one is to do your professional networking in your industry. If you are in the gardening industry for example, you should look for other webmasters in the same industry. Links from their websites or blogs will tell the search engines that your webpages are also about gardening. If most of your links are coming from US based websites with US-centric contents, this will also signal that your content is also for US audiences.

Aside from obtaining links from the websites of people you know, you could also get them by doing guest posting. This is the reason why you really need to negotiate to have a link pointing back to your website every time you do your guest posting. As suggested in the guest posting section of this book, you should choose the websites that you guest post to. They should be related to your niche, they should have access to a market that does not currently go to your website, and they should have a good search rankings. It is ideal if you could get your guest posts from websites with better search engine rankings in keywords that you are interested to compete in.

Marketing in forums and other online communities

Aside from social networks and the search engines, you will need to work with other types of websites that have a big online community. To do this, you will need to look for the types of websites where your average target audience spends a lot of his in. This could be a forum, a membership website or an online app.

If this website has lots of contents, you could also ask to guest post in it. Some blogs for example, has a high following of people that post a lot of comments. With this type of blog, the community it mostly concentrated in the comment section. You may use this section of the website to communicate with your prospect website visitors. Ideally, you should add useful comments in this section to answer other commenters' questions. You could then suggest links for suggested sources of information. In the process, you could also add your own content in here.

Forums are also great sources of traffic. However, forum members tend to be avid internet users. Because of this, they are warry about salesy people online. Before you can convince others to go to your website, you should first gain their trust. In the forum culture, this usually means that you need to contribute content to the forum while following the forum rules. Many forums have point and ranking systems. Active members tend to get more points, increasing their ranking in the website. This gives them certain perks that less active members do not have.

When you have developed a strong relationship with the people in the forums, you can now start promoting your own content. Even if you are already a trusted member in the forum, you should still only suggest your content in the context of the conversation in the forums.

You could also consider looking for Q&A websites. Websites like Quora and the once popular Yahoo Answers, are examples of websites like these. Q&A sites can either be general, like in the case of Quora, or specific. Specific Q&A websites allow only answers related to the topic. There are some Q&A websites for example that focuses on questions related to solving Windows Personal Computer problems. If your content is related to solving PC problems, this may be a good community for you to work with. There are also some that only allow questions about fitness. You will need to find a Q&A website that fits your niche. Only work with it if it has an active community. You can check this out by going straight to their website and checking out the website activity.

Using ads to get traffic

When your website is ready to accept traffic, it's time to start use paid methods to pump traffic into it. It is common to make the mistake of relying solely on organic means of getting traffic. This process takes too long. Let's say you work hard to build your content base and your social media presence. After your done setting everything up for getting organic traffic, the newsfeeds algorithm changes for Facebook, making all your previous efforts futile. A similar event happened to many affiliate marketers back when Google launched its Panda and Penguin updates. The majority of people who depended only on organic traffic were affected the most when pages were penalized.

To learn why you need to use paid means of getting traffic, let us first discuss the differences between free and paid traffic.

Free versus paid traffic

As mentioned above, free traffic is known in the industry as organic traffic. Any visitor coming to your website because of your free efforts in social media and search engine optimization can be considered organic. In the beginning, this will be your primary source of traffic. In fact, it is highly encouraged by affiliate marketing experts that you master the skill of gaining free traffic first.

Free traffic however, is harder to get than most beginners think. The first big factor that works against free traffic is competition. Regardless of what niche topic you choose, there will always be people who will be competing with you. They will compete with you in competing for the attention of your target audience.

If you are promoting a special type of food supplement in your website for example, there will be other people who will be promoting the same product. And you are trying to attract, the same group of people that you are attracting. In the online world, it is easy to track what your competition is doing. You simply go to their websites or their Facebook pages to see what type of promotions they are running. When you become successful, you should expect that your competitors will also be doing the same thing.

With paid traffic, there will also be some competition. However, the number of competing websites will not be as high those competing in free traffic channels. In most websites, there is usually a place for ads, separated from the other types of content. In Google's search result pages for example, the ads are usually located at the top part of the search results. Before the organic search results, you will see two to four ads placements first. Because it is seen first by the search engine user, they are likely to click on it first.

The second big factor to consider when deciding whether to use paid traffic sources, is the speed of business progress. Because of the high level of competition with organic marketing methods, it usually takes an affiliate websites some time before a significant amount of traffic starts coming in. This can be a problem for affiliate marketers with a small capital. The sales come with the traffic that you funnel towards your website. The more traffic comes in, the higher the chances of sales will be. In the beginning, you will only get between 0-10 people coming into your website daily if you rely only on passive and organic means. This is the amount of traffic that you should expect if you are only adding one article in your website and posting one or two contents in your social media channels per day.

The amount of traffic that you get through organic means depends on the number of users you can reach in social media and your search ranking in Google. In the beginning, you will not fare well in both of these marketing factors. With less than 10 people coming to your website daily, you cannot expect to get a substantial income from your affiliate website.

Paid campaigns enhance organic marketing efforts

You should not approach your paid campaigns as separate from your organic marketing efforts. Any success you experience with your paid marketing will also trickle down towards your organic marketing channels. If you make a Facebook ad for instance, some people who do not click on your ads may choose to click on your page and follow it, instead. Some people who do not click on your call to action button in your landing page may choose to surf around your website and they may choose to return at a later date. While behaviors like these do not show as a success in your ad campaign tracking tools, they still have a positive effect on your business.

Using Ads to Get Traffic

Getting few daily visits does not mean that your business model will not work. It just means that you are not getting enough traffic to make the system work. It also means that you are not reaching your target audience with the organic traffic marketing that you are using. You will eventually reach these people with organic marketing methods however, it may take you years to reach your goal.

There are multiple ways to get the amount of traffic that you want. However, the best and fastest way it so use paid methods. Using this method can be risky, especially if you do not know what you are doing. The risk is highest in the beginning when you have no experience of using the advertising platform. You can prepare for your first marketing campaign as much as you can through books and YouTube tutorials but you will learn most of the best practices in marketing with experience. Even if you have decided to use ads to drive traffic to your website, there will still be a lot of planning needed to make sure that you succeed in carrying out an effective and efficient campaign.

First, you need to choose a platform where you will use ads. There are various online platforms to choose from including Facebook Advertising and Google AdWords. These two are probably the biggest mainstream advertising platforms and they are the most recommended for beginners. These two stand out because of the number of people that their platforms can reach. Google AdWords can be used to create ads for search engine result pages, websites using Google AdSense and apps that are using mobile AdSense ads. If your marketing message is better delivered using videos, you can also use AdWords to put up ads in YouTube.

You can target your ads based on the search terms used by people. Text and banner ads shown in website hosting AdSense can be targeted using the type of content in the said website and the information that Google has on the person using the website. For instance, you can make your ads appear only in financial websites to promote your financial affiliate programs. You can also make the ad target market narrower by targeting people only from specific countries.

With mobile becoming the primary way of using Google, the AdWords platform also allows advertisers to target users based on the type of device they are using. If the product you are promoting can only be used through mobile, you can make your ads show only on mobile devices.

Most importantly, Google has a variety of free tools that allows you to monitor and learn from your ad campaigns. For instance, you can use Google Analytics to track the number of visits you get from an ad campaign. With this tool, you can also use this tool to track how these people moved around your website and whether they clicked on any of your affiliate links or not.

Facebook Ads on the other hand standout because of the wealth of information that Facebook has about their users. Just like Google AdWords, Facebook ads can also be used to target people based on the device and the type of network they are using (Wi-Fi or mobile data). The primary types of information used targeting in Facebook though are the person's interests and basic demographics. Basic demographics refer to information like the person's age, gender, location and occupation. Facebook allows advertisers to use these types of information for ad targeting. Advertisers can then use the person's interests to make the targeting narrower. The interests of a person are based on the contents that they engaged with in the network. A person who follows basketball stars and teams for example, will be matched with ads that are targeted to people who are interested in basketball. That pretty much sums up the basic way of ad targeting in Facebook.

Tracking success and refining your campaigns

Your success in affiliate marketing will depend on how you adjust your ad campaigns to make them more effective and efficient. To do this, you will need to use two important tools. The first one is Google Analytics. This tool will tell you how people arrived in your website, what pages they viewed while they were there and on what page they left. If the visitor viewed more than one webpage, additional information like the average time spent on the website will be available.

You can use Google Analytics to decide whether your ads campaign is bringing enough traffic or not. You can also use it to track the movements of your users within your website. Most importantly, you can use this tool to check whether the users you've targeted click on your affiliate links or not.

The next best tool for tracking your ad campaigns is Facebook Pixels. Similar to Google Analytics, Facebook Pixels requires that you use a tracking code in your website. With this tracking code, you will be able to track the website users who come from Facebook. By tracking these people, you will be able to create a custom audience made up of Facebook users who go to your website. By using this feature, you will be able to create ads targeted towards people who are already visitors of your website.

For example, you could create a page that will redirect people to the landing pages of the affiliate link. You could then use Facebook Pixel to track this page. Next, you will need to distribute a link to this page around the website, which will serve as your proxy affiliate link. You should promote this link as you would promote your affiliate website. When people from Facebook click on that link, they will be redirected to the affiliate landing page. But before that, they will first pass through the proxy page, allowing Facebook Pixel to track their activity. Back in Facebook Pixels, you can create a Custom Audience made up of only those people who clicked on that link. This way, you will be able to create ads or boosted Facebook content specifically targeted towards people who clicked on your Facebook link in the past.

Another feature unique to Facebook ads is the ability to create a Lookalike Audience. This type of audience is created by using the qualities of a previous group you've created. Let's say you have a Facebook page with 100 likes. You want to increase the number of likes to your page using a Facebook promotion. You can create the Lookalike Audience feature to target people who are similar to the people who liked your page.

You could also make a Lookalike Audience group from the data you've gathered from Facebook Pixels. First, you will need to set up Facebook Pixels in the pages that you want to track. Next, you will need to create a custom audience made up of people who visited the page tracked by Facebook Pixel. Lastly, you can create a Lookalike Audience based on the custom audience group you've created. The people in the Lookalike Audience group will be new users who have similar characteristics of people who clicked your affiliate link. This type of audience is likely to click on your affiliate links in the future.

While this all sounds great in theory, the reality is that it will take you multiple tries to create the best type of audience group in your Facebook ad campaign. Even if you already have a successful campaign, you should not stop tracking. Keep tracking your campaigns and making adjustments. You should then test these adjustments to keep improving your ads targeting system.

Starting your first campaign

An ad campaign will only become successful if you do the necessary preparations before you start doing it. Follow these steps to increase the likelihood of success in your first campaigns:

Define your advertising goal

All your decisions and the actions you make should be based on one advertising goal. In most cases, your goal will be related to increasing sales. For instance, you could create a goal of sending more traffic towards a specific affiliate link.

Identify the target audience of your advertising

The next step is to identify the types of people you need to reach. You need to create a profile of your target audience based on the affiliate product that you are promoting. If you are promoting a high-end electronic shaver for example, your target will be men who are obsessed with grooming. If you are promoting luxury handbags on the other hand, your target will be women who are interested in fashion and luxury items.

To begin with, try to think of real people you know who are interested in the product you are promoting. Using these people as your inspiration, try to identify the defining characteristics of your target audience. You should include basic information like age, gender and location. You could also include specific information like interests and preferences of the people you are targeting. For example, you can target people with specific hobbies or with important responsibilities.

Identify the platform where you will put your ads

You do not have to create ads in all of the advertising platforms online. This will cost a lot of money. Instead, you should only look for the platform where your target audiences are found. If your target users are searching for the product online, you can choose to use Google AdWords so that your ad will be shown in the search result pages. On the other hand, if the product you are promoting is visually appealing, you can put your ads in highly visual social networks like Instagram, YouTube or Pinterest.

If you are targeting professionals, you could use networks that can target this kind of information. LinkedIn and Facebook for instance are able to group people based on their occupation. You could use these networks to target people of specific professions.

If you are just targeting anyone from a specific location, you also have the option to use CPM advertising. CPM or cost per mille is an advertising scheme where in the advertisers pay per 1000 impressions on an ad. With this type of advertising scheme, you will be able to show your ads to thousands of people. The targeting tools of this kind of advertising are less accurate than that used in Google and Facebook ads. This is more suited for affiliate marketers who are offering products with no specific target buyers in mind.

After choosing your advertising platform, you should learn as much as you can about it before making your first ad campaign. You could begin by reading about how others experienced creating their first campaigns. You can go online to learn about how to do a campaign.

After learning how to do it through people's blog posts, you can learn further by making a mock campaign. Go to your chosen ad platform, create an account and test out their interface on creating your first campaign. You will not be charged until the ad goes live.

Create a plan for the overall user experience

Before you make your first campaign, you should first plan what kind of user experience you will give your audience. In this step, you should draw up how you will make use of the traffic that you will get from the ad. If the affiliate program will allow you, you can make the traffic go straight to the affiliate link's landing page to minimize the chance that the visitor will bounce. Many affiliate programs allow this kind of traffic scheme however, they do specify not to use ad keywords that may compete with their own ads. An affiliate program for a website called ABC.com for example, will usually not allow you to use the words ABC.com. If you choose to use this path, you should use a redirect page to go between the ads and the affiliate landing page. This will allow you to track the number of users that your ad brings to the link. It also allows you to use Google Analytics and Facebook Pixel to track the users.

If the affiliate program does not allow ad traffic, you can still make use of ads. However, you will need to send them to your own website first. If the ad link goes directly to the affiliate landing page, the ad only needs one click for it to be successful. If you need to make them pass through your website on the other hand, you will need to get an extra click from the users to make the ad successful. First, they need to press the ad link and then, then will need to press the affiliate link on the website. To make this ad scheme successful, you will need to create a great landing page in your website that will receive the traffic sent by the ad.

Create your advertising creatives

Now that you have chosen the platform where you will publish your ads, the next step is to create the creatives or visual marketing materials. First, you will need to decide on the type of ad that you will use. Search result pages only allow text ads to show while Facebook allows a combination of image and texts. Ads for mobile are also mostly just text ads while ads published in websites are mostly in the form of banners.

After deciding on a type of creative, it is time make them. Text ads are the easiest to create because they do not need an image to become live. You only need to decide on what your ad will say and then input the statements in the ad creation process. Text ads in the internet usually come in a specific format. The biggest part of the ad is the title and it states what the ad is offering the online user. Below it, there is usually subtitle in smaller fonts. This part explains further the offer made in the title of the ad. Lastly, the last part of the ad is the URL or Domain name where the ad will go when someone clicks on it. Text ads are usually used by cost per click networks like Google AdWords.

Next to text, the second type of ad contains images. These are more commonly known as banner ads because they are usually square or rectangles in spaces around the content. You can create them yourself using Adobe Photoshop or any other image editing tool. You can also use free tools like Canva.com to craft it. If you do not want to make your own ad creatives, you can choose to have it made with websites like Fiverr.com.

When creating ad images, make sure that the offer is clear by adding text over the image. Remember to state a clear offer to the intended audience. With the fewest number of words possible, tell the target audience what you are offering or what problem you are trying to solve. You can use a straight statement that says what product or service you are offering or you can start the ad text with a question. Also include the name of your website. This way, you will be putting the name of your website out there.

With images, you can add whatever you want in the ad. However, ad images with people tend to have better click-through rates than those that only contain images of things. However, there is no way of knowing the effectiveness of an ad image for sure before launching it. The best strategy is to try out multiple images and track the methods of each.

Create a landing page

Next to the contents of the ads, the landing page is the most important part of the entire ad process. If the landing page is convincing, the entire user experience that comes with the ad will convert a high percentage of visitors. Otherwise, the ad campaign will lead to losses.

When creating a landing page, think of how you can convince the ad visitor to buy the product. This usually begins with a description of the product and statement of the benefits that comes with using the product or service. Ideally, you should also add features like testimonials from other users of the product as well as video reviews showing people using the product or service.

Throughout the page, there should be a call-to-action button with the affiliate link. The call to action button usually comes with a text component. Many affiliate marketers use words like "Buy Now" or "Visit Website". Make sure to modify the words that you use here so that they catch the eye of the visitor. You could also test different colors of the call to action button or link. Together with the call-to-action button, you should also include a short descriptive paragraph that tells the users what to expect when they click on the button. By adding this paragraph, you are making the process of going to the website of the user easier for the visitor. Most people try to avoid buttons when they do not know what it does. By explaining what the button does, you will be able to set the right expectations to the prospect buyer.

Just like your ad text and images, you should also try out multiple ad landing pages to see which ones are most effective. You could changes different factors to see how they perform when traffic passes through them. You can change the words that you use in the landing page. You could also change other factors like the images and color scheme of the page. After experimenting and getting enough data, stick to the landing pages with the highest success rate.

Remove distractions from landing page

The average webpage has between 30-40 links, going to various pages inside and outside of the website. You should remove these links from your landing pages. The only links in your landing page should be your affiliate link. You should also remove any other distraction that has nothing to do with the product or service that you are offering in the page.

By removing other distractions from the page, you will be able to prevent the user from doing any other action other than to click on the affiliate link in the call-to-action buttons.

Emphasize the benefits of your products by telling a story

The most successful affiliate marketers are master storytellers. They use their storytelling skills to establish the importance of the product they are using. Marketers like Darren Rowse and Pat Flynn for example, use the storytelling method to tell audience about their online projects. In the process, they also talk about what products they use and how these products help them in reaching their goals.

By using storytelling to talk about products and services, marketers are able to connect with the audience without sounding like they are selling something. You can also do this with the products you are using. Instead of just making a list of the benefits of the product for example, you could talk about how you discovered the product. You could also talk about your contrasting experiences before and after using the product. For example, you could talk about how bad your experience was before you discovered the product. You could then explain what the differences were when you started using the product. Your story will have more credibility if you show an image of yourself with the product.

When you run out of stories to tell, tell other people's stories

There will come a time when you exhaust most of your own stories. While they will still be in the internet for new fans to see, you will need to keep serving new content to keep people coming back to your content. To do this, you could discover other people's stories in your niche. Let's say that you have an affiliate website that promotes fitness products. You started your website by talking about how you personally lost weight and started a healthy lifestyle. A year after creating your website, you are running out of things to say about your personal journey. You know that if you stop making content, the traffic will begin to dwindle, decreasing the earning potential of your website.

To be able to create more content, you could look for other people who are undergoing the same journey. You could ask them if they would like to be featured in your website. You could do it in a form of an interview so that you will be able get answers for the important questions. For example, you could look for gym trainers and tell their story in their website. They could talk about their experience in the fitness industry and provide tips to people who are trying to lose weight. You could also talk about the products and services that they would recommend. You could then post an affiliate link of these products.

By creating the stories of other people related to your industry, you will be able to help them promote their own businesses. You will also be able to tap their market when the people you feature share the content about them in their personal social media accounts.

Do the math to check the profitability of an ad

Before you actually launch your first ad campaign, you should first check the cost and reward aspects of the ad. You will need to learn how many sales you will need to make in the particular campaign to break even. If you begin by creating an ad campaign with a $100 budget for example and you get $5 for each sale you create for the affiliate marketer, this means that you will need at least 20 sales to break even. You can lessen the required number of sales that you need to deliver by promoting products with a higher commission. Ideally, you want to increase the commission with products with better commission rates rather than promoting more expensive products. An ad with the same budget but pays out $20 per sale will only require you to make 5 sales to break even. All your sales after the fifth sale will go directly to your profits.

After learning how many sales you need to make, you can run a small scale campaign to test the conversion rates of your content. For example, you can start promoting an affiliate link with a $20 budget in your chosen ad platform. If the ad conversion rate in the $20 campaign looks promising, you could go on with a full scale campaign by increasing the budget or the duration of the ad. Let's say that a $20 campaign brought you 100 visitors and 2 conversions. If each sale makes a $10 revenue, then the ad campaign will just breakeven.

In this case, you need to make some changes to increase the conversion rate of your overall user experience. One thing you can do is to change the ad targeting. You will need to use the tracking tools discussed above to find targeting mistakes that may be affecting the success rates of your ads. You could also check the landing pages of your ads as well as the landing page of the advertiser. Some landing pages for example, use call-to-action buttons that are too small. Sometimes, these buttons may also be in the wrong color or the text included in them may not be inviting enough to click. These factors need to be changed to increase the likelihood of success. Make sure that the call-to-action button is always visible to the audience. Also make changes with the text in the button. Sometimes changing the call-to-action button from "Buy Now" to "Check Prices" may increase the click-through rate of your page.

Chapter 13 Quiz

Please refer to Appendix L for the answers to this quiz

1. How will you be paid for your guest posts?

    A) Guest posting does not pay
    B) Based on the number of words
    C) Based on the amount of traffic that your content gets
    D) Through affiliate sales generated by the guest post

2. What page should you use to contact a website administrator?

    A) Front Page
    B) Exit Page
    C) Contact Us Page
    D) Blog Page

3. What is one positive effect of guest posting?

    A) Positive SEO effects due to backlinks
    B) Increase in popularity
    C) Social Media popularity
    D) More sales

4. What do you call video journal entries in websites like YouTube?

    A) Vines
    B) Skype
    C) Vlog
    D) Blog

5. What tools can you use to become a vlog guest without going to the studios of vloggers?

    A) Skype
    B) Telephone
    C) Audio Recorder
    D) Text-to-Speech Technology

6. What is the biggest search engine in the world?

    A) Google
    B) Yahoo
    C) Amazon
    D) Bing

7. What do you call the artificial intelligence software used by search engines to collect information about websites around the web?

   A) Search Engine Crawler
   B) Sear
   C) Search AI
   D) Search Engine Bug

8. What is one factor that establishes your website's identity to search engines?

   A) Social Media Profile Links
   B) Video Content
   C) Color Scheme
   D) Domain Name

9. What do you call the second phase of SEO wherein you optimize each article in your website?

   A) Page-level SEO
   B) Site-level
   C) Site Mapping
   D) Search Analytics

10. What do you call the practice of using keywords and phrases unnaturally in an article in the hopes of ranking higher in search engine results?

    A) Crawling
    B) Keyword Splicing
    C) Keyword Stuffing
    D) Search Engine Optimization

Inspiration #14

"Success seems to be connected with action. Successful people keep moving. They make mistakes, but they don't quit."

Conrad Hilton

Chapter 14

Analysis Of Ten Traffic Sources

The success of an affiliate marketing business depends on a variety of factors. How good is the demand for the affiliate products you are selling? How tough is the competition you are up against? What are your profit margins? How many daily visitors is your website getting? All of these play very important roles in your journey towards affiliate marketing success. However, there's one factor that you should be focusing your time and efforts on if you want to maximize the results you'll generate from your website. And that factor is the quality of your traffic sources. There are levels when it comes to the quality of traffic sources. In a nutshell, some visitors are more valuable than others.

Traffic source refers to where your visitors are coming from. These are the websites that are sending visitors to your own website. If somebody clicks on a link on Facebook and he is directed to your website, then Facebook is a traffic source. If someone searches on Google and ends up visiting your website, then Google is a traffic source. If a blog puts a backlink to your website in one of its posts and a reader clicks on that link to arrive at your website, then that blog is a traffic source. Basically, any digital property that sends visitors to your website is a traffic source. It doesn't matter if it's a search engine, a blog, a forum, or an app.

I say it again; traffic sources differ from each other when it comes to the quality of the visitors they are sending to websites. For example, the general consensus is that traffic coming from search engines are much better compared to traffic coming from social media sites like Facebook and Twitter. This is true most of the time but there can be exceptions depending on certain situations. It's important that you are aware of all the sources of traffic out there and how they rank against each other in terms of their value and quality. These are the core concepts we are going to discuss in this chapter.

The Connection between Traffic Source and Affiliate Marketing Success

The quality of your traffic sources is directly proportional to your success as an affiliate marketer. This is not an exaggeration. The better you become in attracting your target customers, the more affiliate commissions you are going to earn. It's as simple as that. This is especially true in the context of the affiliate marketing model. Always keep in mind that as an affiliate marketer, the people you are pulling towards your websites are consumers looking for particular products and services. That is these people are ready to purchase whatever product or service you are promoting.

There is a direct connection between traffic source and affiliate marketing success. With that said, you should be more discerning when it comes to choosing which traffic sources you are going to focus your efforts on. There are literally dozens of potential traffic sources out there. It would be impossible to try and target all of them. So what you need to do is find the ones that can provide the best value for your affiliate marketing business. You have to zero in on the sources where you think your customers are coming from. For example, if your target market is composed of tech-savvy young adults, you are logical in assuming that social networking sites are where your target customers hang out. With that said, it would be a great strategy to allot a good amount of your marketing campaign on social media ads.

The same concept can be applied on any traffic source. Think of the affiliate products and services that you are promoting. Then think of the places online where your target customers are more likely to hang out. **You build your marketing strategies based on these two things.** To come up with the suitable marketing plan, you have to do extensive research on how to reach your target customers. Market research is an activity you will be engaging in for as long as you are in business. Online markets are always changing and evolving so you should be updated of the latest trends and developments. Being clueless of these changes can be disastrous for your affiliate marketing business.

When choosing a traffic source, there are several factors that you must consider. These factors allow you to determine if the particular traffic source is worth pursuing. In this chapter, we are going to look into these factors one by one.

1. The cost of the traffic source.

Every source of traffic comes with a price. Even the ones that are often described as free traffic comes with a cost. For example, search engine traffic is often described by online marketers as free traffic but this is not exactly true. In a sense, you are getting free visitors from Google but these free visitors became possible through your SEO efforts and content marketing methods. Performing SEO and writing content are not exactly free. You need to spend time, money, and other resources in performing them. My point here is that there is no such thing as free traffic. There is always a price attached to it no matter how small.

Traffic sources vary when it comes to the cost of generating traffic from them. These cost differences are not written in stone so they ebb and flow depending on the underlying situation. People often say that paying for search engine traffic is cheaper than paying for social media traffic. But what if you spent $100 dollars on Adsense ads and $50 on Facebook ads, does that statement remain true? Obviously not because you actually paid more for search ads than social media ads. As I said earlier, cost differences between traffic sources vary depending on the underlying situations.

But of course, we have general ideas on how much it costs to generate traffic from a particular source. And these are the figures that you need to look into in deciding if a particular traffic source is worth pursuing or not. So basically, the question you have to ask yourself is this: Am I willing to spend that amount of money to get traffic from this source? For example, are you willing to spend $200 on an Adsense ad to generate, say, five thousand unique visitors to your affiliate marketing website? Or, are you willing to spend another $200 to attract visitors from Facebook? Or, are you willing to spend $500 to rent advertising space on a website for the duration of one week?

Here's what I'm trying to tell you here. The cost of generating traffic from a particular traffic source is dependent on how much you are willing to spend on that source. Some affiliate marketers spend thousands of dollars on Adsense ads and a few hundred dollars on Facebook ads. Other affiliate marketers take the opposite strategy by spending thousands of dollars on Facebook ads and a few hundred dollars on Adsense ads. The situation has been completely reversed. This happens all the time in the affiliate marketing industry. It's just a matter of finding the traffic source that works well for you and spending majority of your budget on that source.

So, when you look at a traffic source and start thinking if you should try generating traffic from it, you think about how much it will cost to generate that traffic and how much return you are going to get from your money's worth. For example, you want to give Facebook ads a shot. You plan on setting aside a budget of $200 for your first ad. But before you purchase the ad, you need to learn about the potential returns from the ad. Are the returns worth $200? Let's say that the ad generates ten thousand visits for your website. Is that worth $200 for you? If that's a good return for you, then by all means go and purchase the ad. But if you think the return isn't worth it, you are more than free to not push through with the ad. In a nutshell, to pursue a traffic source more often than not depends on the personal preferences of the affiliate marketer.

2. The amount of traffic available.

Some sources send more traffic than others. For now, the largest mover of web traffic is still Google and the other lesser-known search engines (Bing, Yahoo, and Ask). Search engines still rule the game but social media sites are quickly catching up. In fact, there are some experts who believe that it's just a matter of time before social media sites will surpass the amount of traffic that search engines generate. Looking at the way more and more people are using social media sites for content instead of using search portals, it's not that difficult to believe that this may happen any time soon.

Online traffic is pretty much unlimited. There's no limit to the number of visitors you can attract to your website. The question is which traffic sources will bring you the maximum number of visitors. Is it Facebook? Is it Google? Is it Instagram? Is it direct advertising? You should be asking yourself these questions before you embark on your traffic generation campaigns. To find answers to these questions, you need to consider factors like the type of product or service you are promoting, the type of audience you are targeting, and the number of people using the platforms that drive online traffic. For example, Facebook now has more than two billion active users. This is without a doubt a huge source of traffic but are people on Facebook the kind of people who would be interested in your product or service? Always think of this before you pursue a traffic source.

3. Restrictions, regulations, and rules.

Majority of traffic sources have policies and regulations in place wherein they make restrictions on certain topics, products, and services. A very good example of such restrictive policies is Google Adwords' prohibition of advertisements that are related to alcoholic beverages, drugs, adult content, and gambling. If you attempt to create an ad promoting any of these topics, it will either not be approved or you get banned for it. This is why you should always read an advertising network's policies and regulations before you start creating an ad using the platform. These restrictive policies are not exclusive to advertising networks like Google Adwords. Every digital platform today that can be used for marketing purposes has these restrictive policies.

It's important to be aware of these policies and regulations to prevent mistakes that can hurt you and your business. For instance, a huge number of advertisers using Google Adwords had their accounts suspended and banned for breaking the network's content policies. **If you plan on generating traffic from advertising networks, this is a mistake you shouldn't make** because you are going to need Google Adwords. It's the biggest advertising network so if you want your ads to reach the widest audience possible, Google Adwords is the network you should be using. The same can be said about other traffic sources like social media. If you want to generate traffic from them, then make sure that you don't break any of their restrictions and regulations.

4. The overall quality of the traffic source.

When you sit down and try to determine which traffic sources you should target, you take into account the value of each source to the type of business you are trying to promote. You then rank the traffic sources based on their quality and value. The traffic sources that are on top of your list will become your priorities. This is the best way in ensuring that the traffic sources which provide you with the most value are accorded their fair share of time, money, and resources. If you think social media will provide you the best value, then the largest chunk of your traffic-generation budget will be devoted to social media marketing.

The general consensus is that search engines are the best sources of traffic. This may be true most of the time but there are exceptions. There will always be exceptions. This is something that you should always remember about generating web traffic. Just because your friend Jerry gets most of his web traffic from search engines doesn't necessarily mean you should do the same. Some online marketers prefer social media traffic over search engine traffic. The point here is that it all depends on the type of affiliate marketing business you have and what works for your campaigns. If search traffic brings you the greatest number of customers, then search traffic is for you. If social media brings you the greatest number of customers, then social media traffic is for you.

5. The targeting options available (e.g. gender, browser, devices, languages, categories, etc.)

One of the biggest advantages of online marketing is that you often have the power to choose the specific kinds of people who will be receiving your content and messages. This is called targeting and it's very powerful because it allows you to reach the people who are most likely to be interested in whatever product or service you are offering. For example, let's say that you are selling a fantasy novel for teenagers and young adults. It's your plan to focus your marketing campaigns on Facebook. If you are to create an ad on Facebook, you would want that ad to be seen by teenagers and young adults. Fortunately, Facebook allows you to target this audience by customizing your ad so that it will be delivered to the news feeds of Facebook users who are between the ages of 14 and 18.

That's just an example. You can customize the target ages in any range you want. Not only that, you can also target your audience based on gender, interests, and demographic location. That's how powerful targeting can be. All advertising networks have targeting algorithms in one way or another. You should take advantage of these programs whenever you can because they make it a lot easier for you to reach your potential customers. Of course, targeting will only work well for you if you have a clear understanding of your market. Targeting is only effective if you know what kinds of people will be interested in buying your product or service. If you're interested in learning how to leverage the power of facebook advertising to market your products, take a look at Facebook Marketing For Beginners - Learn The Basics Of Facebook Advertising And Strategies In 5 Days And Learn It Well

6. The niche or audience.

In deciding whether you should spend money and resources on generating traffic from a source, you must also consider your niche and audience. The visitors you are attracting should match the type of products and services that you are promoting in your affiliate marketing website. So in a sense, it's about making sure that you are not wasting your time and efforts on bad and unsuitable traffic. **To determine if a traffic source is appropriate for your niche or audience, you need to have an understanding of that source's user base**. This is especially true if you are planning to generate traffic from social media sites or specific websites and blogs.

For example, if you are planning to drive traffic from Instagram, you have to know what kinds of people use Instagram. Generally speaking, Instagram users are young and tech-savvy individuals who are caught up on pop culture, trends, music, movies, beauty products, and fashion. So, if you are running a website that promotes fashion and beauty products, Instagram may be a great source of traffic for your business. If you are running a business that offers tips and advice on real estate, Instagram won't be a good fit for your business. Facebook or LinkedIn or even YouTube would make for better choices.

The main takeaway here is that the best source of traffic for your affiliate marketing website depends on the various considerations we have discussed above. You need to take the time to weigh all of your options. Don't drive traffic for the sake of driving traffic. You have to identify if the traffic you are generating is providing the best value for your time and money. This is especially true if you plan on spending a lot of resources on advertising. You have to make sure that your budget will not go to waste. Your success in generating traffic will greatly depend on how well you have planned your traffic-generation campaign.

Without further ado, let us now take a look into the various methods on how to attract high-quality traffic to your affiliate marketing website and business. If you want to maximize the number of visitors you get, these are the strategies you should be using. I am not in any way saying that you should use all of them. My advice for you is to experiment with them and find the ones that generate the best results for your business. After identifying the methods that get you the most traffic, you should make such methods the priority of your campaigns. It takes time to test out these techniques so don't rush. Slowly but surely is the name of the game.

Inspiration #15

Our greatest glory is not in never falling, but in rising every time we fall.

Confucius

Traffic Source #1 - Banner Ads

Majority of websites today employ a form of banner advertising in one way or another. Almost all advertising programs like Google Adsense generate the biggest chunk of their revenue from banner advertising. With that said, banner advertising is without a doubt the most ubiquitous form of online advertising out there. Remember those square and rectangular advertisements populating almost every website and blog that you visit? Those are banner ads. Those banner ads are either directly rented by an advertiser or delivered by an advertising program and network like Google Adsense.

Banner advertising is also often commonly referred to as display advertising. This term is usually used to differentiate banner advertising from text-only advertising. The goal of a banner ad is to promote another website. If a website visitor clicks on the banner ad, he or she is redirected to another website or landing page. The banner could be just an image (png, jpg, jpeg) or a multi-media object (flash, HTML). Banner ads have evolved through the years. The simple image-based ads of yesterday have given way to complicated banner ads created using various programs and software. Some banner ads combine images, animations, and even videos.

Based on how they interact with the intended audience, banners ads can be grouped into any of the following two categories:

1. Static Banner Ads – These are simple images and visuals that a website visitor can just click on to be redirected to the intended website or landing page. The ads don't move nor interact with the visitor in any other way. These are much easier to create and they are usually cheaper as far as advertising costs are concerned.

2. Animated or Dynamic Banner Ads – These are banner ads that feature moving images and animations. They are usually created using Flash software, JavaScript programs, or any other program. Many advertisers prefer animated or dynamic banner ads because these are flashier which means they are more effective in getting the attention of website visitors. However, some webmasters don't use animated or dynamic banner ads for the same reason. They say that these are too intrusive and they divert the attention of readers from their content to the ads.

Aside from generating traffic, what else can banner ads do for you?

Well, there's a lot actually. Banner advertising is the perfect tool for building brand awareness. Brand marketing is all about making yourself available in as many places as possible right? Think of Coca-Cola putting their logo and name on every imaginable thing. That's the core of building a brand. That's the approach you should take when marketing yourself online. And banner advertising can do a lot for you in this regard. To maximize your exposure, I highly recommend that you take full advantage of advertising networks like Google AdWords. AdWords displays your banner ad in websites and blogs that its algorithm thinks are relevant to what you are advertising.

Banner advertising is also an efficient tool for lead generation. If you are in the business of generating leads, then banner advertising should be among the top priorities in your marketing kit. Whether you are trying to attract new subscribers to your newsletter or you are looking for potential clients for a service you are offering, banner advertising can help you in finding good leads. What a lot of marketers do is create a sales page or a lead page which serves as the destination point for their banner advertisements. People who click on the banner ads are redirected to these simple but highly optimized lead pages. The biggest advantage of directing people to a lead page is that they are immediately confronted with an offer that they find difficult to refuse. They have to take quick action or the offer slips away from their hands.

How about click-through rates?

The click-through rate is the measurement pertaining to the number of times that a banner ad is clicked in the context of how many times the ad was viewed and displayed. With that said, **the click-through rate is calculated by dividing the number of clicks that the ad got over the number of times that the ad was viewed or displayed**. For example, let's say that the banner ad was viewed one hundred (100) times. If out of those 100 views, the ad was clicked five (5) times, then the banner ad has a click-through rate of 5%. Needless to say, the click-through rate depends on how effective the banner ad is on attracting a visitor to click. In most cases, a click-through rate between 5% and 10% are already considered as high and excellent. Majority of banner advertisements have click-through rates of below 5%.

The good news here is that banner ads are among the ad types that enjoy the highest click-through rates in the online advertising industry. In short, banners are very efficient in generating clicks if you play your cards right. Creating a good banner ad is a combination of making a catchy image and communicating the value that the ad has in store for the viewer. **The ad should contain an image that piques the interest of the viewer. The ad should also communicate to the viewer what the ad is all about.** For example, if you are promoting an online store selling art supplies, the image in the ad should easily inform the viewer that if he clicks on the ad, he will arrive at a website about art supplies. *If your ad meets these two important criteria, your click-through rate should be higher than average.*

How to Create a Banner for Advertising

Creating a banner ad is not as difficult nor complicated as you might think. You don't have to be a professional designer to create one. There are even tools, applications, and resources online that you can use to make one like Bannersnack. A lot of these tools and apps are free to use so you have nothing to lose. It's even easier to create a banner ad if you are using an advertising network like Google AdWords. The network offers you with tools, guides, and other resources to help you create your banner ads. When designing a banner ad, make sure that it can help in achieving the goals you have in mind. For example, if you want your banner ad to attract and entice viewers to click and subscribe to your newsletter, then you have to design the banner ad in such a way that it communicates this purpose. The banner ad shouldn't be misleading in any way.

Here are the core steps in creating a banner ad.

1. Identify your goals. Don't start creating a banner ad unless you have clearly identified what you want to achieve from it. This is very important. A very common mistake among new advertisers is that they assume that as long as their banner ads are flashy and professional-looking, these will get the clicks they need. Nope. Banner advertising isn't solely about being flashy and colourful. The banner ads should've been designed with the proper goals in mind. For example, if you want to attract subscribers to your newsletter, your banner ad should contain a call-to-action like "Click Here to Subscribe", "Subscribe Here", or "Click Here to Learn More". If you want your banner ad to attract customers to a store selling beauty products, the ad should contain images of the most popular and trending beauty products in the current market.

2. Choose the sizes of the banner ads. Another common mistake among new banner advertisers is assuming that larger is always better. They think that the larger the banner ad is, the more clicks it will generate. Well, this is not always the case. Sure, bigger banners tend to get more views but this doesn't mean they get more clicks as well. The size of the banner ad depends on various factors like the type of product or service you are promoting, the type of website you are advertising, the budget you have available, and the type of websites where you want your ad to appear in. You have a lot of options when it comes to banner ad size. The most used ad sizes are as follows:

- 300 x 250, medium rectangle
- 336 x 280, large rectangle
- 728 x 90, leaderboard
- 300 x 600, half page
- 468 x 60, banner
- 234 x 60, half banner
- 120 x 600, skyscraper
- 160 x 600, wide skyscraper
- 970 x 90, wide skyscraper
- 200 x 200, small square
- 250 x 250, square

3. Decide if you are going to use static or animated banner ads. The biggest difference between a static ad and an animated ad is that animated ads are much better in attracting attention due to their dynamic nature. However, you should understand that animated banner ads aren't applicable on everything. There are some products and services that are better promoted with static ads. So, choosing between a static or animated banner ads depends on the product or service you are promoting. Advertising budget is also a major consideration. Needless to say, animated banner ads are usually costlier which means you need a larger advertising purse if you are going to implement mostly animated ads.

4. Design the images yourself or hire a graphics designer to do it for you. If you have decent design and programming skills, you should try making the banner ads yourself. The biggest benefit of making the banners yourself is that you have full creative control over the campaign. You can do everything your own way. However, if you don't have the technical skills to design and make the banner ads yourself, I highly recommend that you hire a skilled and experienced professional to do it for you. It's not that hard to find freelance designers and programmers these days. There are thousands of them out there. You just have to find them. Start with freelancing platforms like Upwork, Fiverr, Craigslist, LinkedIn, etc. You can find talented designers with very affordable rates in these sites.

5. Test the banner ads if they are working and displaying properly. Before you start using the banner ads, make sure to test them several times to make sure that they are free from bugs and that they are displaying without any problems. The only way to test the ads is to make them live for a sample or test website. You then visit that website using a different device to check if the ads are there and if they are displaying correctly. Click on the ad to see if it redirects to the right website.

6. Launch the ads. After testing the ads several times and seeing no issues, you can now fully launch them on any website or advertising network you signed up for. Even after launching the ads, you should make the habit of regularly checking on the ads and their codes to see if they are functioning properly. Sometimes, even if your ads are malfunctioning, your advertising budget is still running. That means you can potentially lose a lot of money from ads that aren't functioning properly. That's a double whammy if you ask me. You don't get the clicks you are looking for while losing money in the process. This isn't a good scenario. So make it a point to regularly check on your ads.

Pricing Models: How Much Does Banner Advertising Costs?
The cost of banner ads is characteristically calculated based either on a per click basis or on a per mille basis. Paying for a banner ad on a per click basis means you incur cost every time a viewer of the ad clicks on the ad. The cost of a click varies depending on the ad and the network hosting the ad. It could be a few cents. It could also be more than a dollar. On the other hand, if the banner ad runs on a per mille basis, you incur cost every time the ad is viewed a thousand times. This is why it's also referred to as "cost per thousand". For example, if the cost per mille is $5, your advertising expenses will be $10 if your banner ad was viewed two thousand times.

The cost of the banner ad is also significantly affected by the ad's size. Naturally, larger ads are more expensive because they occupy more space in a website. The location of the ad also affects overall costs. This is especially true if you are directly purchasing banner ads from website owners. Banner ads that appear above the fold are more expensive compared to ads that viewers are only able to see if they scroll down. Above the fold refers to the visible parts of a website when a user visits the website. Above the fold banner ads are more expensive for the simple reason that they are prominently displayed in the website.

The Pros and Cons of Banner Advertising
Visit any website that contains advertising and it's likely that one or two of the ads you see are banner ads. Banner advertising has been around for a long time but their popularity has never really waned. There's a reason why most advertising platforms like Google Adsense and affiliate marketing companies go out of their way to provide you with banners to use in your marketing campaigns. That

reason is the fact that banner ads are effective and powerful. With that said, if you are planning your own marketing and promotional campaign, you should seriously consider using banner ads. But before you do, you need to be aware of the pros and cons of banner ads.

Pros of Banner Advertising

1. Ease of setup and use. You can create a banner and send it to the website you've contracted for advertising in the span of just a few seconds. That's how quick the process especially if you have a banner image ready. You don't need any technical knowledge about HTML, Flash, or JavaScript. Basically, what you need to have is a destination URL and the banner image location. This is if you are directly dealing with the websites where your ad will appear. The process is a little bit more different if you are using an advertising network like Google Adsense. In this instance, you only design the look of the banner ad. Delivery of the ads to websites is the responsibility of the advertising network.

2. Banner ads are less intrusive compared to other forms of online advertising. If used properly, banner ads can actually help in adding value to the content of a website because they refer the reader to relevant websites with similar content. Hence, most people don't have any major negative reactions to banner ads. This is also the same reason why banner ads tend to have higher than average clickthrough rates. Online people hate ads like pop-ups and fly-ins because these are too intrusive. You don't have this problem if you are using a well-designed and properly sized banner ad.

3. Banner advertising allows you to perform more accurate split testing. Split testing is the process of experimenting with two sets of ads with the goal of determining which ad type will get better results. For example, you create banner ad A and banner ad B. You launch both banner ads then track their results and performance for a set period of time. You then take down the ads so that you can analyze the performance of the ads. Find the ad that got the better results and use that ad again. Banner advertising is usually image-based which is why it's the perfect type of ad for split testing.

4. You are in control of the ads. Banner advertising offers you control over the ads that you create and distribute. If you are doing direct banner advertising, you get to choose the websites where your ads will appear. If you are using the services of an advertising network like Google Adsense, you lose some of the control but overall, you still decide what your ads contain and how they look like to viewers. Being in control also means you can change the design and look of your banner ads whenever you deem it to be necessary. If you are not getting the results you expected, you can pause the ads so that you can implement the necessary changes.

5. Banner ads are not that expensive compared to other forms of online advertising. This is for the simple reason that banner ads require less resources to create, they occupy less space, and they are less complicated. In most cases, advertising networks charge less for them compared to other types of online advertisements. The only type of advertising that can claim to be less expensive than banner advertising is textual advertising. Be that as it may, the differences in pricing are not that much. If you want to get the most out of online advertising but you are operating with a very tight budget, I highly suggest that you purchase ads composed of a combination of banner ads and textual ads.

6. You have access to a wide variety of ad designs. This is the beauty of image-based advertising which is basically a category which banner advertising falls into. You have all the flexibility to come up with different designs and formats for your ads. You can create the images yourself or you can avail of the services of a professional graphics designer. You have a lot of options. Some advertising networks even go out of their way to help you design your banner ads. For instance, Google AdWords provides you with tools and resources to help you come up with the right designs for your ads. Other advertising networks do the same for their advertisers.

7. Banner ads are universally accepted by all ad server solutions. This is very important if you plan on taking the services of advertising networks. Before your banner ad can display properly in websites and other digital spaces, it should be fully accepted and compliant with the ad server. The good news is that all ad providers and networks today offer banner advertising services. That said, you don't have to worry about your ads not displaying properly or not linking to your own website. Ad servers are the foundation of advertising networks. A server is the lifeblood of the network. Without the server, the ads can't be delivered to where they are supposed to be displayed.

Cons of Banner Advertising

1. Banner ads are the usual victims of ad blocking programs and software. If you are not familiar with ad blockers, these are basically online programs or applications that block and prevent ads from displaying on the websites and blogs that you visit. These programs are usually free, easy to download, and even easier to install to a browser. If an online user has an ad blocker installed to his browser, this means that most if not all your banner ads will be blocked and prevented from displaying. Ad blockers have gotten better over time so their success rates range from 95% to 99%. This can be a huge issue if you plan on generating a sizable numbers of visitors via banner advertising.

2. Competition among banner advertisers is very tough. And it's likely to get tougher in the coming months and years as more entrepreneurs and businesses get in on the action. With more banner ads entering the pool, it will get harder and harder for you to get your ads in front of your target market. It doesn't matter what niche you belong to, the increase in competition is basically the same. The number of banner ads will continue to double and triple with the passage of time. To get ahead of the competition, you have to be willing to increase your budget so that you can reach more people. You have to understand that banner advertising is very similar to a bidding process. Advertisers with bigger budgets tend to get the best results from their banner advertising campaigns.

3. Online users are starting to have ad blindness towards banner ads. Ad blindness is a growing problem in the online advertising industry. Simply put, online ads like banner ads aren't as effective as they used to be. There are a few reasons why ad blindness occurs. One, online users are getting smarter in the sense that they can easily spot ads and separate them from content. They see the ads but they are indifferent towards them because they know that these are paid ads. Another reason for ad blindness is the ubiquity of banner ads. Almost every website these days has some type of banner advertising. In short, they are everywhere. They are too common that online users ignore them every time they come across them.

How to Get the Most Out of Banner Advertising

1. Use the most effective and standard banner ad sizes. To identify the most effective banner sizes, you have got to listen to the experts. For example, Google Adsense says that the most effective banner sizes in their advertising programs are Leaderboard, Half Page, Medium Rectangle, and Large Rectangle. There's absolutely no reason why Google Adsense should lie so you should take their advice and put them to action. Other advertising networks advise their publishers about the banner sizes that work well for them. You should listen to them because they have the same goals as you are. And that is to get the best value from your money and ad campaigns.

2. Keep it simple. It's amazing how a lot of online advertisers think that the more complicated their ads are, the more results they can generate. That's not the case at all especially today wherein there's an overload of information and content. It's still best to keep your banner ads simple, clean, and clear. Get rid of all the unnecessary bells and whistles. You need to focus on the communication aspect of the ad. The ad should be able to quickly tell the viewer what it's about and what's in it for the viewer. For example, if your ad is about art supplies, the ad should inform the viewer that he/she will find content about art supplies if he/she clicks on the ad. Being direct and straightforward is the keyword here. You have to get the attention of the viewers in three seconds or less.

3. Use buttons properly. Buttons on banner ads can be very effective if they are implemented properly. They can be annoying and intrusive if used improperly. Buttons play an important role in increasing a banner ad's clickthrough rate. The best place to put a button is on the lower right side of the banner ad just below the ad's main content. Use contrasting colors so that the buttons can be easily identified by the viewer. Furthermore, if you are using several versions of your banner ad, make sure that the buttons are consistent in all of them. I also suggest that you split test various versions of the buttons to determine which types and formats of buttons get the most clicks from viewers.

4. Clearly define the frame of the ad. Why is this important? One way of improving a banner ad's clickthrough rate is to make sure that the viewer knows which or where to click. If your banner ad has undefined frames, it may be difficult for the viewer to identify where he should point his mouse. This leads to a lot of clicks that go nowhere. A lot of online marketers advise using undefined frames because this technique helps in making the ad blend well with the website content. However, this is only applicable for textual ads because they are very similar to the content. But when it comes to banner ads which are mostly image-based, you need to clearly define the frames so that viewers know where the ad starts and where it ends.

5. Make your text instantly readable. There is no single way to create a banner ad. It could contain text, images, buttons, or a combination of all of these things. For the banner to work, it should contain a headline and a tag line if necessary. The general rule is that if you have both a headline and a tag line, the font sizes of the two texts have to be different. This makes it so much easier for the viewer to read. Again, you need to use contrasting colors. The color of the text should contrast with the color of the background so that the text can be easily read by the viewer. Most banner advertising experts advise that you use clear font weight, short sentences, and short lines. The copy within your ad should be four lines or less. If you go beyond four lines, your banner ad will look cluttered and spammy.

6. Make the ad visually blend with the sites where it's featured. If your ad visually blends into the digital spaces where it's featured, you have better chances in getting the viewer's trust. If viewers trust your ad, they are more likely to click on it. You can easily create an ad that blends if you are directly dealing with the sites where it will be displayed. You know exactly what the sites look like so you have an idea about the colors and fonts that you are going to use in your ad. However, if you are feeding your ad into an advertising network like Google AdWords wherein you don't have the power to pick where your ad will be displayed, it's difficult to create ads that blend. So what you need to do is look at the common themes and designs of websites in your niche to help you come up with ads that visually complement such themes and designs.

7. Make sure that your banner ads are consistent with the brand you are trying to develop and build. Your banner ads will be shown in numerous places online so it's a powerful way to hype up your brand. To avoid confusing your target audiences, you should be consistent with your banner ad designs and themes. Imagine if Coca-Cola used a lot of colors aside from red in its branding strategies? It wouldn't have worked right? If you see a Coca-Cola ad, the color red is everywhere. That's what you should be doing with your banner ads, not just with the colors but with other aspects like buttons, fonts, and logos.

8. Instill a sense of urgency in your banner ads. Have you ever wondered why online marketers are so fond of associating timetables with their products and services? Jerry is selling his ebooks for $3 for two weeks only. Matthew is offering discounts for his graphic design services until the end of the month only. Larry is offering a free download of his game app for 24 hours only. And so on and so forth. Why do they do these? Because it creates a sense of urgency and encourages the customer to avail of the product or service before it's too late. You can apply the same concept into banner advertising. This is very powerful if you are selling a product or a service in the destination URL.

9. Only choose graphics and images that enhance your ad message. When choosing a graphic or image for your banner ad, it should meet the following criteria. One, the image should enhance your message. Two, it should be directly related to your product or service. And three, it should complement the brand that you are trying to build. For example, if you are promoting outdoor products like tents, hiking shoes, and trekking poles, the graphics and images you are going to use in your banner ads should contain scenes and imagery that are related to the outdoors. The images will instantly inform the viewer that the ad is about being outside and enjoying nature.

10. Keep the file size of your ad small and minimal. Banner ads are like websites. If your banner ad takes too long to load, the viewer will become disinterested. The general rule is that the banner ad should be under 150 kb. This is the size that Google Adwords recommends for its advertisers. It makes complete sense because the smaller the size of your ad, the faster it loads. Your ad needs to load fast in a page before the viewer loses interest and scrolls down the page. With that said, banner ads that loads slow lead to lost opportunities. You will be losing a lot of potential customers of your ads are not loading fast enough.

11. Use the correct file formats. Using the wrong file format scan completely screw the look and design of your banner ads. Most of the time, JPG, PNG, JPEG, and HTML5 files are your working deliverables. You should be aware of the differences between these formats and how they can affect the overall look and performance of your banner ads. If you are working with a freelance designer, he will most probably be working on your banner ads using Adobe Photoshop, Adobe Illustrator, Google Web Designer, or Adobe Animate. Make sure that you inform him about the particular file formats that you need.

12. Make your banner ads stand out from the crowd. If your ads are similar to a lot of other banner ads out there, it will be difficult for the ads to get the attention of online users. Sometimes, it's necessary to go against the flow to make yourself stand out. That is you need to find ways to separate yourself from the crowd. This could mean using the least used colors, fonts, or formats. However, you should strike a good balance between being unique and being consistent with your branding goals. Try to be different but not too much in the sense that your ads start losing their branding message.

13. Change the banners frequently. It's never a good idea to use the same banner too often and for too long. This develops ad blindness which means people will start ignoring your banner ads because they've seen it these so many times. Such a behavior is completely understandable. If you've seen a movie numerous times, you will get tired of it to the point that it becomes annoying. It's the same with online banner ads. With that said, you need to create various versions of your ads then use them following a rotation schedule. This keeps the banner ads fresh in the eyes and minds of viewers. Just a simple change in font or background color can completely make an ad look different.

14. Involve the audience in your ads. What do we mean by this? It means you need to create banner ads that talk to the audience. The audience should be able to relate to the ad copy. Think of the advertising process as a conversation between you and your audience. What would you like to tell him? What does the audience want to hear from you? These are the types of questions you should be asking yourself in designing and writing the copy for your banner ads. The most effective ads are the ones that are able to connect to the needs and wants of the audience. This is something you should always remember when planning your banner advertising campaigns.

Inspiration #16

Believe in yourself. You are braver than you think, more talented than you know, and capable of more than you imagine.
Roy T. Bennett

Traffic Source #2 - Solo Ads

Before anything else, we need to clearly define what solo ads are because a lot of new online entrepreneurs are often confused about the method. Honestly, I never understood why this is called solo advertising. But it's basically email list hiring. You find someone who has an email list that might be beneficial to your affiliate marketing business. You then enter into a deal by renting the email list. The particulars of the deal depends on your negotiations with the owner of the email list. You can rent the list for a single email blast campaign. Or you can rent it for a series of email blasts. How much the deal costs depends on the size of the email list, the type of affiliate products or services you are promoting, and the reputation of the owner of the list.

A Quick Illustration of How a Solo Ad Works

Let's say that you run an affiliate marketing website where you promote and sell all sorts of self-help and self-development books. You decide to set aside some of your marketing budget with the intention of spending these on solo ads. What you should do is search online for individuals who are in the self-help and self-development niche and who also happen to maintain their own email lists. These individuals can be bloggers, gurus, coaches, and writers. What's important is that they have an email list or a subscriber list which they built through a newsletter. Contact these individuals and inquire if they are interested in renting out their email lists to you.

Before you contact these individuals, you should come up with your business proposals first. What are you going to offer to them in exchange for the chance to use their email list? What kind of value can you provide for them? Write down and polish your proposals so that you are ready to send them when the email list owners ask what value they can get from you. An example of a deal would be as follows: you create the message and content that is sent to the email list. You pay the owner of the list $500 for every email blast. So if you rent the list twice, you are going to spend $1000.

This is just a simplified example. There are various types of deals that you can enter into when renting an email list. You need to be creative with your negotiations. Renting an email list can be expensive because owners of the lists have a lot of risks to contend with when they agree to carry your marketing messages. For example, the paid marketing messages can alienate some of the people in the list. It doesn't matter if the products or services you are promoting in the campaign are relevant to their needs and wants. Sponsored email blasts tend to rub a lot of people the wrong way. The point here is that the model can be risky for the owner of the list. This risk drives the prices for solo ad campaigns. That said, you must be ready with your budget when sending in your proposals especially if you are sending them to reputable and influential people in your niche.

Where to Find Solo Ad Lists

There's a good number of places where you can find people or companies who are renting out their email lists for advertisers and marketers. I am not going to name specific individuals or companies because what works for one person may not going to work for another. Solo ad marketing is about finding the lists that matches well with your affiliate marketing business. Only you can go through this process. However, I'm going to recommend that you try your luck within online marketing communities and forums. These are the places where you can usually get in touch with people who accept solo ads. Many of the members of these forums and communities are in the business of building lists and renting them out to interested parties.

And don't forget Google. Just a quick search for "solo ads" will provide you with countless resources and websites where you can get in touch with solo ad providers. In fact there's a ton of them out there that sifting through the crowd can be difficult if not frustrating. There are two rules you should follow when choosing which solo ad providers you should deal with. One, the provider should have a list that's relevant to your affiliate marketing niche. If you are selling weight loss products, then the list's members should be composed of people genuinely interested in losing weight. And two, the provider should have some sort of reputation. That is he has no record of scamming clients.

You need to be very careful because it's very easy to build lists using bots. Providers can show you huge lists but in reality, majority of those in the lists are bots or manufactured accounts. With that said, you should only purchase solo ads from reputable and reliable sellers. Read reviews about their services. Contact them directly and ask all the questions you need to ask. How did they build their lists? Where did they source out the members in their lists? Have they worked with other marketers in your niche before? These are just some of the questions you can ask a solo ad provider.

The Pricing Models for Solo Ads

When purchasing a solo ad from a provider, you should fully understand the pricing model that will be followed. You usually have the choice of either picking a fixed price agreement or a performance-based agreement. The fixed price model involves paying the solo ad provider a fixed amount regardless of the performance and results of the campaign. The fixed price can be paid on a per solo ad basis or on a time basis. For example, you pay the list owner $100 for every solo ad you purchase. Or you pay the list owner $100 every week for your solo ads. The biggest drawback of the fixed pricing model is that there's no guarantee that you will get your money's worth.

The alternative to a fixed price model is the performance-based model. With this model, the amount you pay for the solo ad is dependent on various variables. The cost of the solo ad depends on the performance of the ad. For this reason, a lot of affiliate marketers prefer this model in paying for their solo ads. Now, performance is measured using various metrics. The performance of a solo ad can be measured based on how many clicks it got, how many people opened the message, or how many people actually bought the product or availed of the service being promoted. Let me touch on these metrics a little bit.

1. Pay per Click – You pay for every click that your solo ad gets. For example, let's say that the agreement needs you to pay 50 cents for every click that your solo ad receives. You rented an email list with 10,000 members. If 2,000 of these members click on the solo ad, this means that the ad will cost you an estimated amount of $1000. That was computed by multiplying 2,000 by 50 cents.

2. Pay per Open – You pay for every member of the list that opens the solo ad sent to their email address. Again, if 2,000 members open the ad and the rate per opened email is 50 cents, your payment for the solo ad will be $1,000.

3. Pay per Conversion or per Sale – The solo ad will only incur you costs if members of the list is successfully converted into a customer. For example, let's say that the solo ad promoted a product worth $50. For every conversion or sale, the owner of the list will receive $5. Let's assume that 2,000 members of the list converted or bought the product. This means that the solo ad will cost you $10,000 (2,000 x $5). That seems a lot of money to pay for a solo ad. Yes it's a huge expense but keep in mind that you've made $100,000 in sales (2000 x $50).

There's no general consensus on the question of "Which of these pricing models are the best?" Some affiliate marketers prefer pay per click models. Some prefer the pay per open and pay per conversion models. At the end of the day, it all depends on the model that suits your kind of affiliate marketing business. For that reason, it's best that you experiment with the different pricing models to see which models will work well for your brand.

Pros of Using Solo Ads

1. You can potentially get a huge email list very quickly. I'm saying this in the context of if you are planning to build your own email list for your affiliate marketing website. So basically, in purchasing solo ads, you are using other email lists as leverage in building your own email list. It's a very powerful strategy that works for a lot of affiliate marketers. It worked for them so there's a good chance that it's going to work for you as well. Just remember to only purchase solo ads from email list builders who are in the same niche as yours.

2. Solo ads have SEO benefits. Every solo ad you create will contain a link to your affiliate website, blog, sales page, or any digital platform associated to your main website. This has both short-term and long-term benefits to your business, SEO-wise. Links contained within emails may not have direct significant effects but they set off a chain of events that can lead to more backlinks and exposure for your website.

3. It is a quick way to generate a good number of website visitors especially if your affiliate marketing website is so new that it only gets a few visitors a day. With a solo ad, your website will receive the initial exposure it deserves. Let's say that you purchased a solo ad from a list builder who has a list with 20,000 members. Imagine if half of the people in the list clicks on the solo ad and are redirected to your website. That's a quick 10,000 visits your website will receive in a very short period of time.

Cons of Using Solo Ads

1. Solo ads can be very costly especially if you purchase them from very prominent and influential marketers and list builders. Some big list builders charge hundred if not thousands of dollars per solo ad. Even the small and medium-sized list builders often have high rates. Making matters worse is that some solo ad sellers take advantage of the cluelessness of some beginners to overcharge them for their services.

2. There is no guarantee that your solo ads will convert into new subscribers or sales. This is understandable because everything will depend on the quality of the email list you rented for the solo ad. Generally speaking, the conversion rates of solo ads are pretty good. They are in fact higher than the average rates in other online marketing methods. This is for the simple reason that solo ads are delivered to the target audience via their inbox, the least place for people to find ads. But conversion only happens if the people in the list are genuinely interested in the contents of the solo ad.

3. Solo ads can be very disruptive. People who are not aware about how solo ads work may look at them as spam. This isn't good for your ad copy because people might just delete it without even opening it or worse, they'll send it to the spam folder. This means you will be paying for the ad copy only for it to be tagged as spam by the recipient.

How to Get the Most Out of Your Solo Ads

1. Split test your solo ads using various versions of it. The main goal of split testing is to test out different versions of your solo ad to identify which version will get the best results. The version that gets the best results will be the one you are going to use in majority of your solo ad campaigns.

2. Make sure that your solo ad seller is reliable and reputable. Purchasing solo ads is one of the cheapest and fastest ways to generate targeted traffic towards your affiliate marketing website. Unfortunately, there are a lot of bogus and shady solo ad sellers out there. You don't want to be caught up with these bogus operators. Make sure that the seller is legit before you enter into a deal with him. Here are some of the signs that a solo ad seller isn't legit:
- Their promises are too good to be true.
- They don't have a sales page.
- They offer ridiculously low prices for their solo ads.
- They don't have someone who can vouch for them and their services.
- They may have some testimonials but these seem fake and manufactured.
- They don't have testimonials altogether.
- They don't have a sales page or official website.

3. Start off small and work yourself up the ladder. Don't make the common mistake of purchasing big solo ads right from the start. You will either get burned or you end up with conversions that are way below your expectations. Think of your first solo ad purchases as tests and experiments. They will serve as your lessons as you learn more about how solo ads work and how you can optimize the results you generate from them. On average, solo ads that cost you $15 to $80 per purchase are a good place to start.

4. Write a high-quality email copy for your solo ads. The content will be received by the recipients in their email inbox so make sure that you write the content with this in mind. Don't make the copy too long because most people don't like reading long emails. Also, don't make the copy look too complicated. Avoid using too much images and graphics. A single image is often more than enough to accompany the ad copy. Make the ad copy simple, clear, and direct to the point. Don't beat around the bush.

5. Keep making adjustments to your solo ads. Don't expect to create a flawless ad copy the first time. You will make mistakes that need fixing. You should never stop in improving your solo ads. Get rid of the things that aren't getting results and scale or improve the ones that are getting results.

Traffic Source #3 - Google Adwords

Google has recently changed the name of their advertising platform from Google Adwords to the much simpler Google Ads. There are a lot of reasons why you should be using Google Ads. Whether you want to bring in new visitors to your affiliate marketing website, increase your online sales, or simply get more people to sign up with your newsletter, Google Ads has all the tools you need to get these done. Google Ads takes the guesswork out of online advertising. And you have several ad types to choose from.

How Google Ads Works

Signing up with Google Ads is easy and free. If you have a Gmail account, you can easily create a Google Ads account in just a couple of minutes. Google provides you with everything you need to get started. There are tons of tutorials and guides on the platform's help section. I suggest that you go through these guides to make sure that you will be using the platform correctly. The most important things you need to learn are the platform's advertising basics, how to set up a Google Ads campaign, and how to improve your results.

Your ads will be shown in three main areas. One, your ads will be shown alongside search results if someone performs a search for your main keywords on Google. Two, your ads can be shown in Google's digital properties like YouTube. And three, your ads will be shown in websites that have enrolled in Google's Adsense program. This last one is the most important because it provides you with the chance to reach as many of your target audience as possible. However, if you want to maximize the reach of your ads, you should customize and optimize them so that they get the chance to be shown in all three possible areas.

What's the Pricing Model for Google Ads?

How much does Google Ads cost? The answer is "it depends". There are several variables that affect how much you are supposed to pay for your ads. However, it's worth mentioning here that you are always in control of your budget. You are only going to pay for the ads that are working. That's right, you only pay for ads that pay off. This is because Google Ads follows the cost-per-click and cost-per-impression pricing models.

In other words, Google Ads is going to charge you only if someone views your ad, clicks your ad, or completes a call-to-action. You call the shots in all of your advertising campaigns. This basically means that you can pause your ads whenever you want. Your spending will also be automatically paused. There's no added obligation or burden when you decide to pause and adjust your ads. The pricing model of Google Ads is as flexible as they come. Because you set your own advertising budget, you set the price that you are willing to pay when someone clicks or views your ad.

As I have mentioned earlier, the specific amount that you pay for your ads are affected by several variables. *The competition for the keywords you are targeting is the most significant variable.* If there are a lot of people targeting the same keyword, it's normal for ads targeting the keyword to be more expensive. You could be paying anywhere from one cent to five dollars for a click. There are premium Google Ads that can cost the advertiser up to $50 per click.

Pros of Google Ads

1. Google Ads has a much wider scope and reach compared to other advertising networks. This is by far the biggest benefit you will get from Google Ads. The platform has the capability to take your message to the right people at the right amount. Your ad can be displayed in a plethora of digital spaces like websites, blogs, forums, and even social media sites like YouTube.

2. You can measure your success. Google Ads has some of the most comprehensive analytics tools in the market. You can track the performance of every ad that you run out there. Google's Analytics program is tied in with your Google Ads account so that you can easily gather and analyze the data that you need with regards to the performances and results generated by your ads.

3. Google Ads generates results much faster than SEO. This is very important especially if your website or business is completely new and you need to find a way to get your foot through the door. Google Ads helps you get in the front page of the search results if you use the right keywords. This will jumpstart the number of people visiting your website.

4. Google Ads increases your brand awareness. It's much easier to build your brand these days because of the internet. It's even much easier if you use advertising platforms like Google Ads for leverage. It enables you to inform a huge number of people about your business in a short period of time.

5. Google Ads allows you to test your ads and find the ones that generate the best results. The platform has tools and resources that enable you to run two ads at a time with variations so that you can track and measure how each variation performs. This is called split testing and it's easy to do with Google Ads because of their comprehensive Analytics tool.

6. You can create ad campaigns based on the specific demographic that you want to target. You can customize your ads based on age, hobbies, occupation, income, location, gender, and interests. Of course, the targeting will not always be accurate but at least you can be sure that majority of those seeing your ads have a semblance of interest in your message.

7. You can schedule your Google Ads so that these reach the right audience at the right time. In short, you get to decide the time and day when you want your ads to start running. It depends on the activities and habits of your target audience. For example, if you are targeting college students, maybe it's a good idea to run your ads early in the morning and at night wherein they are not busy with their classes and studies.

8. Google Ads comes with its own keyword research tool. Google has the best and most accurate keyword research tool because they have the better search data. The keyword planner is built right into the advertising platform so that you can access and use it with ease if you are brainstorming for more keyword ideas to use in your ads.

Cons of Google Ads

1. People trust natural results over ads. This is a drawback but it's something that can be said about all types of online advertising. This is a con in the sense that if a person searches on Google and he gets ads and organic results, he will likely choose the organic results over the ads. This is something you should always keep in mind when creating ads with Google Ads.

2. High-value keywords can be very competitive and expensive. The rates for ads on Google Ads depend on the keywords you are using and the targeting options you pick. Be reminded that Google uses a bidding structure which means that keywords being targeted by a lot of advertisers tend to be a lot more expensive. If you are in a very competitive niche, then this means you will have to spend more money on your campaigns.

3. Adverts have limitations. For example, if you are going to use a textual ad, there's very little words and sentences that you can use on the ad. This can be very problematic if you are trying to market a product or service that's a bit difficult to explain in just one or two sentences. But you can hurdle this limitation by being creative in writing your ad copies.

How to Get the Most Out of Google Ads

1. Start with a small budget. A lot of people who use Google Ads for the first time often make the mistake of spending too much money from the start. This is very risky for the simple fact that you are still learning the ropes. A botched ad campaign can easily cost you a lot of money with very little results. With that said, it's highly recommended that you start with a small budget. Even if you make mistakes, you will have minimal losses.

2. Educate yourself about quality score (QS). Knowledge about quality score can help you in improving the performance of your ads. The quality score helps you in estimating how much you are supposed to pay per click or per impression for your ads. Quality score is the metric that Google uses to rank ads in their system. The score ranges from 1 to 10 (with 1 being the lowest).

3. Always do your keyword research before creating an ad. The keywords you use in your ads determine the sites where they will appear in. If your keywords include the term "soccer", your ad will likely appear in sites whose content are related to soccer. Google has its own keyword research tool and keyword planner that you can use for free.

4. Take advantage of geotargeting and ad scheduling. Geotargeting and ad scheduling can make the difference between a successful ad campaign and a failed one. Geotargeting enables you to only target people from specific locations (i.e. countries, states). Ad scheduling, on the other hand, allows you to decide what time of the day or night your ad will run. These two strategies help you in controlling your ads.

5. Make your ads mobile-friendly. This is very important today considering the fact that more and more people are using their mobile phones to access the internet. If people view your ads on mobile phone, how does the ads look? Are they big enough? Is the ad copy appropriate? Expect a lot of your ad views to be coming from mobile devices. Make sure that these views count by making your ads mobile-friendly.

6. Make your landing page relevant. This is especially true if you are directing viewers of your ads to a sales page or a lead page. The ultimate goal of pay-per-click marketing which is a huge part of Google Ads is to not just get a click but a sale as well. If you are directing clicks to a landing page, make sure that that landing page immediately provides the visitor with what he needs. If it's a product, the product should be prominently highlighted.

7. Optimize your negative keywords. Negative keywords are the keywords that you don't want to be associated with your ads. For example, if you have an ad promoting badminton rackets, a potential negative keyword would be "badminton shuttlecocks". This is a negative keyword because you are selling rackets, not shuttlecocks. The good news is that Google Ads enables you to enter these negative keywords into your campaign so that your ads won't appear in sites that contain your negative keywords.

8. Decide whether your ad is going to appear in the search network or in the display network. The search network refers to Google's search results. If a person searches on Google, the results page will include not just the search results but also relevant ads. The display network refers to the sites that display Adsense ads by Google. These include digital properties of Google like YouTube.

9. Perform a lot of split testing to determine the types and designs of ads that work well for your affiliate marketing business and website. Split testing is a strategy that the best online advertisers use. Fortunately for you, Google Ads makes it very easy for you to perform split testing. You can ran two ads simultaneously and track their performances and results for a similar period of time. When then period elapses, you collect the data and analyze which ad performed better.

10. Keep changing your ad formats. There's this thing called ad blindness wherein online users get too used to your ads that it becomes very easy for them to ignore your ads. To keep your ads fresh and interesting, you should make use of a variety of formats and designs. And don't just stick to a single theme for the ads. You should regularly change things to prevent ad blindness among your target audience.

Traffic Source #4 - YouTube Ads

There are several reasons why you should be using YouTube to drive traffic to your affiliate marketing website. I'm going to mention to you the two most important ones. One, YouTube is the second largest search engine in the world. And two, more than two billion videos are streamed on the platform every single day. In other words, the video-sharing platform is a marketer's paradise. If you want to build hype around something, whether it's a product or a service, YouTube can significantly help you with it. There are two major methods on how you can use YouTube as a promotional tool for your affiliate marketing website.

The first method is to create your own YouTube channel and promote your product or service by making videos on your own. This is going to take a lot of your time and resources. You need to be comfortable in front of the camera. It's also a bit more difficult to get viewers because people on YouTube tend to be averse towards videos that are promotional in nature. With that said, you need to come up with an angle on how to make videos that aren't blatantly promotional. You need to be creative about it. Use videos to tell stories that viewers can relate to while subtly injecting your product or service into the video. It takes a lot of practice to master this technique.

The second method of marketing through YouTube is to take advantage of the video platform's advertising program. Keep in mind that YouTube is owned by Google which means that advertisements in the site are delivered by Adwords, the advertising program by Google. So if you want to create ads that will appear in YouTube, you must create an account with Adwords. If you don't already have an account, you should register right now. It will only take a few minutes of your time. If you are a new sign-up, Google might offer you some credits that you can use for free for your first ad campaigns.

In this chapter, our focus will be on YouTube advertising. How do you create ads that will get a lot of attention from people who regularly watch videos on YouTube? That's the core question we are going to answer in this chapter. So let's roll.

How to Create a Video Ad for YouTube

Before anything else, you need to link your YouTube channel with your Adwords account. This will only take you a few minutes. After successfully connecting the accounts, you can start developing your YouTube video ad campaign. The first thing you should do is create the marketing video you are going to use and upload it on YouTube. Once it's live, allow it some time to generate a few views and for it to get picked up by YouTube's algorithms and recommendations system.

To set up your advertising campaign, sign into your Adwords account, click on the Campaign button then select Video from the dropdown menu. Just follow the steps and input the details and information that are asked from you. You should give the campaign a name so that you can easily identify it from your other advertising campaigns. You also need to choose the format for the ad. Here's a quick overview of the formats you can choose from:

1. TrueView Ads – These are the standard video ads on YouTube. TrueView ads are further divided into two categories. These are video discovery ads and in-stream ads. Video discovery ads are the ones you see at the homepage, at the search results pages, and at the related videos sections. On the other hand, in-stream ads are the ads that play before a video starts. In-stream ads can also play in intervals within a video. Have you experienced watching a YouTube video and an ad suddenly appears for a few seconds? Those are in-stream ads.

2. Pre-Roll Video Ads – These are very similar to in-stream ads in the sense that they are played either before a YouTube video starts or within the YouTube video itself. However, pre-roll ads are very different because you can't skip them unlike in-stream ads. A pre-roll ad plays out in its entirety before you can watch the YouTube video. A pre-roll ad can also appear in longer YouTube videos. For example, if a YouTube video is ten minutes long, a pre-roll ad might appear and play at the halfway mark.

3. Bumper Video Ads – These are very short video ads that are often just six seconds long. These ad spots quickly play before YouTube videos. They are very short which means viewers are less likely to skip them. Bumpers aren't really great for promotional campaigns because you really can't send a proper marketing message in just a few seconds. For this reason, most online marketers use bumper video ads as teasers for their longer and more complicated video ad campaigns.

After choosing the video ad format for your campaign, it's time to put your advertising budget in order. This is one of the biggest benefits of using Adwords for your video advertising. You have control over your campaign budget. You can determine the maximum price you would like to pay for each view of your ad. You can adjust your maximum price whenever you want.

The final step in creating the ad is targeting. This involves defining the types of people you would like to view the ad. You can define your audience based on several options such as gender, age, location, interests, and even viewing history. For example, if you are promoting beauty products in your video ad, then it makes sense that you target female viewers.

The Pricing Model for YouTube Ads

So how much does it cost to run a video ad on YouTube? Again, I have to remind you that ads on YouTube are served by Adwords so the cost-per-click and cost-per-impression pricing models are in effect. You have control over your budget but the per click and per impression costs of your ads depend on various factors. These factors include the ad format you used, the competition in your niche, the length of your ad, your budget allocation, where your ad will be displayed, and the type of audience you are targeting. Advertisers pay incrementally more for focused target audiences. All these factors come into play when Google determines how much you should pay for your ad campaigns.

Generally speaking, per click and per view costs for YouTube ads range from $0.10 to $0.30. Some ads can cost the advertisers more than $1.00 per click or per view but these costs are quite rare. Again, these costs can be flexible and be under your control. You can pay more or pay less for each click and view by adjusting your budget. Simply speaking, the more money you feed into your campaigns, the more expensive the ads become. The more money you spend on the ads, the more people the ads reach.

Pros of YouTube Advertising

1. YouTube ads have a very wide reach. The latest count shows that YouTube has nearly two billion active users. This represents almost one-third of all people in the internet. These users watch an estimated five billion videos every single day. Needless to say, YouTube is the perfect place to advertise your affiliate marketing site if you want to maximize the reach of your marketing message.

2. With YouTube advertising, you have a lot of targeting options to choose from. These targeting options include topics, niches, demographics, keywords, placements, and categories. With targeting, you will get your money's worth as long as you have targeted the right people. Always keep in mind that your YouTube ads will be created and delivered through Google Adwords. This means you have access to all the tools and resources in the advertising network.

3. YouTube ads are very affordable. With YouTube advertising, you pay per click, per view, or per thousand impressions. Typical ads in the video-sharing platform cost between $0.10 to $0.30 for every view. The rate for each view depends on factors such as your targeting, your video quality, the video's length, and your overall budget.

4. It's easy to track the performances of your ads. This is for the simple reason that your YouTube ads are created using Google Adwords. Adwords has the best ad-tracking system which allows you to track and measure the performances of your ads. Not only that, you can also use YouTube Analytics to understand how viewers are interacting with your videos.

5. There's the viral factor. It's a well-known fact that it's a lot easier for videos to go viral. As the biggest video-sharing platform today, YouTube is the best place to post videos that you want to go viral. YouTube makes it very easy for users to find your videos through its tagging and recommendation systems.

Cons of YouTube Advertising

1. You have little control over the content where your ads will appear in. This is something that you should always take into account when using an ad network like Google Adwords which serves your ads to videos on YouTube. YouTube even got into some trouble a few years ago when advertisers decided to halt their advertising campaigns when they realized that their ads were appearing alongside terrorism videos and hate speech videos. Since then, YouTube has installed measures that helped curb this problem. But the system is not perfect so there will always be the possibility that your video ads will appear alongside videos that you don't want to associate yourself with.

2. It's a challenge to hook viewers and entice them not to hit on the "skip" button. As you know, the ads that play within videos on YouTube can usually be skipped by viewers. With that said, you only have a few seconds to capture their interest and keep them watching. This is easier said than done though. The goal is to make your videos unique and interesting. You also have the option of making your short ads unskippable but you need to pay for them at a premium.

3. Majority of YouTube users find ads to be very annoying. To be fair, this is true for all types of ads regardless of where they are being showed. YouTube ads, in particular, are extra annoying because they are very intrusive. Some of the ads automatically play while you are in the middle of watching a video. This can turn off a lot of people.

4. Poor customization options. This is one of the main drawbacks of video advertising. You need to play along to the themes and designs of the host platform which in this case is YouTube. Your business website design and branding will not reflect on your YouTube ads.

5. Low security for your content. The video-sharing website cannot safeguard your original videos and ads from illegal downloads and copyright infringements. People stealing your content can be very damaging to your business and brand.

How to Get the Most Out of YouTube Advertising

1. Choose your YouTube ad formats wisely. There's a reason why YouTube offers a wide variety of ad formats. These have different uses. Each ad format has its own pros and cons. There are factors that you must consider in choosing which formats you are going to use. These factors include the kind of affiliate product you are promoting, your target audience, your advertising budget, etc.

2. If you are going to use both in-stream ads and discovery ads, you should segment them into different campaigns. These two types of YouTube ads are very distinct from each other. In-stream ads are those ads that play before, during, or after a video. On the other hand, discovery ads are the ads that appear next to videos. Discovery ads appear either on the search results or on the recommended videos alongside a video. Most YouTube advertising experts recommend that you have a different strategy and budget for each ad type.

3. Take full advantage of YouTube's targeting options and features. You must pay close attention to the kinds of people who would be interested in watching what you are offering. Who are these people who are consuming your messages? What are their needs and wants? What are they looking for? These are just a few of the questions you need to answer to decide on your targeting options. Targeting the right people is one of the most important keys to success in YouTube advertising.

4. Consider video remarketing. What is remarketing? This is a term used for the online advertising strategy of following your website's visitors in other places. For example, a person visits your affiliate marketing website and spends some time browsing through your products. To remarket that website visitor, you create a video ad which will play when that same visitor leaves your website and goes watching videos on YouTube. Have you ever wondered why you keep seeing ads in YouTube or Facebook for products and services that you've browsed in other sites? That's remarketing in action. It's a very powerful affiliate marketing strategy that can significantly increase your sales.

5. Add interactive elements into your YouTube ads. YouTube ads have seen a lot of improvements during the last couple of years. One of the most notable of these changes is the ability of advertisers to add interactive elements into their ads. For example, you can directly link up your affiliate marketing website with a TrueView ad. Or you can add clickable call to actions in your ads. You should capitalize on these interactive features to improve your clickthrough rate and conversion rate.

6. Tell stories with your ads so that you can easily connect with your target audience. Ads are annoying. That's a fact. You can make your ads less annoying to viewers by using a story angle which makes the ad about the audience. This way, viewers will see themselves in the ad and they can relate to it.

7. Inject a sense of humor into your ads. Ads can be entertaining to watch if these are funny. The most well-known ads are the ones that made people laugh. A good sense of humor can make any type of ad interesting. If it's original and really funny, it has a good chance of going viral. Having a video go viral in YouTube is like winning the lottery. You get an avalanche of views and new prospects in a short period of time.

8. Inspire viewers to take action. A great strategy in creating adds that will resonate with your audience is to present a serious problem and then show them that by supporting your affiliate marketing business, they can help solve that problem. You are basically asking your viewers to help you make a difference in providing solutions for a serious problem. For even better results, you can try to partner with organizations and charities in creating your ads. It's a win-win situation for all the parties involved.

Inspiration #19

Whatever you hold in your mind on a consistent basis is exactly what you will experience in your life.
Tony Robbins

Traffic Source #5 - Facebook Ads

Facebook's advertising program is without a doubt the best social media advertising program today. Facebook is the largest social media platform out there which also makes it the biggest market if you plan on promoting a product or service through social media. It also happens that it's very easy to set up ad campaigns on the platform. You don't have to be that technically savvy to run and manage an ad campaign on Facebook.

If done properly, Facebook advertising can bring in a lot of traffic and new customers for your affiliate marketing business. The program comes with micro-targeting features that enable you to reach your exact audience based on demographics, location, behavior, hobbies, and interests. This means that Facebook advertising is great for your budget, conversion rates, and return on investment.

How Facebook Advertising Works

Before you can use Facebook advertising, you must have a Facebook business page. Keep in mind that a business page is completely different from a profile page. If you don't have a business page, you should make one right now. Just go to your Facebook homepage, click on the "Create" tab on the upper right corner, and select "Page". Just fill in all the necessary information and you are good to go. Once you have the page live, you can start creating ads right away.

To get started with a new ad campaign, log into your Facebook Ads Manager account and select the Campaigns tab. Click on the Create tab to begin with your campaign. Facebook will then ask you what your objectives are in creating the campaign. There are eleven marketing objectives (as at Dec 2018) that you can choose from. These are as follows: brand awareness, traffic, app installs, lead generation, conversions, store visits, reach, engagement, video views, messages, and catalog sales. After choosing your objective, you must name your campaign. Naming your campaign is very important especially if you are running several campaigns at a time.

From here, you just have to follow the instructions and guides provided by the platform. A very important step you should not ignore is the targeting process. Targeting is about choosing the audience who will get to see your ads. You can target your audience by location, age, gender, and language. When customizing your targeting options, Facebook provides you with an audience size indicator which gives you a sense of how many people your ad can potentially reach. For a more detailed treatment of this topic, see Facebook Marketing For Beginners - Learn The Basics Of Facebook Advertising And Strategies In 5 Days And Learn It Well

The Different Types and Formats of Facebook Ads

1. Photo Ads - This is one of the easiest ads to make on Facebook. You can just post a photo in your business page and have it boosted. Photo ads are great for driving people to your website and for raising awareness about your products and services. Photo ads are among the ads that you can make directly from your Facebook business page.

2. Video Ads - You have the option of creating bite-sized videos that will only take a few seconds to watch or you can create long-form videos that are more than one-minute long. You can even create looping GIFs for your ads. Videos enable you to deliver more meaningful content in a much faster way through videos.

3. Stories Ads - Yes, you can create ads that are delivered as a Story. One of the biggest benefits of a Story ad is that it seems more personal in the eyes of the viewer. In short, Story ads get you closer to your target audience. They are more authentic and you can be creative in designing the content that are shown through your Stories. Story ads are effective because they are fast, authentic, and helpful.

4. Messenger Ads - You can also design ads that are displayed through Facebook's Messenger app. This is different from email marketing in the sense that you don't directly send marketing messages to people. Your ads are simply shown in the Messenger app when the messages being exchanged in a conversation are relevant to your ad. That said, Messenger Ads are not that intrusive as you might think.

5. Carousel Ads - If you are promoting several products, carousel ads are perfect in showcasing your products at the same time. Carousel ads allow you to show up to ten photos or videos in a single ad. Each photo or video even comes with its own link. This means that you can link each product to the specific product page in your website that describes and sells it. You can use carousel ads in Messenger and through the Audience Network.

6. Slideshow Ads - This is almost similar to a video ad. Only this time, you are using slides of several images. You can add sounds and text to the ads to make them more interesting and more interactive. Slideshow ads are much cheaper than video ads and they load much faster. They play very well on most connection speeds.

7. Collection Ads - These ads are designed to turn viewers into buyers. Collection ads can help you get your conversion rates up. A collection ad contains a primary video or image with four smaller photos below it that are arranged in a grid-like layout. People viewing the ad will be seamlessly taken to a sales page if they click on any of the accompanying images.

8. Playable Ads - If you are promoting mobile apps, this is the ad you should be using. Playable ads provide people with an interactive preview of the mobile app. This means that they get to use the app before they can install it. This is the perfect ad for mobile apps especially for apps in the gaming niche. Let people play with the game to help them decide if it's something worth buying or downloading.

How Much Does Facebook Ads Cost?

You decide how much you want to spend on your ad campaigns in Facebook. There's a minimum for some of the ad formats but these are really small. Don't worry, you will be notified if there's a minimum while you are in the process of creating your ad. The bottom line here is that you are still in full control of how much you are going to spend on your Facebook ad campaigns. If you want to spend just $5 a week, that's cool. If you want to spend $50,000 a week, it's all up to you.

Facebook requires you to set up a budget when you create an ad or a campaign. In order to control your costs per results generated, you must come up with a bidding strategy. If you don't want to bid, Facebook will do it for you by spending your ad budget evenly throughout your ad's run time. Facebook also offers two ways on how you can ensure that you don't spend more than your budget. One, you can set your campaign spending limit. Your ad campaign will freeze once you have reached your campaign spending limit.

Two, you can also set your account spending limit. This is similar to the campaign spending limit but it applies to all the campaigns in your account. For example, let's say that you are running three ad campaigns and your account spending limit is $1000. Once all three ad campaigns reach total costs of $1000, all of the ads in all three campaigns will stop running. If you want to make sure that you don't run the risk of spending more than you can afford, I highly suggest that you set your account spending limit. You can still set your campaign spending limit even with the account spending limit in place.

Pros of Facebook Advertising

1. Facebook advertising is the most targeted form of online advertising. This is not an exaggeration. You can advertise to people by location, behavior, interests, and age. If you know who your customers are, you can customize your ads through targeting to ensure that these are viewed by the right people. Targeted ads help you generate the best possible results from your ads.

2. Facebook advertising is very affordable. As we have mentioned earlier, you can spend $5 a week if you want. Even with small amounts, you can still reach a significant number of people. For example, a $5 budget can still reach 1,000 people or even more if you play your cards right. Since your ads are shown prominently within Facebook, every penny you spend on your ads is worth it.

3. Creating an ad on Facebook is lightning fast. Unlike other online advertising platforms where it can take so long to set up an ad, creating an ad on Facebook can take just a few minutes. You can post an image on your business page, boost it, and the ad will go live in a matter of minutes. Because of the fast delivery of ads, you also get instant results. Hundreds of people will immediately see your ads in their newsfeeds and sidebars.

4. Facebook advertising is measurable. One thing that Facebook is very good at is delivering statistics to its advertisers. Every ad you run is measurable because you can view the number of clicks, likes, shares, impressions, or conversions that it received. You can access all of these information through the Facebook Ads Manager. The data is presented to you in a clear and concise layout so that you can easily see and understand if your ads are generating results or not.

5. You have access to a large mobile audience. Facebook is one of the most popular websites that are accessed by people through mobile phones. It follows that if you want to reach a lot of people through their mobile phones, then Facebook advertising is the way to go. What's great is that Facebook's advertising program provides you with tools and resources that you can use to optimize your ads for a mobile audience.

6. Facebook has extensive analytics. The social network takes its analytics seriously. It offers its advertisers a comprehensive reporting system for ad performance. Everything is laid out clearly for you. You don't have to spend a lot of time going through confusing statistics and data. Facebook churns through the data and presents you with easy-to-interpret information.

7. Massive exposure for your ads on a global scale. Facebook has users from all corners of the world. As of this writing, Facebook has more than two billion active users. This is essentially your market. Because of this large user base, your ads will go a long way even if you are working with a very minimal budget.

Cons of Facebook Advertising

1. The Facebook algorithm actively limits the visibility of branded messages. This is understandable on their part because they want organic posts to be the ones being displayed in the news feeds of users. Since branded messages are often filtered out, this limits the presence of your ads.

2. Increasing competition. The number of businesses using Facebook to advertise their products and services is growing by the thousands every single day. This means that the likelihood of your advertisement standing out greatly diminishes. It becomes more and more difficult to get the attention of your target customers and audience.

3. Negative comments are everywhere. Most of the time, users in Facebook will be able to leave comments on your ads. Expect to get a lot of negative comments especially if you are selling a product or service. A lot of these comments will be coming from trolls or even from people who have never tried your product or service. With that said, it might be necessary for you to do some comment moderation in your ads. This can be time-consuming.

How to Get the Most Out of Facebook Advertising

1. Target the appropriate audience. Don't make the common mistake of attempting to reach as many people as possible from numerous demographics. Of course, you would want your ads to reach a lot of people but more views doesn't necessarily mean more sales or conversions. It's the quality of the audience that matters the most. If you are reaching the right people even if there's less of them, you will generate better results.

2. Get the landing page right. Whether your ads are redirecting to your Facebook business page or to an outside website, see to it that the landing page is optimized to welcome the visitor. A good landing page is instrumental in helping you reach your goals. Remember that ads are merely meant to get the attention of people. It's in the landing page where you convince the person to buy your product or avail of your services.

3. Make your ads clear and simple. Don't beat around the bush because you are competing with thousands of other advertisers. You only have a few seconds to attract the attention of a potential customer. Make it count by making sure that the person gets an idea of what you are offering the moment he or she lays an eye on your ad.

4. Be consistent with your ad campaigns. Just focus on the ads that are working well for you and keep on improving them. Trying too many things at the same time can eat away at your time and resources. For example, you should use the same theme or images across your ad copies and landing pages.

5. Mine for information using Facebook's analytics features. There's so much that you can learn just by looking at the data and statistics surrounding your ad campaigns. You will get an idea about the types of ads that are resonating with your target audience. You will also see how and where your ad viewers are coming from. You can mine all these information to make improvements on your ads.

6. Start with a small budget then slowly build the budget up as you get better in running and managing your ad campaigns. Starting small allows you to learn and experiment with very little risks. If your campaign does not go as you expected, at least you used a small budget. As you learn and gain more experience, that's when you slowly increase your spending.

7. Observe your competition especially the most successful ones. This is a matter of watching and learning. What are they doing that make them so successful? How are they running and managing their ad campaigns? How are they targeting their customers? Find answers to these questions and implement them in your own campaigns.

8. Tell stories with your ads. Storytelling is an integral part of human communication. The better you are in telling stories, the more effective you are as a communicator. When developing your ads and writing your ad copy, you should infuse stories into them. It's easier for people to relate to your ads if there's a story being told. Even better if you make your target audience part of the stories you are telling.

9. Monitor the performance of your ads and adjust them in real time. This is one of the biggest advantages of advertising on Facebook. You can tweak, modify, and customize your ads even if these are still live. Your modifications are applied in real time. This means that you can easily change the look of an ad in just minutes.

10. Have a long-term strategy for your ads. You must have a long-term plan with regards to the progression of your ads. This is the best way for you and your business to stay relevant within the Facebook platform. Every decision you make with regards to your ads should be geared towards achieving your long-term goals.

Inspiration #20

Most of the important things in the world have been accomplished by people who have kept on trying when there seemed to be no hope at all.
Dale Carnegie

Traffic Source #6 – Instagram Ads

Instagram is now owned by Facebook so the photo-sharing network's advertising program is very similar to that of Facebook. However, you can only create ads on Instagram if you have converted your account to a business profile. There are a few ways on how to create ads on Instagram. You can make the ads using Instagram yourself or you can create the ads using the tools and resources on Facebook. The types of ads that you can create on Instagram are very similar to that of Facebook. I suggest that you read our Facebook section to remind yourself of these ad various ad formats.

There are three ways to create and run ads that appear on Instagram. These are as follows:

1. Create ads directly from Instagram. This is very similar to boosting a post on Facebook. After creating a post on Instagram, you can convert the post into an ad by promoting it. You can also promote not just posts but Instagram stories as well.

2. Create ads using your Facebook business page. You can link your Instagram account with your Facebook business page. When you create ads or promotions for your page, these can also appear in Instagram.

3. Create and run ad campaigns using Ads Manager. You can design Instagram ads through the Ads Manager by simply selecting Instagram as the placement. This is unique in the sense that you can use it to create Instagram ads even if you don't have an Instagram account.

The Pricing Model for Instagram Ads

So how much does it cost to advertise on Instagram? Again, Instagram is owned by Facebook so the costs of advertising on Instagram are very similar to the costs of advertising on Facebook. With that said, we refer you to our chapter about Facebook advertising. However, the quick answer to the question is this: the average cost-per-click on Instagram is around $0.5 to $1. Of course, the costs will be much higher in very competitive industries in Instagram like fashion and beauty products. Some Instagram ads can cost up to $5 per click.

It's also a well-known fact that Instagram ads are more expensive compared to Facebook ads. This is for the simple reason that Instagram has a much simpler interface which means that ads are exposed and displayed to more people. On average, an ad on Instagram will cost the advertiser between $0.70 and $1. However, you should always keep in mind that the amounts you pay for your ads depend on various factors.

The Pros of Instagram Advertising

1. Instagram is one of the fastest growing social networking sites today. Just recently, the site breached the one billion members mark and it's still going strong as far as new sign-ups are concerned. That said, Instagram is not one of those social sites who go popular then die a slow death. Putting up ads on Instagram is a great investment given its popularity and the fact that it doesn't seem to be slowing down any time soon.

2. Instagram ads are not that intrusive compared to other types of social media ads including Facebook ads. Being non-intrusive means that the ads are less likely to annoy their targeted audience. Instagram ads, if designed properly, look like normal Instagram content. This is why Instagram ads tend to convert better compared to Facebook ads.

3. The engagement rate for Instagram ads is much higher than the engagement rates in other social media platforms. Again, this is for the simple reason that ads in Instagram look like standard posts and content. Engagement rates for ads in social sites are usually better when there are very little distinctions between ads the content that people see in their feeds.

4. Instagram ads are great for building brand awareness. When you promote a post on Instagram as an advertisement, it will appear in the news feeds of your target audience without being too out of place or disruptive. Unobtrusive ads are very powerful in building hype around your business and brand. There's a reason why thousands of companies and brands are using Instagram. The payoff for their advertising efforts are too good to ignore.

5. Instagram users are using the app to purchase products online. It's estimated that at least one-third of Instagram users have used the platform to purchase a product online. Keep in mind that Instagram currently has more than a billion users. This means that around 300 million users have in one way or another bought a product or availed of a service through Instagram. Instagram allows you to create ads with call-to-action buttons like Shop Now or Contact Us.

6. It allows you to learn about the likes and dislikes of your core customer base. Instagram is a great tool for understanding the ever-changing likes and dislikes of your followers and customer base. When creating normal posts or ads, you get to gauge the reactions of your audience through their likes and comments. You can determine what kind of content and ads they are drawn to. This helps you in improving your posts and ads.

7. You can use Instagram to fuel your other marketing campaigns and efforts. What does this mean? I've mentioned earlier that you can use Instagram to understand the needs and wants of your target audience. Well, you can use the information you gathered from your Instagram campaigns to improve your marketing efforts in other platforms. For example, if you are also advertising through Google Ads, you can use the information from your Instagram ads to improve the performance of your Google Ads campaigns.

8. You can see your return on investment because sales and leads through Instagram Ads are trackable. Instagram uses the same Ads Manager as Facebook so it has all the tracking capabilities of Facebook. You can look at everything like link clicks, likes, comments, shares, and other actions that your audience used to interact with your ads. You get to see how many results you achieved and at what cost.

The Cons of Instagram Advertising

1. You have a limited audience especially if you are targeting an older crowd. Instagram has more than a billion active users but these are primarily composed of young people between the ages of 18 and 29. This means that if you have a product or a service that targets an older audience, then Instagram is not the best platform to advertise your product and service. Another important thing you should know about Instagram is that around 60% to 70% of its users are women. Again, this can be problematic for you and your affiliate marketing business if you are promoting products and services that are mostly used by men.

2. Instagram is a visual-based networking site which means that if you want to create text-heavy ads, it's not the best platform for you. If you run an affiliate marketing business with a heavy amount of text or written content, Instagram is not the best fit for your business.

3. Links on Instagram are not that effective. First of all, you can only put a link to a post if you are a business account and that you are boosting the post. Ordinary users are not allowed to place clickable links in their posts. This is an issue because it creates the impression among regular users that Instagram posts aren't supposed to contain clickable links. So when they come across Instagram ads that contain clickable links, they are almost blind to the links.

How to Get the Most Out of Instagram Advertising

1. Take advantage of Instagram's zoom feature and use this in your ads. Instagram users can zoom in on content in their feeds. This is a great opportunity for you to make your ads more attractive and interactive. Most Instagram users access their accounts and feeds through smartphones. That said, you should create ads that users can easily zoom in on.

2. Only promote as ads your best content. You don't have to promote every piece of content you post in your Instagram account. This will not only bloat your advertising expenses, it will also alienate your core audience. It's never a good idea to flood your feed with ads. With that said, you should only select a few of your best content to promote as ads. This will increase your engagement which means more people will get to see your promoted content.

3. Make your ads look like regular content. The best way to make people notice your ads on Instagram is to create ads that blend in with your regular content. In short, don't make the ads look like ads. Your target audience is more likely to respond to your ads that look like regular content as opposed to blatant product or service promotion. You should always incorporate images of actual people in your ads. Posts that contain actual human images tend to get more likes compared to other types of content.

4. Use a call-to-action in your ads. When you create an ad on Instagram, you have the option to add a call-to-action to the image of your ad. You can place the call-to-action on the bottom right corner of the ad. Taking advantage of the feature can significantly increase your ad's engagement rate.

5. Be familiar with all the ad types so that you can choose the right formats for your business. Take the time to learn about the various features and functions of the different ad types (photo ads, carousel ads, video ads, marquee ads). Knowing about the differences between these ad types should help you decide which ad types will suit your business product or service.

6. Consider partnering with influencers in Instagram. This is a very powerful marketing strategy that can do wonders for your brand if you do it right. What you need to do is get in touch with popular Instagram users who create content that's related to your niche. For example, if you are selling beauty products, then you should look for Instagram influencers in the beauty niche. Contact them and propose a partnership.

7. Test your ads. Testing is one of the most effective techniques in online advertising. It helps you in developing your ads that perform well. The good news is that Instagram makes it very easy to test two ads and find out which ad works better. The social network allows you to duplicate your existing ads and tweak them to test different elements like images, captions, texts, and call to actions. To find out the ads that generate the best results, be sure to analyze the reports and statistics that Instagram provides you.

8. Keep your ad copy short and direct. It's no secret that social media users have very short attention spans. You only have a few seconds to get their attention. That said, it's important that you write ad copy that's short and direct. Always keep in mind that Instagram is an image-heavy platform. People use Instagram because they want to look at visual content. Putting too much textual content in your ads will bore them and drive them away. In short, always keep your captions to a bare minimum.

9. Use relevant hashtags. Using hashtags accomplishes two things. One, it makes your content look like regular content which means people will be more likely to interact with it. And two, hashtags expose your ad to more people. Using the proper ads can attract a good number of views for your ad especially if the hashtag is quite popular or is trending on the site.

10. Create ads that inspire people. This is especially true if you are creating video ads. Have you ever wondered why the best ads are the ones that inspire people? It's for the simple reason that the ads touch us and we feel the urge to share the message of the ads. Inspiring ads go viral much easier compared to other types of ads. Even if you are not creating video ads, you should still incorporate an inspirational message in your ads.

Inspiration #21

Perseverance is the hard work you do after you get tired of doing the hard work you already did.
Newt Gingrich

Traffic Source #7 – LinkedIn Ads

LinkedIn is a great place to find more leads for your business. This is especially true if you are not just interested in finding new customers. You are also looking to attract potential business partners. You see, LinkedIn is a social networking site for business professionals. The latest estimate is that the site now has more than 500 million users. That's a lot of members. Keep in mind that a huge percentage of this user base are professionals and entrepreneurs. If you want to turn some of these into customers or business partners, you should definitely set aside a budget for LinkedIn advertising campaigns.

How LinkedIn Advertising Works

Obviously, you must have a LinkedIn account before you are able to use their advertising program. So if you don't already have a LinkedIn account, go visit their website now and sign up then come back here. The platform is free and the sign-up process will only take a few minutes of your time. Make sure to fill in all the details so that you will have a 100% complete profile. With your account verified and complete, you can start creating your LinkedIn ads.

Before you can get started, you also need to create a Campaign Manager account. You can also create one in just a few minutes. This is the account you are going to use in managing and optimizing your advertising campaigns on LinkedIn. The account comes with a lot of features and functions aimed at helping you get the most out of your campaigns. It provides you with dynamic visual reports that recalculate and display the data that match your filter and search settings. The account also provides you with detailed analysis of the actions that your campaigns generated including shares, likes, clicks, follows, and comments. Last but not the least, the account provides you with informative data about the demographic categories of the LinkedIn members who viewed or interacted with your ads.

After getting a Campaign Manager account, you can now start creating your LinkedIn ads. There are three types of ads you can choose from. These are Text Ads, Sponsored InMail Ads, and Sponsored Content Ads. You can use a mix of the three ad types if you want. Here's a quick overview of the three types of ads on LinkedIn:

1. Sponsored Content - These are the ads that appear in the news feeds of LinkedIn users. This option offers you with three core benefits. One, it helps you in getting your message across to targeted users through a variety of devices such as desktop computers, laptops, tablets, and smartphones. Two, you can use rich media in your ads so that these will stand out in user news feeds. And three, Sponsored Content ads can help you in testing your messaging and optimizing them in real time. That's right. You can optimize your LinkedIn ads in real time.

2. Sponsored InMail - This ad is designed to help you deliver relevant and personalized content to users through the LinkedIn Messenger service. You can use this ad in both desktop computers and mobile phones.

3. Text Ads - Use these to drive new customers to your business through a pay-per-click advertising format. There's a lot that you can do with Text Ads. Creating an ad takes just a few minutes of your time. You can choose the specific professional audience that you want to reach. You can set your own budget without long-term commitments nor contracts. Furthermore, you only pay for the ads that generate results for your business. You pay either on a per click or per impression basis. Last but not the least, you can track the number of leads you're getting from your ads using conversion tracking.

What's the Pricing Model for LinkedIn Advertising?

LinkedIn follows a flexible and dynamic pricing model in the sense that the amount you pay for your ads is up to you. You can start with any budget you want and you can pause and stop the ads any time you want. To get the most out of your ads, you should set a total budget, a daily budget, and maximum bids. Setting up your maximum bids makes sure that you are not going to pay more than the price you bid.

Another important matter you should know is that your ads are sold through an auction. There are other advertisers in LinkedIn who are targeting the same audience as you. Needless to say, the tougher the competition is, the more money you have to spend to reach more of your target audience.

You get to choose your ad pricing. You can pay through cost-per-click, cost per 1000 impressions, and cost per send. The cost per send pricing model only applies to Sponsored InMail ads.

The Pros of LinkedIn Advertising

1. You have access to a professional audience. This is very important especially if you run an affiliate marketing business that sells products or services that are geared towards professionals and entrepreneurs. It's also a great way to find reliable business partners.

2. You have several ad types to choose from. We've discussed earlier the three main types of ads that you can create through LinkedIn's advertising program. You can choose from Sponsored Content, Sponsored InMail, or Text Ads. You can use all three formats if you want.

3. LinkedIn allows you to define your audience using specific categories. Your ad can be delivered to LinkedIn users depending on their resumes and company profiles. You can define your ads by generation, geography, gender, schools attended, language, industries, groups, and keywords.

4. You get what you pay for. It's no secret that LinkedIn ads are among the cheapest advertising programs today. The minimum budget for an ad campaign is a measly $2. Keep in mind that LinkedIn users are highly targeted so even if you have a small budget, it can still go far in reaching your intended audience.

5. LinkedIn wall updates display much longer compared to other social networking sites. This means that more people will be able to see your ad in their newsfeeds. This is because LinkedIn has less users but a huge majority of these users share many things in common.

6. LinkedIn ads are great in increasing your conversion rates. Studies have been done on how helpful LinkedIn is in improving conversion rates and most of these studies come to the conclusion that LinkedIn is indeed a very powerful tool in increasing conversion rates.

The Cons of LinkedIn Advertising

1. Limited audience. This is without a doubt the biggest drawback of advertising on LinkedIn because a huge percentage of its users are professionals and entrepreneurs. If you want to appeal to a much younger audience, LinkedIn is just not the right platform for you.

2. If you are going to avail of LinkedIn's Sponsored InMail ad option, you run the risk of being accused of spamming the inboxes of LinkedIn users. This is a very tricky strategy because you need to provide something of value to the recipient because if you are not able to do that, you will likely be tagged as a spammer.

3. A lot of LinkedIn's users are just looking for jobs. They are not interested in products or services. This can be very problematic for you who is spending premium for ads that are delivered to the news feeds of these job-seeking users. You should always remember this important fact when designing your ad campaign and when you are choosing which users to target.

How to Get the Most Out of LinkedIn Advertising

1. Make sure that your ads have very compelling visuals. Writing a good headline is good but you need to complement it with a great visual to attract the attention of your target audience. LinkedIn itself has tested various ads in their system and they found out that ads with visuals get more clicks compared to ads with no or uninteresting visuals.

2. Test everything. Don't just stick to a single ad design or format. It doesn't matter if you are promoting a product or a service, you need to test variations of your ads to determine the ones that generate the most results. Test and improve. This should be your strategy especially if you are planning to run a series of ads.

3. Bid above the suggested range if you want a lift in your clickthrough rate. Keep in mind that ads within LinkedIn follow the bidding system. The more you put in your ads, the more chances they have in being seen by your target audience. Experts suggest that you bid at least 10% above the range. This can increase your clickthrough rate by up to 15% and your conversion rate by up to 27%.

4. Keep your ad copy short, simple, and direct. Always remember that you are competing with hundreds of other advertisers on the platform. You should condense your message in just a few clear sentences. You only have a few seconds to get the attention of your audience. Get rid of jargon that might confuse your readers.

5. Track and evaluate the performances of your ads and ad campaigns. This is something that a lot of new LinkedIn advertisers take for granted. Never underestimate the power of tracking the performances of your ads because this is the only way to determine if your ads are working or not.

Inspiration #22

I am not a product of my circumstances. I am a product of my decisions.
Stephen Covey

Traffic Source #8 – Twitter Ads

Twitter is on the top five most influential social networking sites today. It boasts of millions of active users every hour. You are missing out on a huge market if you are not using Twitter to promote your affiliate marketing business. One of the good things about Twitter is that it has a smart user base. Twitter users are well-known for being more discerning and more interactive when it comes to content that they are truly interested in. With that said, Twitter is the perfect platform to reach out to your target market.

All you need to get started is to create an account with Twitter. Signing up will take just a few minutes of your time. You can start designing your ad campaign right after you confirm and verify your account. You can launch ad campaigns and tailor your ads depending on your goals and what types of people you want to reach. This is why Twitter can be a great platform to promote your affiliate marketing business.

How Twitter Advertising Works

To get started, you must decide on your objectives in buying ads from Twitter. What is it that you want to achieve? Twitter makes it very easy for you to choose which objective you should target. You can choose from tweet awareness, tweet engagement, follower growth, traffic for your website, and app downloads.

After choosing your objective, the next step is to decide on your audience. What types of Twitter users would you like to reach with your ads? Twitter has specific targeting features that allow you to pick the audience for your ads. You can target Twitter users based on their geographic location, their interests, gender, the devices they use, and the celebrities they follow. This is a crucial step in the process. The more accurate you are in targeting your audience, the better results you can generate.

After choosing your audience, you now have to start bidding and setting your campaign budget. Like most online advertising networks and programs, ads on Twitter are managed through an auction. You decide how much you are willing to pay for each interaction generated with your ad. For example, how much are you willing to pay for a click, a new follower, or a referred visitor to your website? There's no minimum to how much you want to spend on each campaign. You get to choose the daily budget for your ads. However, for best results, Twitter specifically recommends that you start with at least $30 a day if you want your ads to reach audiences throughout the day.

How Much Does Twitter Ads Cost?

The fortunate thing about Twitter Ads is that they can accommodate both small and big advertising budgets. Whether you are a small business or a major corporation, you can advertise your products and services on Twitter. As I have mentioned earlier, there is no minimum requirement for Twitter Ads. You only spend what your budget can afford you. You have complete control over how much you want to spend on your ads. How much you spend in your campaigns are set by you.

When you set up your advertising campaign, you choose the amount you are willing to spend on your ads on a daily basis. It could be $10 a day, $30 a day, or $1000 a day. However, there's this thing called "billable action". The "billable action" refers to the action you want to generate from your audience based on the objective you chose. For example, if your objective is to get more followers, the "billable action" would be when a Twitter user follows you after seeing your ad on his or her Twitter feed. If your objective is to generate traffic for your website, the "billable action" will be when a user clicks on your ad and visits your website.

But here's the thing, the price for each "billable action" is not fixed. Remember that Twitter ads are managed through an auction. This means that what you pay for each follower generated by an ad is not the same as the amount being paid by other advertisers. You could be paying more or less for each "billable action" compared to other advertisers. As an advertiser, you will be bidding on available ad space for the audience you want to reach. How much you pay depends on the following factors:
1. The quality of your ad
2. The number of other advertisers targeting the same audience as you
3. The size of the audience you want to reach
4. The amount you are willing to bid

The main takeaway here is that ultimately, you have the choice if you want to spend $10 a day or $1000 a day for your Twitter ad campaigns. I would highly recommend that you start with lower budgets when advertising on Twitter. Slowly increase your campaign budgets as you learn more about how the thing works. This will save you a lot of time and money.

Pros of Advertising on Twitter

1. You have multiple types of ads to choose from. Again, these ad types depend on your objectives. You can run a promoted tweet which is pushed in the timelines of people who don't even follow you. You can promote your account so that it appears as a recommended account in the profiles and feeds of users.

2. Twitter enables you to narrow down your target audience. You can precisely target users based on their geographic locations, interests, genders, and the people they follow. You can even target users based on keywords they use in their tweets. For example, if you are promoting a website that sells soccer gear, you can set up an ad so that it appears next to tweets that contain the keyword "soccer" or "soccer equipment".

3. You only pay for performance. When you promote a tweet or an account, you only pay when you have achieved your objective. For example, you only pay if your ad generates new followers or if users click on the ad and are redirected to your main website. In short, you only pay when people take action on your ads.

4. Twitter has a keyword targeting feature. This is a very precise tool you can use to go after very specific people on Twitter. The feature allows you to target users who have used a certain word or hashtag in their tweets. Keyword targeting also allows you to reach users who haven't posted but interacted with tweets containing the keywords or hashtags. For example, if you are targeting the keyword "trail running", your ad can reach the feeds of people who liked tweets that contain the keyword "trail running". This is how powerful keyword targeting can be.

5. Low cost per clicks. You can literally pay a few pennies for every action generated by your ads. This is because the price of every action on your ad is determined through an auction. It has everything to do with how much you are willing to pay for each action. The competition for advertising on Twitter is not that saturated so ads there are fairly cheap compared to advertising costs in other well-known social networking sites like Facebook, YouTube, and LinkedIn.

Cons of Advertising on Twitter

1. Twitter is lacking when it comes to analytics. Unlike social networks like Facebook and Instagram that provide their advertisers with detailed analytics and statistics for their ads, Twitter has really poor analytics. Yes, Twitter does provide you with some sort of analytics but these are not as detailed nor in-depth compared to other social networking sites. The bottom line here is that Twitter's analytics reporting is not as vigorous.

2. Your ads can easily get lost in the Twitter stream. How the Twitter stream works can be very detrimental for your ads. Since the stream changes too fast, your ads can get lost in the clutter. Because of the constant stream of information, a person can easily miss your ads.

3. It's hard to prove if you are getting a return on your investment (ROI). This has something to do with Twitter's clunky analytics and reporting system. It's really difficult to measure the actual results you are getting from your ads. For example, it's nearly impossible to prove if someone actually purchased an item after clicking on your ad.

4. Limited account service if you are just a small advertiser. If you are just a small business owner, it's unlikely that you will have access to Twitter representatives who will instantly answer your questions, help you troubleshoot problems, or assist you with your advertising campaigns.

How to Get the Most Out of Twitter Advertising

1. Keep in mind that a huge majority of Twitter users are young, tech-savvy, and educated. Why did I mention this? Well, because if you are going to create advertisements for Twitter, make sure that these are ads that will relate well to young, educated, and tech-savvy audiences. You should design ads that will be relevant to these young audiences.

2. Remember mobile users. Up to 80% of Twitter's active users access the social network through a mobile app. Needless to say, you should make sure that your Twitter ads are easy to read on smaller screens. If you include links in your ads, see to it that the links redirect to mobile-friendly websites.

3. Create ads that look natural. Do not be too pushy when designing your ads. Twitter ads usually appear in the feeds of users and if these ads are too pushy or too salesy, users often ignore them and skip over them. They won't respond to the call to actions associated with your ads. When you design your ads, treat them as if these are regular posts in your news feed. The more natural the ads look, the better chance that people will engage with them.

4. Avoid using too many hashtags on your ads. This is especially important if you are putting links in your ads. Hashtags are clickable which means that they compete with your links in getting the attention of viewers. If a person clicks on the hashtag instead of clicking on your link, then that's potentially a lost customer. Most advertising experts recommend that you use not more than five hashtags in your ads. For best results, your hashtags should number between two and three. Some advertisers don't even use hashtags in their ads because hashtags can be very distracting.

5. Encourage viewers to interact with your ads. Aside from including call to actions in your ads, you should actively encourage people to engage with your ads. One good way to do this is to ask questions in your ads. Asking a question lets people feel that they are part of the conversation. It's easier for them to relate to the ad this way. It compels them to answer, click share, or like the ads.

6. Experiment with multiple tweets per campaign. This is one of the good things with Twitter advertising. You can experiment with multiple ads at the same time in one campaign. This enables you to test various ad ideas to determine which ideas will generate the best results. For example, maybe you want to know if your image ad should contain a white or black background. You can test and experiment with both colors to find out which color is better in attracting attention.

7. Try putting deadlines in the offers that you are promoting in your ads. This is a strategy that creates urgency. This is a very powerful technique if you are promoting products or services. What a lot of online marketers do is set up a discount or promo for a selection of products and services. They then set up a deadline for the discount or promo. For example, customers can get a 30% discount for a particular product only if they avail of it in the next seven days. Creating urgency increases the conversion rates of your ads.

8. Get in touch and partner with Twitter influencers. These are social media celebrities who have sizable followings on Twitter. You can leverage their reach to drive attention to your ads. Only partner with influencers who are in the same niche or industry as your affiliate marketing business. For example, if you are selling vegetarian cookbooks, then it makes complete sense that you partner with an influencer who posts content about vegetarianism and vegan diets on Twitter.

9. Target specific keywords. One of the most common mistakes that Twitter advertisers make is not targeting very specific keywords when putting together their Twitter ad campaigns. If you want to grab attention from the proper audiences, you should target specific keywords in your ads. If you are selling sports memorabilia, then you should be targeting the keyword "sports memorabilia" in your ads.

10. Tweet at the right time. The time you choose in posting your ads depends on the type of audience you are trying to target. You need to find out the best time for you to tweet. What are the time periods wherein your target audience tend to be online?

Traffic Source #9 – Bing Ads

Bing may not be as big as Google but you should not count it out if you want to reach as many people as possible online through advertising. Bing claims to generate 12 billion searches around the globe every single month. In the United States alone, Bing powers at least one-third of desktop searches. That's a lot if you think about it. Advertisers are often too focused on Google that they fail to see how big Bing can be.

What I'm trying to say here is that you should not put all your search advertising budget on just one basket. Don't just focus on Google. You should also spend some advertising money on Bing. In using Bing Ads, your advertisements can appear in Bing, Yahoo, and MSN. And yes, you also have the power to target your ads to different geographic regions, demographics, and other factors.

How Does Bing Ads Work?

It's easier to understand Bing Ads if you see how they look. What I need you to do is visit the Bing website and perform a quick search for any term or keyword. The resulting page will contain not just results but ads as well. These ads may appear before the list of results, beside the results, or in between the results. So basically, if you create an account with Bing Ads and set up an ad campaign, your ads will appear in these search results.

How Much Does Bing Ads Cost?

How much you are going to spend on your ads is completely up to you. It's you who decide on the bid amount for the particular keywords that you are going to target. In short, you get to decide on the price that you are willing to pay every time a person clicks on one of your ads. It's easier to explain this through an example. First of all, it's important that you understand that an auction determines which ads will be shown on the search results page. Needless to say, if your ad is relevant to the search query and you invested a good budget on the ad, then there's a good chance that your ad will win the auction.

Let's say for example that your bid for every click your ad gets is $1. If your ad gets shown in the search results of Bing after a person made a search, it's understood that you pay $1 if your ad gets clicked upon. Bing makes the decision if your ad is eligible to appear on the results page based on your bids and the relevance of your ads to the search query. Let's do the math here. If your ad gets shown in the results page and the ad generates 10 clicks, this means that the campaign will cost you $10.

However, it's not always the case that every click will cost you $1. This is just the maximum amount you are going to pay for every click. This means that a click will cost less than $1. It could be 80 cents, 50 cents, or even lower depending on the competition for the keywords you are targeting.

Pros of Bing Ads

1. Bing ads have less competition and they offer cheaper cost per clicks (CPC). Not only are you going to save a good amount of money, it's also easier for your ads to appear in the search results because the competition is not that saturated compared to Google. In short, you get better ad positions and at less costs.

2. Bing Ads has great device targeting options. Bing Ads allows you to target people based on the device that they are using. You have the option to target desktop users, tablet users, and mobile phone users. You can exclude one or two of the types of people depending on the devices they are using. For example, let's say that you have designed an ad directed towards mobile phone users. You can customize your ad so that it will only appear in the feeds of mobile users and not in the feeds of desktop and tablet users.

3. Bing Ads is very friendly to local and small business owners and marketers. You can easily target your ads so that they will be displayed when someone searches in your area. This makes it easy for you to target people based on their locations. If you are selling car parts in a particular city, you can purchase Bing Ads that target people searching for car parts in your area.

4. Bing Ads is cost-effective because you pay only when some clicks on your ad. If your ads don't get any clicks, then you are also not obligated to pay for the ads. You are going to pay for the ads depending on the actions taken by viewers of the ad.

5. You can avail of personalized advice from experts on Bing advertising. There are experts who will help you drive more leads and attract more engagement from your ad viewers. You can ask them question. You can seek help on how you can make your ads more engaging.

6. There's no minimum fee. It's completely up to you how much you are going to pay for your ads. Signing up with the program is also free and there are very little barriers you must go through. You can actually set up an account in under an hour. It's advisable that you get started with a small and limited budget to get a taste of the market. As you learn more, you slowly increase the amount you spend on your advertising campaigns.

Cons of Bing Ads

1. The audience for your ads can be very limited. This is for the simple fact that Bing is not that big as Google. Google still controls more than 50% of the search market. This means that you miss out on a lot of opportunities if you solely rely on Bing Ads to promote your affiliate marketing business.

2. Bing Ads does not allow you to make use of broad match negative keywords. Just to refresh your memory, negative keywords are keywords that seem to be relevant to your website but they are not actually relevant to what you are promoting. Using negative keywords allows you prevent your ads from showing in irrelevant searches. Bing Ads isn't that good in this aspect of advertising.

How to Get the Most Out of Bing Ads

1. Track your ads so that you can determine which ones are working well and generating results. Bing Ads has its own tracking interface so you should make use of it whenever you can. The interface provides you with information about your ads and your campaigns. If you are not satisfied with the information you are getting from the interface, you can set up your Bing Ads account with Google Analytics.

2. Take advantage of automated rules. This is an exclusive function that enables you to automate some of the processes involved in creating ads on Bing such as budgeting, bidding, and selecting keywords. Setting up these automatic rules can be frustrating at first but these will benefit you in the long run. Taking advantage of automated rules allow you to manage huge advertising campaigns with less hassle.

3. It's important to take into account the time zones associated with your target audience. The idea here is that you should activate your ads during the times wherein you think your target audiences are active online. It would be a waste of time and money if your ads go live while most of your target audiences are asleep or are offline. Taking time zones into account is all about maximizing the reach of your ads.

4. Take the time to monitor your competition. You need to be constantly looking for ways on how to stay ahead of the competition. How do you make sure that it's your ads that appear in the search results and not those of your competitors? You observe what they do and what's working well for them. You then try to replicate their success by implementing their strategies on your own ads. You should also take advantage of the Auction Insight Report, a competitive analysis tool by Bing Ads. The tool provides you with very valuable information about how your advertisements are performing compared to the ads by your competitors.

5. Target mobile and tablet devices. In this day and age, a large percentage of the searches being performed online are done using mobile devices. You should be ready for these mobile searches. The idea here is that you should design ads that will look nice in mobile and tablet devices. If a person searches on Bing and your ad is among those displayed in the search results, does it stand out or does it look big enough if the person is looking at it through a small smartphone screen?

6. Take advantage of the close variant matching feature of Bing Ads. What this means is that you have the ability to match your most important keywords to related variations. Close variant matching is an intuitive strategy to connect people with the businesses and brands they are searching for on the Bing search engine.

7. Go local with your ads. Another good thing with Bing Ads is that it has some features that enable you to customize your ads for local SEO. Going local means that you target search queries on Bing that are coming from your location. For example, let's say that you are selling motorcycle parts in Los Angeles. Needless to say, you would like people searching for motorcycle parts in Los Angeles to be redirected to your affiliate marketing website. With local ads, you can reach these queries because your ads will be shown in the search results page.

Inspiration #24

If you can tune into your purpose and really align with it, setting goals so that your vision is an expression of that purpose, then life flows much more easily.
Jack Canfield

Traffic Source #10 - Outbrain Amplify

If you have a content-heavy website or blog for your affiliate marketing business, I highly recommend that you seriously consider promoting it via Outbrain Amplify. Outbrain describes itself as a "premium discovery platform". The company helps marketers connect with their target audiences through personalized recommendation systems and programs. Outbrain has partnered with thousands of online publishers from major media corporations to small bloggers. With that said, you have the potential of reaching a lot of people if you advertise with Outbrain Amplify.

How Outbrain Amplify Works

Before we proceed, it's important that you are aware of the core business model of Outbrain. It's a platform that connects advertisers with publishers. Publishers are the sites and blogs that display Outbrain ads on their sites. Advertisers are those who pay to advertise in the sites of these publishers. In this context, you are one of these advertisers. In using Outbrain as an advertiser, you make it easier for your target customers to discover your website and whatever affiliate products you are selling. When you set up an advertising campaign with Outbrain Amplify, your content will appear as recommendations in the pages of websites that signed up with Outbrain as publishers.

Outbrain Amplify utilizes a complex set of algorithms and their patented Interest Graph to pair your website's content with users who might find your content relevant and engaging. Outbrain's algorithms were specifically designed to deliver content that people would like to read based on their online activity and the sites that they visit. Using Outbrain can do a lot of things for your business and website. It can drive organic traffic. It can build exposure for your products and services. And it can increase your leads, sales, and conversion rates.

How Much Does Advertising on Outbrain Amplify Cost?

Let's talk about Outbrain's pricing and billing model. Outbrain basically follows a cost per click (CPC) pricing model. Needless to say, you will be charged based on the number of clicks that each of your ad campaigns generate. Here's the good news. You get to set your own CPC and your campaign budget. You are in full control of your budget and spending at all times. You only spend what you can afford because you can set a cap for your budget.

To illustrate how budgeting and spending works through Outbrain Amplify, let's illustrate it through an example. You signed up with the program and you are ready to run your first campaign. When creating your campaign, you will be required to set your campaign budget. Let's say you set your campaign budget to $50 and your cost per click to 50 cents. This means that you will pay 50 cents for every click that your ad gets until the $50 runs out. With the $50 budget, you can receive a maximum of one hundred clicks.

When your campaign reaches the maximum clicks and your budget runs out, your ads and content will automatically stop showing in the sites of publishers until you replenish your budget or you create another campaign.

Pros of Advertising Through Outbrain Amplify

1. The platform is very easy to use. You can create your ads in just a few minutes following their 4-step launch process. You will be guided and assisted along the way. There are also tutorials on how you can create, design, and customize your campaigns. Outbrain is among the easiest advertising platforms to use. You don't have to be that technically-savvy to use their tools and resources.

2. It's easier for your ads to reach your target audience. Always keep in mind that Outbrain is a content discovery platform. Their main service is to help content creators deliver their content to their target audiences. This is why Outbrain develops and uses algorithms that make it easier and faster for marketers to connect with their audiences. They also make use of behavioral data to capture the attention of audiences.

3. You get your money's worth. As we have discussed earlier, Outbrain follows the cost per click pricing model. You only pay for your ads only when viewers and readers click on them. You only pay for clicks, not views or impressions. When a reader clicks on your ad, it means that he is interested in your content. It means that he is showing interest in whatever you are trying to promote. For this reason alone, ads delivered through Outbrain Amplify tend to have higher than average conversion rates.

4. Outbrain Amplify is very effective when it comes to native advertising. What is native advertising? This is the technique of utilizing ads that match the look, feel, and design of the digital space in which they appear. Unlike other types of ads like banner ads, native ads don't look like ads at all. They flow well with the themes and content of the websites where they are displayed. They are non-disruptive and their main purpose is to provide additional content and additional value not only for the host website but for the readers and viewers as well.

5. The platform has an easy to use dashboard. You can track, measure, and optimize your advertising campaigns straight from your Outbrain Amplify dashboard. This makes it easy for you to customize your ads in real time. If something is not going as you expected, you can always modify your campaigns to try and improve the results the campaigns are generating.

6. Outbrain Amplify is safe and secure. This is one of the most important selling points of Outbrain. They are very serious when it comes to maintaining values of quality, security, brand safety, and transparency. Keep in mind that when you sign up with Outbrain, you will have to provide some of your most sensitive information like name, address, and online banking/payment details. However, you are assured that Outbrain will keep all of your information safe.

6. Outbrain Amplify offers responsive designs for their ads. This means that you can create ads that respond to the designs and layouts of the websites where they appear in. The ads also respond and adapt depending on the type of device that the reader is using. The responsive ads can change their formats and looks in response to whether they are being viewed through a mobile phone, a tablet, or a desktop computer or laptop.

Cons of Advertising Through Outbrain Amplify

1. Your ads can potentially be displayed in low-quality websites. Let me remind you that Outbrain partners with both major media outlets like CNN and small websites like obscure blogs. It can really hurt your business or your brand if your website or content gets featured in a low-quality publisher and partner. Unlike other advertising platforms like Google Ads, Outbrain does not allow you to prevent your ads from showing in specific websites and URLs.

2. Outbrain's partner websites are still limited in numbers. Outbrain has been around for quite a few years and it has amassed a good number of partners and publishers who display Outbrain ads in their sites. But this number is not that large if you compare it to other major online advertising platforms like Google Ads. My point here is that your Outbrain ads may not reach the number of people you'd expect to reach.

3. A lot of the advertisers on Outbrain today are using tactics that can be described as clickbait. In fact, this problem is so rampant that some publishers and advertisers have pulled out of the program. Many advertisers on Outbrain are creating exaggerated and misleading headlines for their ads. As a result, a lot of these ads look spammy. This can hurt your business and your ads since your ads will often be appearing alongside these spammy and clickbaity content.

4. Outbrain's customer service is not that reliable based on the experiences of a lot of advertisers there. It can be difficult to get hold of a knowledgeable customer representative if your ads are not working or if there's something wrong with your ad campaign. With that said, it can take a little bit of time before your ad issues can be addressed. This can be really problematic if you are running and managing time-sensitive ads.

How to Get the Most Out of Outbrain Amplify

1. You should submit your planned ad campaign at least a week before you are going to launch the ads. This is because every piece of content that you submit to the Outbrain network is manually reviewed by Outbrain's review staff. This is to make sure that your content is up to the network's standards and that you are not breaking any rule or policy. In other words, timing is everything.

2. When planning an ad campaign, it's better if you focus on promoting a single URL. This doesn't mean that you should run a single ad. You can run several ads. It's just that all of them should point towards the same URL. Even Outbrain's staff recommends that you use a single URL for your campaigns instead of multiple URLs.

3. Test out multiple ad images and headlines. When you are creating an ad campaign around a single URL, Outbrain encourages you to submit six to seven variations of images and headlines. What Outbrain does is test out these variations so that they can determine how to optimize the ads and generate better results from them. This has been shown to effectively boost clickthrough rates. When submitting images and headlines, make sure that these are relevant and interesting for your target audience.

4. Try to differentiate your campaigns depending on whether the ads are for mobile users or desktop users. Some ads may work well for mobile while other ads are more effective on desktop. It's also worth mentioning here that Outbrain Amplify's algorithms often prioritize mobile traffic over desktop traffic. You should take note of this important difference when you are creating your ads.

5. Implement the Outbrain pixel in the website where your ads redirect to. Installing the pixel in your website enables you to track the conversions of your ads right in your Outbrain Amplify dashboard. The data and other information you gather through the pixel will help you optimize your ads for custom audiences. This in turn will increase your conversion and engagement rates.

6. Watch your daily budget and lower your bids if necessary. If your campaign is capping its daily budget for several days in a row, this means that you are not getting the maximum numbers of clicks and conversions that you could potentially get. What you should do is adjust and lower your bids to accommodate more clicks for your daily budgets. You will be getting more daily clicks at the same costs.

7. If a campaign is performing well below your expectations, something is definitely wrong. When this happens, some advertisers adjust their campaigns. However, it might be better if you start a new campaign instead of adjusting the existing campaign. Just cancel the current campaign and start all over again. Adjusting the campaign will simply regurgitate the same poor results. So terminate the campaign and start anew.

Inspiration #25

It is during our darkest moments that we must focus to see the light.
Aristotle Onassis

Chapter 15

7 Ways To Track And Optimize Your Traffic Sources

Many affiliate marketers are so caught up on traffic generation methods that they fail to take a closer look at the actual sources of their website visitors. This is a huge mistake because knowing where your traffic comes and how they interact with your website provides you with helpful insights on how to further improve your traffic. You should set aside some of your time and resources in tracking and analyzing your traffic sources.

It's not that difficult to track and measure your traffic sources. The good news is that there's a nice variety of tools that you can use to perform such a task. In the following chapters, we are going to discuss the best of these traffic-tracking tools. We are going to explain what these tools are and how you can use them to track your traffic sources. These tools are Google Analytics, ClickMagick, Voluum, ClickMeter, Trck.me, LinckTrackr, and Improvely. If you are serious about understanding your traffic sources, these are the tools you should be using.

There are several reasons why you should be constantly tracking your traffic sources. These reasons include the following:

1. Tracking enables you to take a closer look at your traffic sources so that you can ensure diversity. When we say diversity, we are alluding to the necessity that your website should be coming from several sources, not just one source. The more sources of traffic you have, the better it will be for your affiliate marketing business. Traffic diversity is essential to maintaining a healthy and sustainable business website. The danger of generating traffic from very few sources is that your business can easily fail if these sources suddenly stop sending you traffic and customers. As the saying goes, you should never put all of your eggs in the same basket. Diversify whenever you can.

2. Tracking helps in maximizing the effectiveness of your split-testing experiments. Allow me to remind you that split-testing is the strategy of running ads with variations at the same time to see which types of ads will generate the better results (i.e. higher conversion rates, more clicks, more views. Tracking allows you to pinpoint various data points. These include where the largest chunk of your visitors are coming from, which types of ads are getting the better results, and of course the conversion rates of your campaigns.

3. Tracking helps you in identifying emerging trends. Constantly monitoring your traffic sources is instrumental in helping you identify emerging trends which you can then further exploit to generate more traffic for your affiliate marketing website. In the process of tracking your traffic sources, you will come across data and information that allows you to sort of predict what the future holds for your business website.

4. Tracking assists you in identifying where your real audiences are coming from. It's a lot easier to analyze your traffic if you have been closely tracking them for a while. With the information you have gathered during the tracking process, you can break down your traffic sources in smaller categories so that you can address them more accurately. Breaking down your traffic sources into smaller categories leads to more actionable insights.

5. Tracking helps in determining the return on investment for your marketing campaigns. Most of the time, your online marketing campaigns will be focused on driving specific types of web traffic. The most effective way for you to determine the ROI for these campaigns is to identify and track the incoming traffic from specific sources.

6. Tracking can help you in identifying algorithm changes. Yes, you can spot algorithm changes and the effects of these changes in your traffic levels if you are constantly monitoring your traffic sources. Although algorithm changes are often associated with Google, other search engines and majority of the drivers of online traffic are regularly modifying their in-site algorithms. You can only spot these algorithm changes if the changes are publicly announced or if you are constantly monitoring your traffic from specific sources.

The point here is that tracking your traffic sources is something that you should be doing. It should be a part of your marketing plans and campaigns. Tracking allows you to become smarter and more logical with your marketing campaigns. It's all about working smarter and not harder. It's about honing your marketing strategies to ensure that you are getting your money's worth. Without further ado, let's take a closer look into some of the best tools that you can use to track and analyze your traffic sources. Let's start with the big fish which is Google Analytics.

Inspiration #26

It's not about perfect. It's about effort. And when you bring that effort every single day, that's where transformation happens. That's how change occurs.
Jillian Michaels

Tracking Tool #1 – Google Analytics

In the simplest of terms, Google Analytics is a tool developed and owned by Google that help website owners analyze their traffic. The implications of Google Analytics are huge considering the fact that Google commands majority of the internet's traffic flow. The latest estimate is that nearly 100 million websites are using Google Analytics. If you are not using the tool right now to track and analyze your website's traffic, then you are missing out on a very powerful too. What's amazing about Google Analytics is that it's free. That's right. You don't have to pay a penny to use it.

How exactly does Google Analytics work? Simply put, all you need to do to get started is to place several lines of code into your website. This code acts as an online tracking device that records the activities of anyone who visits and interacts with your website. Google Analytics aggregates the information it gathered about your visitors and then present this information is clear and simple reports. Google Analytics aggregates the information it gathered by four levels: user level, session level, pageview level, and event level.

There are a lot of things you can do with Google Analytics. You can use it review the effectiveness of your online marketing and advertising campaigns by tracking the quality of landing pages and the conversion rates of the same landing pages. The impact of Google Analytics on the performance of your marketing efforts can be huge if you learn how to take advantage of the various features and functions of the platform.

The Key Features of Google Analytics

1. It provides you with accurate and detailed web traffic reports. At the most basic level, this is the bread and butter of Google Analytics. The tool will provide you with important information like how many people are visiting your website each day, where are they coming from, and how much time they spend browsing through your website. You also have the ability to track traffic trends on your website. This allows you to make decisions that use these trends as leverage.

2. It helps you identify the keywords that people use in finding your website and its contents. These are referred to as keywords referrals. This is very important if one of your major goals is to attract organic traffic from search engines. You need to be aware of the words and phrases that people type into search engines when they look for your website. Needless to say, you need Google Analytics when designing your SEO strategies. In fact, nearly all of your SEO efforts will depend on the data and other information that you get from the reports that Google Analytics provides you.

3. It provides you with information about the third-party websites that are sending traffic to your affiliate marketing website. But first, what are considered to be third party websites? These are the websites other than search engines which are referring traffic to your website. These could be blogs, forums, and social media sites (i.e. Facebook, Twitter, Instagram). Google Analytics tracks these third-party websites and provides you with information about the number and quality of traffic that these sites are sending towards your own site.

4. Google Analytics allows you to create your own customized dashboards depending on the types of data and information that you care about the most. For example, if you care most about traffic levels, keyword referrals, and conversion rates, then you should make these more prominent in your dashboard. Adding them to your dashboard makes it easier for you to access and analyze the reports provided to you by Google Analytics.

5. It helps you visualize how your visitors are interacting with your website. This is something that Google Analytics has nearly perfected. The platform's flow visualization graphics give you a ton of information about the movements of your viewers as they browse through your website. You'll get a clear idea of how your audiences are engaging with your content. It also provides you with tips on how you can drive your engagement rates higher so that people will spend more time in your website.

Pros of Google Analytics

1. Google Analytics is completely free to use. It's the most comprehensive traffic analytics platform today and you don't have to pay to use. It really doesn't get any better than that. There are no hidden charges. You can use every tool and resource within Google Analytics for free. All you need is a Google account to access the analytics service.

2. It helps you pinpoint the links and pages in your website that your visitors click the most. This is one of the biggest reasons why a lot of webmasters use Google Analytics to track and measure engagement. The tool will provide you with reports that show which pages and links in your website are getting the most attention from visitors. Are visitors browsing your products page? Are visitors reading your "about" page? It allows you to measure whether your optimization campaigns are guiding the right amount of traffic to the right pages.

3. It's instrumental in helping you understand what visitors don't like about your website. You get to understand what kind of first impressions you make among first-time visitors of your website. For example, let's say that you've installed Google Analytics in your website for some time and the reports are showing that your website has a high bounce rate. The bounce rate is the measurement of the visitors who immediately leave your website after dropping by. With that said, a high bounce rate means that you are not making a good impression among your visitors. Google Analytics helps you in identifying the reasons why you have such a high bounce rate. Needless to say, if you know the reasons for the high bounce rate, it's easier for you to come up with the necessary solutions.

4. It helps you determine where you rank in search engines. It's not enough to know how search engine optimization works and how you can apply it to your website. You also need to know if your optimization methods are working to your advantage. You need to know if your optimization methods are improving the rankings of your website in search engines. This is where Google Analytics come into place. It assists you in knowing this important information.

5. It assists you in setting your goals and planning how you can achieve such goals. When setting up you advertising and marketing campaigns, it's important that you set goals for such campaigns. However, setting your goals is not an easy. You need to make sure that you are not understating or overstating your goals. Google Analytics helps you in coming up with realistic goals. And of course, on top of setting your goals, Google Analytics also helps you in planning the strategies you are going to implement in achieving such goals.

Cons of Google Analytics

1. The overall theme and design of the platform can be a little bit overwhelming and confusing. Even for seasoned online marketers, the platform can look complicated. There are so many dashboards and too many things to look at and manage. It takes time for you to get used to the platform's various features and functions.

2. The user interface is constantly being updated. This is not bad per se because the platform has to be updated because of the changing online environment. It's a drawback in the sense that the constant changes can lead to a lot of wasted time, money, and resources on your part. These changes may involve the introduction of new features which means there's always something you need to learn. The changes may also involve the removal of a feature which means you have to discard some of the things you've learned because they are no longer applicable.

3. If you plan on availing of the platform's premium services, it's very expensive. The platform's premium version costs $150,000 a year. That's a humongous amount that only major corporations and medium-sized businesses can afford. If you are just a small affiliate marketer, the platform's premium services will be out of reach.

4. All visits to your website that has been connected with Google Analytics must execute a Javascript file in order for the platform's tracking services to function properly. If the Javascript file has not been executed when a person visits your website, the visit is not counted by the platform. If this happens too often, it can really cloud the accuracy of the reports you get from Google Analytics. The effect of the Javascript file on your website can be significant if your website gets a lot of heavy traffic. The script can slow down your website's loading and compromise some of your website's features and functions.

How to Get the Most Out of Google Analytics

1. Learn everything you can about the platform before you start making important business decisions based on data you get from the platform. The good news is that Google Analytics has a lot of guides and tutorials on how you can use the platform. The FAQ (Frequently Asked Questions) and Help sections also contain in-depth articles on how you can use the tool. Don't just read the on-site content that Google Analytics provides you. You should also take the time to read guides and tutorials written about the platform by outside parties.

2. Never stop monitoring your website's bounce rate if you want to increase your website's conversion rates. This is one of the things where Google Analytics is very good at. You can use the tool to determine why people are leaving your website. Decreasing your bounce rate will likely increase your conversion rate.

3. Utilize audience data when creating custom segments. Google Analytics has features that allow you to classify your visitors into custom segments using various demographic data like gender, age, and location. For best results, you should draw the data from the audience reporting feature of Google Analytics.

4. Identify pages in your website that are taking forever to load. Google Analytics can help you in identifying these pages because such pages often have high bounce rates and low traffic. Take the time to identify these slow-loading pages and fix them as soon as possible.

5. Have your top Google Analytics reports directly emailed to you. You can set up a Google Analytics email report and have your most important reports sent to you on a schedule. The reports sent through email are concise and easy to interpret. You don't have to dig through a lot of data to understand the reports.

6. Examine how visitors engage with your website. In using Google Analytics, you should not just focus on the numbers. Knowing how many visitors you have is important but it's more important if you know what these visitors are doing when they get to your website.

7. Use calculated metrics. These types of metrics are more complicated so it takes time to learn them. Use these only when you have considerable experience using Google Analytics. These metrics give you the power to customize your analysis and measurement.

8. Set up custom alerts so you will always be aware about what's happening with your website and with your campaigns. Custom alerts will notify you about important things like dipping traffic, dwindling conversions, and diminishing revenues.

Inspiration #27

Success is no accident. It is hard work, perseverance, learning, studying, sacrifice and most of all, love of what you are doing or learning to do.

Pele

Tracking Tool #2 – ClickMagick

ClickMagick is a click tracking and marketing optimization platform. In other words, it's a tool you should consider using if you want to understand your traffic sources and how they are engaging with your website and marketing campaigns. It enables you to create tracking links which will then help you determine who clicked on your links and which clicks led to sales. It's the perfect tool for affiliate marketers who wish to understand how their website visitors are interacting with their links and content.

Unlike some other tracking tools, ClickMagick is hosted in the cloud. It's completely web-based so there's no need for you to install anything on your computer. You don't have to worry about upgrade glitches, server crashes, database corruption, and hosting problems.

The Key Features of ClickMagick

1. Automated alerts for winners of your split-tests. With other tracking platforms, you need to constantly pore over the status of your split tests to determine which types of ads and campaigns are generating the best results. If you use ClickMagick, you will receive alerts about the winners of these split tests.

2. Link cloaking. This is a process that plays a very important role in affiliate marketing. It allows you to obfuscate your affiliate IDs and make the links much shorter. The same benefit applies if you look at link cloaking in the context of tracking traffic sources. The visitors you are tracking are more likely to click on your links if these are cloaked and shorter.

3. Several kinds of pop-ups. With ClickMagick, you can use at least five different types of pop-ups on any site. These pop-ups are as follows: exit directs, exit pops, delayed, and on load. You can use these to collect leads, offer bonuses, and motivate your traffic to respond to your marketing messages.

4. An active notification bar. ClickMagick comes with a piece of technology that allows you to put a customized notification bar on any website. This is a very powerful tool in driving your conversion rates higher.

5. Advanced retargeting. Through ClickMagick's retargeting features, you can follow your potential customers anywhere on the web. You can add a pixel on all of your tracking links.

6. Traffic quality score analyzer. ClickMagick analyzes the traffic that's going to your affiliate marketing website. The platform also assigns a quality score on all of your tracking links.

7. Automatic bot filtering. Outside bots can screw the accuracy of your tracking systems. ClickMagick filters these bots to prevent them from interfering with your tracking links.

Pros of ClickMagick

1. You can use ClickMagick to track all kinds of links and ads. You can use it to track direct response ads, social media ads, links in social media sites, solo ads, email ads, banners, media buys, and pay per click ads.

2. You can use ClickMagick to track your entire sales funnel. This means that you can track your visitors from the time they opt in to your funnel all the way to the last downsell or upsell.

3. It's very affordable. With just a small monthly fee, you will gain access to all of the features and functions of ClickMagick.

4. ClickMagick offers a 14-day free trial period. This applies to all types of accounts on the platform. This means you can get a free trial on their three core plans (starter plan, standard plan, and pro plan).

5. ClickMagick has more than two dozen features and functions that you can utilize for your tracking programs. Many of these features can't be found anywhere.

6. You can upgrade, downgrade, or cancel your account at any time. For example, if you want to upgrade your account from a starter plan to a pro plan, it can be arranged within a day. Furthermore, upgrades, downgrades, and cancellations won't cost you a penny because you won't be charged for the changes.

Cons of ClickMagick

1. The platform is a bit complicated so it will take you some time to get your head around it. Some of the platform's features and functions can be completely new to you. With the dozens of functions and settings, the tool can be daunting to master.

2. There are issues when it comes to setting up a custom domain. If you are not using a popular hosting company like GoDaddy, it might be difficult for you to set up your own custom domain.

3. ClickMagick doesn't have a live chat support. This is a huge problem if you require immediate solutions to serious issues down the line. Not having a live chat support basically means that it can take some time before your problems can be addressed.

How to Get the Most Out of ClickMagick

1. Avail of the platform's 14-day free trial and use that time to educate yourself and experiment with the platform's features and functions.

2. If you have a fairly popular website with heavy traffic or if you want to track multiple websites, it's recommended that you avail of the platform's Standard Plan or Pro Plan. These plans have a ton of features that can deal with the requirements of your sites.

3. Always use the platform's automatic bot filtering feature. Bots can meddle with the links and campaigns you are tracking. This is not good because you will be provided with inaccurate and sketchy tracking results.

4. Use the platform's click fraud monitoring and traffic quality analyzers to prevent malicious data from infringing into your tracking reports. ClickMagick does most of the work, you just have to activate the required features and functions.

5. Try comparing the tracking reports you get from ClickMagick with those you get from Google Analytics to see if you are getting consistent tracking reports. Don't worry, ClickMagick is completely compatible with Google Analytics.

Inspiration #28

Strength doesn't come from what you can do. It comes from overcoming the things you once thought you couldn't.
Rikki Rogers

Tracking Tool #3 - Voluum

Voluum is an all-in-one software that specializes in tracking, managing, and optimizing advertising campaigns. Also hosted in the cloud, Voluum develops complicated software that provides users with data analytics insights. Those behind Voluum also develops optimization tools powered by AI (artificial intelligence) that make advertising easier to do and less intimidating. Voluum is huge in the sense that it manages thousands of advertisers. Voluum tracks nearly three billion dollars' worth of ad revenue every single year. There are 230 thousand campaigns running on the tool every month. In short, Voluum is a major player in the online ad-tracking industry.

Voluum offers services in four core categories which they have named as follows: Affiliate, Performance Agency, In-House Media Buyer, and Custom Solution. As an affiliate marketer wanting to track traffic, you can utilize all three categories. But you should focus more attention on Affiliate and Performance Agency.

The Key Features of Voluum

1. State of the art reporting. Voluum is very quick in generating the traffic reports that you need. Most of these reports are generated instantly and in real time.

2. Up to 30 data points. Voluum provides you with reports that contain at least 10 custom data points and 20 standard data points. These reports and data points provide insights about the visitors to your pages.

3. Direct tracking pixel. You can gather data from organic and direct website visitors. This provides you with a broad overview of your online marketing campaigns and the types of results these campaigns are generating.

4. Multiple cost models. Voluum can track most types of advertising cost models. It can track ads that support cost per mille (CPM), cost per click (CPC), and cost per action (CPA).

5. SSL for custom domains. SSL support is very important especially since you are managing an affiliate marketing website. What's great about Voluum is that they directly sell SSL certificates to their users.

6. Custom conversions. This is a feature which enables you to track every action and engagement that users take throughout their lifecycle as a customer or visitor of your website. The data you gather from this feature will help you optimize your campaigns and maximize the value you get from your visitors.

7. Traffic log. This is a comprehensive log of all the visits you are getting. You can download the log as well as the details about the visits in the log.

8. Anti-fraud kit. Voluum takes fraud very seriously. This is why they set up this anti-fraud kit to help you identify fake and invalid visits and views. The kit also takes action against these fraudulent visits to make sure that they don't happen again.

9. Traffic distribution AI. This feature comes in handy if you are running multiple campaigns with multiple sites. The traffic distribution AI optimizes all your sites including landing pages, sales funnels, ads, and other campaign paths.

10. A/B testing for flows. You can perform A/B testing directly from the Voluum platform. This can save you a lot of money and time. Testing helps you in identifying the campaign paths that generate the most results for your website and business.

Pros of Voluum

1. It can handle huge amounts of web traffic. You don't have to worry about your server crashing because of an avalanche of traffic. Not only that, Voluum is super-fast in redirecting your visits and clicks.

2. The software is regularly updated. There are more than twenty people that manage and run the software every day. If there's a bug or if the system goes down, things are fixed immediately.

3. You can customize your plan. As of this writing, Voluum offers three plans. These are Basic, Advanced, and Premium. However, you can customize the plan you want by requesting for additional features.

4. You can track all of your campaigns in a single dashboard. This is one of the strongest selling points of Voluum. They have made it very easy to track all your campaigns in one place regardless of whether the sources of your traffic are organic or are from paid campaigns.

5. It has a bevy of collaboration tools. You can create workspaces and shared reports so that several members of your team can work on the projects together.

Cons of Voluum

1. The software is trying to do so many things that their tracking service sometimes looks like just a side-service. They are offering so many services and solutions that it can be difficult to believe that they have their focus on their tracking offers.

2. Their plans are quite expensive. Their lowest-priced plan is the Basic Plan which will cost you $224 a month. Their Premium Plan costs $1124 a month. If you are running a small affiliate marketing website, it will be difficult to think that you can afford such high-priced plans.

3. Voluum only offers a 7-day free trial. Seven days are not enough to test and check if the tracking software performs just as advertised. You need at least two weeks to fully test a tracking software's capabilities and come up with a decision if it's good or not.

How to Get the Most Out of Voluum

1. Get SSL certificates for the domains that you are tracking. Major browsers like Chrome and Firefox are pushing for webmasters to get SSL certificates for a safer internet. Sites without SSL certificates tend to be avoided by a lot of online users in fear that their information can be stolen or used in shady online deals.

2. Take advantage of the 7-day free trial. Although this is a very short free trial and it won't be enough to let you test out all of Voluum's features and functions, it can still help you familiarize yourself with the platform.

3. If you are going to run multiple campaigns, it's best that you delegate the tracking and management of the campaigns to several members of your team.

4. Don't forget to perform A/B tests on your ads and campaigns to determine the strengths and weaknesses of your campaigns.

5. Take advantage of Voluum's collaboration tools. These tools allow you to work on several campaigns by teams and by using a single Voluum account.

6. Use the platform's anti-fraud kit to detect and screen out invalid traffic and bots. Voluum has a complete guide on how to use this feature so you should probably read that guide. It's in their FAQ section.

7. Try integrating your Voluum account with Zeropark. Zeropark is a self-serving advertising platform. Integrating the two accounts provides you access to more tools and resources that you can use to further refine your campaigns.

Inspiration #29

We don't develop courage by being happy every day. We develop it by surviving difficult times and challenging adversity.
Barbara De Angelis

Tracking Tool #4 – ClickMeter

As the name of the tool implies, ClickMeter is a software that specializes in tracking and getting the most out of your links. ClickMeter can be used by agencies, affiliates, advertisers, publishers, and even developers. Needless to say, ClickMeter has many similarities with Voluum, the tracking software that we just discussed in the previous chapter. It provides you with tools and resources that you can utilize to monitor, compare, and optimize your marketing and advertising links in one place.

As one of the most influential tracking software today, the software boasts of clients that range from small businesses to major corporations like Payoneer, iStockphoto, Mindshare, Loreal, and Texas Instruments. The software is also used by non-business organizations like charities and schools (i.e. Capella University).

The Key Features of ClickMeter

1. The software makes use of cutting-edge technology that can be best described as reliable, scalable, accurate, and high-performance. This is courtesy of ClickMeter's team of dedicated engineers and continuous research and development.

2. You can choose from four profiles depending on how you are going to use the platform. You can either use the software as an Agency, an Affiliate, an Advertiser, or as a Publisher. Choose the profile that best suits your affiliate marketing operations.

3. Data collection for every click or view. The data you can collect include timestamps, IP addresses, countries of origin, regions, cities, languages, and browsers. You can even track clicks using custom parameters.

4. Conversions tracking. You can track what led to conversions. What are the events or activities that led to a conversion? This is the question that ClickMeter answers for you. For every sale or download, there's got to be something that prompted the customer to buy into the item.

5. A/B split testing feature. Every tracking software or program should have this very important feature. This is a very powerful strategy especially if you are using landing pages to promote your affiliate products.

6. Spam blockers. ClickMeter comes with a built-in spam blocker that aims to minimize the number of spam that your websites and campaigns receive. These spam blockers also prevent tracking of malicious clicks.

7. Compatibility with Google Analytics. If you are not satisfied with the data you gather from ClickMeter, you can integrate your ClickMeter account with Google Analytics so that you can gather additional data. As I said, the data points of the two platforms are compatible with each other.

8. Link tagging. You can use tags to classify your links. Classifying your links through tagging makes it easier to access links and the reports attached to them.

Pros of ClickMeter

1. ClickMeter has been around for a long time and they have pioneered a lot of the functions and features that are common among tracking softwares these days. As a pioneer in the industry, it also means that the software has reputation. You know that you are getting a reliable tool.

2. You get to choose which type of profile fits your business and your goals. Since we are talking about affiliate marketing here, you should choose the "Affiliates" profile. Or you can choose either the "Agencies" profile or the "Advertisers" profile.

3. The software has more than 100 features and functions. You have access to all these features even if you avail of the program's cheapest plan.

4. They offer a 30-day money back guarantee. If after 30 days of using the software and you think that you are not getting any results, you can request for a complete refund. You can also change the plan you availed anytime.

5. ClickMeter is hosted in the cloud which means it doesn't require you to install a code. After subscribing to the plan, you are ready to go.

6. ClickMeter doesn't collect cancellation fees and signup fees. You can cancel your account anytime you want without worrying about fees. There are also no minimum terms.

7. You can integrate ClickMeter with other tools and software such as Google Ads, Google Analytics, Chrome, Firefox, Shopify, Wordpress, and Backpage.

8. The dashboard allows you to discover at a glance how your marketing campaigns and clicks tracking are going.

9. The software churns through several data points to analyze your tracking campaigns. These data points include list of clicks, world map, top browsers, top cities, top nations, top IPs, top keywords, top sources, and top parameters.

10. You can export your reports in CSV formats to other platforms. For example, you can export the reports to Excel if you want copies that you can easily share with your team or with any other third party.

Cons of ClickMeter

1. ClickMeter only provides email support for their customers. This can be a serious problem if you want to get in touch with customer support as soon as possible. If you encounter an issue, you need to write them an email and wait for their respond. That's not instant support.

2. The plan packages are a bit expensive. Basically, ClickMeter offer three plans: Medium ($29 per month), Large ($99 per month), and Ex-Large ($349 per month). These are considerable amounts of monthly fees considering the fact that some tools that are similar to ClickMeter offer much lower charges.

3. It can sometimes be overwhelming to use their website's interface. This is why if you are a complete beginner when it comes to tracking tools and software, you might want to start with a much simpler software before using ClickMeter.

How to Get the Most Out of ClickMeter

1. For the best value, you should avail of the platform's Large plan. It costs you $99 per month but it's worth it. For one, the maximum number of clicks and views you can track each month number to 200,000. You also get two years of data storage.

2. Choose the profile that suits your business and your goals. As we have mentioned earlier, you can choose from any of the following profiles: Agencies, Affiliates, Advertisers, and Publishers. The profile you pick depends on what you want to do and achieve on the platform.

3. Cloak or mask your affiliate codes. This is easy to do with ClickMeter. Not only will this make your links look more interesting for your audiences, it will also help prevent others from changing your code with another code during the redirect process.

4. Use ClickMeter in conjunction with Google Analytics for more comprehensive reports. The two tools may seem like they offer similar services but they differ greatly. Google Analytics is more on identifying visitor trends in your website. ClickMeter focuses on link tracking, measurement, and traffic source analysis.

5. Don't forget to use tracking pixels. Installing tracking pixels is one of the best ways to track and measure the behavior of people visiting your website or people clicking on your links. It's a lot easier to collect data and analyze them if you are using tracking pixels.

Inspiration #30

Fortune always favors the brave, and never helps a man who does not help himself.
P. T. Barnum

Tracking Tool #5 – Trck.Me

Trck.Me is a lesser known tracking software because it's not that big and influential. But it's a really powerful tool that you might need if you are looking for an affordable and effective tracking software. The software is good enough to be used by major businesses such as Bonjour, Self Image, Leadpage, Sketch, Clover, and Rocket Responder.

The tracking features and functions of Trck.Me are among the most effective in the industry especially for small to medium-sized businesses. With Trck.Me, you can track countless types of channels and links using different verticals.

The Key Features of Trck.Me

1. Unlimited events. I would say that this is the most important feature of this software. There's no limit to the number of events that you can generate from your campaigns. Allow me to remind you that an "event" refers to the action that your target audiences perform when engaging in your campaigns. An "event" could be a click, a view, a download, or a subscription.

2. Unlimited data points. The more data points you can track, the better and more accurate results you get from your tracking campaigns. This works well for Trck.Me because they also offer unlimited events.

3. One year data storage. This is a lot considering the fact that Trck.Me only charges $29 per month for their basic plan. In short, you are getting your money's worth as far as data storage is concerned.

4. Affiliate marketing tools. This is one of the reasons why a lot of affiliate marketers make use of Trck.Me. The developers of the software made sure that it came with various affiliate marketing tools that affiliate marketers can take advantage of.

5. A/B split testing. This is a no-brainer because all tracking software offer this feature. What makes Trck.Me unique is that their A/B testing options are fine-tuned for affiliate marketers. You will get more out of them if you are an affiliate marketer.

Pros of Trck.Me

1. They offer a 30-day money back guarantee. This means you get to use the tool for up to 30 days and if you are not satisfied with the service, you can demand for a full refund. You will get your money back, no questions asked.

2. They have very affordable plans. Trck.Me is one of the cheapest tracking tools today. They offer just two plans. There's the Standard plan which costs $29 per month and there's the Enterprise plan which costs $79 per month.

3. You can upgrade, downgrade, or cancel your account any time you want without any additional fees. This is on top of the 30-day money back guarantee when you sign up.

4. You can make use of your own domain name to or sub-domains to create your short tracking links.

5. It has auto tagging features. What this means is that Trck.Me automatically tags where your visitors are coming from so you don't have to burn your time creating special links for every marketing channel.

Cons of Trck.Me

1. If you want to avail of their social media reach tracking and 25 sub-accounts features, you have to sign up with the Enterprise plan which costs $79 per month.

2. They have weak customer support. It seems like the only way to reach them should you encounter problems with your account is via email. And we all know that email is not a very responsive customer support path.

3. Some sections of their website are outdated. Some of the links in their frontpage are clickable but these lead to error pages. Not a good sign for a website that develops tracking software. They can't even get their own links right. What makes you think that they will be able to track your links properly?

How to Get the Most Out of Trck.Me

1. If you are managing multiple domains and campaigns, it's recommended that you avail of the platform's Enterprise plan. The plan provides you with lifetime data storage, 25 branded domains, 25 sub-accounts, and social media reach tracking.

2. If you are managing a small website, you should start with the Standard plan because it has everything you need given the tracking requirements of your website. If you have plans of upgrading your account to Enterprise, only do it when you have reached a point where the traffic and sites you are managing and tracking are too large.

3. Choose to be billed annually because it can save you a lot of money. If you choose to be billed annually you can save $10 each month from your fees for the Standard plan and $20 each month for the Enterprise plan.

4. Take full advantage of the platform's unlimited events and unlimited data points features. Don't hold back on the campaigns and tracking programs that you implement because there are no limit on events and data points.

5. Use as leverage the software's affiliate marketing tools. Since you are an affiliate marketer, these are tools that are perfect for your marketing campaigns and tracking goals. You should use them whenever you can.

Inspiration #31

If you can dream it, then you can achieve it. You will get all you want in life if you help enough other people get what they want.
Zig Ziglar

Tracking Tool #6 – LinkTrackr

LinkTrackr has been around for a long time. More than eight years to be exact. Their software tools are used by well-known online entrepreneurs like John Chow, Armand Morin, Amish Shah, and Mike Filsaime. That said, the software has a proven track record. Their software makes it easy to track links and gather data on their performances. The tool enables you to track real-time data for every sale, lead, or visit that you generate from your links and campaigns.

The tool's main service is in link tracking. On top of its link tracking services, the software also offers add-on features which can help you step up your affiliate marketing game. LinkTrackr is a SAAS service developed by Kash Media.

The Key Features of LinkTrackr

1. Link tracking and analysis. This is the main service of LinkTrackr and they are very good at it. They make the process very easy. All you need to do is enter your destination URL and give the tracking URL a name. You can then use the tracking link in your ads and promotions.

2. Track sales and leads. LinkTrackr's conversion tracking software is activated by simply adding a piece of code in your website. If placed properly, the code can be used to track multiple sales and leads. LinkTrackr makes use of standard iFrame and JavaScript tracking codes.

3. Cloak affiliate links. LinkTrackr's link cloaker is very simple and very easy to use. Cloaking is one of the most effective ways on protecting your affiliate links from theft and other forms of sabotage. LinkTrackr turns your normal affiliate links into more natural-sounding links.

4. Paid ad tracking. This feature is intended for paid ads and budgeted campaigns that you want to track and measure. Tracking these ads help you determine if you are getting your money's worth out of them.

5. Pay per click tracking. LinkTrackr's PPC tracking tool is very important if you want to track links and ad campaigns from multiple advertising networks. For example, let's say that you are promoting items from Commission Junction and ClickBank. LinkTrackr helps you track these two networks from a single dashboard. This will save you a lot of time and resources.

6. Affiliate sub-ID tracking. This involves passing a tag at the end of the affiliate links you are using. The tags are passed on to the merchants or the advertisers. These tags are also included in your affiliate commission reports. Sub-ID tracking is a bit more complicated so it takes time to learn exactly how it works. But it's something you should learn because it can do a lot of things for you especially if you are using multiple networks in your affiliate marketing business.

7. Pixel tracking codes. LinkTrackr's pixel tracking function has the capability to track multiple leads and sales within the same sales funnel. The tracking service is also very easy to follow and implement. You can also use pixel tracking codes for retargeting and other marketing strategies.

8. Postback S2S tracking. This unique feature allows you to gather accurate conversion data from a lot of third-party websites even without using cookies. This strategy is also referred to as postback URL, callback URL, or S2S pixel.

9. A/B split testing. With proper split testing, you can double or even triple the engagement for your links, ads, sales funnels, and more. LinkTrackr has simplified the split testing process for you. You can even split test more than two links or ads.

10. URL and link rotator. If you are tracking more than one links, it's recommended that you use the URL and link rotator. What it does is rotate the websites and landing pages you are promoting. For example, the first 100 visitors will go to link 1 and the next 100 visitors will go to link 2, and so on and so forth.

Pros of LinkTrackr

1. It's one of the most affordable link trackers in the market today. It's most basic plan only costs $7 a month although this is paid annually. This means that you pay $84 for a year's worth of services. Not bad at all considering the fact that some trackers charge the same amount or even more for a single month. LinkTrackr's most expensive plan is the Extreme plan which costs $47 per month.

2. LinkTrackr offers a 30-day risk-free guarantee. You can use the tracking service for up to thirty days. And if you are not satisfied with it, you can request for a refund. They will give you your money back.

3. LinkTrackr has the capability to help you track every lead and every sale in your sales funnel up to the original click. The tracker still works perfectly even if you have multiple downsells and upsells. As long as the trackers have been placed properly, there should be no problem in tracking the leads and sales no matter how deep they go.

4. LinkTrackr supports major affiliate marketing networks such as Shareasale, Clickbank, Commission Junction, and JVZoo. If you are using these networks, you can integrate them with your Linktrackr account.

5. You can import your commission reports from other networks and add them to your LinkTrackr dashboard. All you need to do is download a CSV copy of the reports from the networks and import then to LinkTrackr. What LinkTrackr does is match your sub-ID from the network to your LinkTrackr. This would provide you with more detailed reports about the sales and commissions you have generated.

Cons of LinkTrackr

1. You pay more per plan if you pay for the services in a monthly basis. For example, let's say that you avail of the Basic plan. If you pay on an annual basis, you pay $84 a year. That's equivalent to only $7 a month. But if you choose to pay on a monthly basis, you are going to pay $17 per month for the Basic plan. That's a whooping $10 difference.

2. There are click limits. LinkTrackr is a hosted SAAS (Software as a Service) which basically means that it shares resources with other users. Because of this, LinkTrackr has to limit the clicks and views that it can provide for its clients. This is not good if you have a highly-trafficked affiliate marketing website.

3. They only accept PayPal as their payment option. This is problematic because not all people have PayPal accounts. Some had their PayPal accounts banned and we all know that once you are banned in PayPal, it's nearly impossible to get another account. So if you don't have a PayPal account, you can't use LinkTrackr. Unless you find a way to get someone else with a PayPal account to pay for your LinkTrackr fees on your behalf.

How to Get the Most Out of LinkTrackr

1. Read LinkTrackr's guides and tutorials before you start using the software. You have to make sure that you are doing things right. Using LinkTrackr is not free so if you botch your tracking campaigns, you might as well be throwing money into thin air. To access the guides and tutorials, just click on the Tutorials tab on the upper right corner of the LinkTrackr website.

2. Get smart with link cloaking. You can prevent affiliate theft by utilizing LinkTrackr's cloaker for all of your affiliate links. Cloakers make your links shorter and more interesting. You can also use your own custom domain cloaker.

3. Try to find a way of naming your individual ads and campaigns. If you are running multiple campaigns, it will be difficult to track them all if these are all over the place. You need to find a way to organize them and name them so that it will be easier for you to identify one campaign from another. In fact, LinkTrackr suggests that you create a standardized naming convention for all your referrals, ad traffic, and organic traffic.

4. Try server postback tracking. What's great about this method is that it does not depend on cookies to track views, clicks, and conversions. It can even be more accurate than pixel tracking. With server postback tracking, a unique click ID or transaction ID is generated by the platform during the initial click. This click ID is passed one from one page to the next until it reaches the conversion page.

5. Always perform A/B split testing. LinkTrackr's split testing feature can instantly split your sources of traffic into different landing pages. Setting up a new split test is as simple as specifying the URLs and assigning a traffic percentage to each of the URLs.

6. Use LinkTrackr's pay per click (PPC) tracking software. If you are using multiple PPC networks, it will be time-consuming to log into each network and download the reports. LinkTrackr's PPC software enables you to get the same reports without having to log into all of the PPC networks you are using.

Inspiration #32

Life is 10% what happens to you and 90% how you react to it.
Charles R. Swindoll

Tracking Tool #7 – Improvely

Improvely is another great alternative for tracking and optimizing your online marketing campaigns. The tool has a comprehensive set of features around conversion tracking, click fraud monitoring, affiliate marketing, agency marketing and reporting. According to Improvely, more than 6,000 online entrepreneurs and marketers currently use their tools and resources. These include companies and agencies like Make a Wish Foundation, Twitch, Unicef, and Atlantic Net.

If you regularly advertise online and you want to determine if you are getting your money's worth from your advertising campaigns, Improvely has the tools necessary to track your campaigns. Improvely works well with major online advertising networks like Google Ads, Facebook Ads, Bing Ads, and Taboola. If you run marketing campaigns using these networks, Improvely can help you track the performance of your ads.

The Key Features of Improvely

1. Detailed traffic reports. Improvely shows you where your traffic, revenue, and conversions are coming from. This provides you tips on how to improve your marketing strategies and generate even better results.

2. Custom-built funnel reports. You can see how your customers engaged with you in the sales funnel. You will get reports about the paths that people took to conversion. The reports will also show where customers dropped off and didn't finish the conversion process.

3. Customer profiles. Improvely builds profiles of the people who visit your website. These profiles contain information about their conversions and their past visits. You can use these information for retargeting.

4. Click fraud monitoring. Click fraud is rampant online because of bots and of black-hat marketers who are trying to game the system. Well, luckily, Improvely has installed measures in its software that detect and get rid of these fake and invalid clicks.

5. Commission tracking. If you are running a marketing campaign for an affiliate website, Improvely is the software you should use in tracking the sources of your commissions. The tool identifies the landing pages, ads, and keywords that are generating the affiliate commissions for your business.

6. Affiliate link cloaking. Link cloaking is very important in affiliate marketing. Improvely makes it very easy to cloak your links. You have full control over the URL that appears in the shown address bar and the text that appears in the title bar of the browser window.

7. Protection for ads and keyword lists. Improvely provides protection for your ads and keyword lists because there's always the chance that someone will steal them. There are other affiliate managers out there who like to snoop around other people's campaigns and steal their ideas. You don't want this to be happening to your campaigns.

Pros of Improvely

1. You have nothing to install because Improvely is a hosted service. There's no software to download and install. Furthermore, you don't have to pay for upgrades in the software. Because the service is hosted in the cloud, you can access and use it from anywhere and from any device (i.e. desktop computer, laptop, smartphone, tablet).

2. It offers protection against suspicious and fraudulent activities. This makes sure that you won't be paying for invalid and fraudulent clicks and views. This protection applies to all of your campaigns even if you are doing multiple campaigns at a time.

3. Improvely shows you where you should focus your marketing efforts in order to maximize your visitors and conversions. The tool also helps you cut down on the ads, landing pages, and campaigns that aren't getting you results.

4. You can instantly test brand new landing pages. You can add and remove landing pages at will without waiting for approval from third parties. Improvely has built-in split testing that's capable of showing you instantly what variations of your ads are performing well.

5. You track everything from a single dashboard. You don't have to sign into several websites to keep track of all your marketing campaigns and efforts. The single dashboard brings together analysis of your traffic sources together in one convenient place.

6. All traffic and conversion reports are updated in real time. This means that when a person visits your website or opts into your landing page, these are immediately tracked and added into the reports.

Cons of Improvely

1. Their advertised 14-day free trial is a bit misleading. The first fourteen day of using the software is only free if you avail of a plan after the trial period ends. If you don't cancel within 14 days, you will be charged for the monthly plan you initially chose.

2. Their dashboard can be intimidating because it contains a lot of features and there are too many things going on. If it's your first time to use a tracker, it's easy to get lost and be confused by everything.

3. Their Large Agency plan doesn't have a fixed price. The plan simply carries the price tag of $299+ per month. Notice the plus sign after the amount. This means that you can potentially spend much more than you expect.

How to Get the Most Out of Improvely

1. Activate and keep a close watch over Improvely's click fraud detection feature. Fraudulent clicks and views can skew your marketing campaigns. Not only will you get inaccurate information, your decision-making process will be compromised as well.

2. Keep separate copies of the customer profiles that Improvely generates for you. It can be very time-consuming to keep digging through the platform to find your customer profiles. It's better to download them, make copies of them, and store them in a separate but accessible place.

3. Take advantage of Improvely's features which enable you to work with teams. This is very important if you are running an affiliate marketing business with employees. Improvely allows multiple individuals to run and manage campaigns on the dashboard.

4. Activate your email alerts for new conversions. Sometimes, you don't have the time to keep on checking your Improvely dashboard for new conversions and reports. Creating an alert for these conversions and reports will keep you updated via email about the latest developments in your tracking campaigns.

5. Export raw data and reports to Excel CSV. You accomplish two things in doing this. One, you will have copies of all your raw data and reports. If something happens to your Improvely account or if your dashboard becomes inaccessible, you will still have in your hands raw data and reports of all the important information you have gathered.

Conclusion

Before anything else, thank you for getting this far. The fact that you read this book up to this point tells me that you are serious about building your affiliate marketing business. That's a good start. The main themes of this book focused on improving your traffic generation methods and tracking your traffic sources. If you went through every chapter and understood everything that you've read, then you are more than equipped to reach the goals you've set for yourself and your affiliate marketing business.

As I have mentioned at the beginning of this book, generating traffic is the cornerstone of building an online business such as an affiliate marketing website. The better you are in generating traffic, the better chance you have in attracting customers. But not all kinds of traffic are equal. Some are better than others. This difference in quality mostly lies in the source of the traffic. It's for this reason that we discussed in detail the most popular sources of traffic in the first section of this book.

If you want the best traffic for your affiliate marketing website, you should focus your attention on the sources of traffic that we have discussed on the first part of this book. I'm not saying that you should try generating traffic from all of them. You just have to find the ones that work well for the type of business you have and focus on those sources. For example, if testing showed that you are getting most of your visitors from social media, then this is a cue for you to spend most of your efforts and resources on social media traffic generation. The same can be said about the other sources of traffic.

Driving traffic is one thing. Tracking traffic is another thing. That's why in the second part of this book, we presented to you and discussed the most common traffic tracking tools that you can use for your affiliate marketing business. Tracking your traffic is essential in the sense that it helps you understand your visitors and customers. What do they want? How are they interacting with your website? Which parts of your website get clicked the most? Why are they leaving your website too soon? These are just a few of the important questions that you can only answer by tracking your traffic sources.

This book will serve as your guide in planning your traffic generation campaigns. Always keep a copy of it accessible so that you can consult with it whenever you need some insights.

With that said and done, good luck with all your traffic generation strategies, your advertising campaigns, and your tracking programs.

Amazon FBA Mastery

Your 5 Days

Beginner To Expert Guide

In Selling Highly Profitable Private Label

Products On Amazon

By

Michael Ezeanaka

www.MichaelEzeanaka.com

Introduction

Today, millions of people all over the world do their shopping online. And one great thing that came out of this whole internet shopping phenomenon is the opportunity given to individual sellers to compete on equal footing against big companies and retailers. Setting up an e-commerce business is not as costly as opening a physical store that requires you to pay for monthly rent, utilities, and so on. You can set up shop in your basement and run your business behind the computer in the comforts of your home.

One of the most popular e-commerce websites and online retailers is Amazon. In fact, according to one study, Amazon is the starting point of 44% of online shoppers, with Google trailing behind at 33%. Moreover, 40% of people who live in the United States buy at least one item every month from the website. No wonder it has become the central hub of online buying and selling.

And if you are specifically thinking of selling your own stuff with your own private label on Amazon, and have them take care of storage and fulfillment to customers, you have come to the right place because this book will teach you everything you need to know about Amazon FBA, which is exactly what you need. Combine your hard work and business acumen with high quality products and Amazon FBA, and you will surely be well on your way to great success.

Without further ado, let's get right into it!

Chapter 1

Amazon FBA Business Model Explained

Before you get too excited and start sending all your products to Amazon, you should first understand what the Amazon FBA business model is all about. Amazon FBA literally stands for Fulfilled by Amazon and it gives third-party vendors access to Amazon's facilities and services. Launched in 2016, Amazon FBA is just one of the different business models that Amazon offers to its partner sellers. If you register to this program, you are taking advantage of Amazon's huge facilities, efficient cataloguing, advanced shipping, and customer service. How cool is that?
Amazon gets half of its sales from third party vendors like you, and 66% of the top 10,000 Amazon vendors use FBA.

How The Business Model Works

You send all your products, whether used or brand new, to one of Amazon's fulfillment centers. These are huge warehouses where they store all the products sent by sellers like you. These fulfillment centers are massive, the largest covers an area of 1,264,200 square feet and is located in Texas. The warehouses are run not only by employees but also by robots. As of 2018, they have 75 fulfillment centers across North America. Add to this the additional 25 sortation centers, where items are sorted to be delivered to different locations, and you get an idea how Amazon can handle such a huge undertaking.
When your products reach one of these fulfillment centers, they will then be sorted and catalogued. You do not have to worry about your products getting lost or damaged in these huge warehouses because they are well taken care of by employees and robots, and everything is computerized. And on the off-chance (which means it is an extremely rare occurrence) that one of your products gets damaged while in the fulfillment centers, you can consider it sold because Amazon will pay for the full retail price of the item.
Now you just wait for someone to buy your item listed on the Amazon website. Amazon will handle the whole transaction when a customer buys your listed product on the website. The whole process is automated, which makes it a lot faster.
Since the items in the warehouse are assigned their unique inventory code, it is easier to find them among the hundreds of shelves lined up inside the huge warehouse. The item will be packaged and delivered to the buyer by Amazon on your behalf.
Once the item is delivered to the customer, Amazon will follow up to ensure that there are no problems with the shipment and that the customer is satisfied with the order. Amazon also handles customer service for FBA items, and also returns and refunds, with your assistance of course.
So what are your responsibilities as a seller? You still have something to do, right? Of course, you do. Amazon FBA just shoulders half of the work so that you can focus your attention and efforts on other things that are also important when managing an e-commerce business.

As an FBA seller, you still have to:

1. Determine the products that you want to sell.

Amazon will not help you choose what products you want to sell, and they also will not source your products for you. You still have to do your research on what products sell well, and where you can source them. You also have to know how much the products are going for online and in physical stores so that you can have a rough estimate on how much profit you will be getting. One important tip to remember is to sell fast-moving items because you have to pay for their storage in the fulfillment center.

2. Monitor your inventory levels.

It is your responsibility as a seller to check if you still have enough products to sell that are in storage. Since these items are in the fulfillment centers, it is easy to lose track of how much you still have because you cannot see them in person, unlike when you keep your stocks in your own place. Although Amazon will let you know if your inventory is running low, it is still up to you to be proactive and ensure that you have enough products to sell.

3. Market and promote your products.

This does not mean you have to pay expensive TV or print ads. Maybe that's how it was many years ago. Online advertising is different. It is a lot less expensive and you need to use the right techniques more than money. If you are a re-seller of brand name products that are already highly-ranked, you may no longer need to do this step because the big corporations already have their own million-dollar ads and billboards. But if you are selling your own custom products or private label products, then you have to do this step and make sure that people can see your products. Remember that Amazon has millions of products listed online, which makes marketing an essential step if you want people to find your items for sale.

What are the benefits of Amazon FBA?

Based on what you have read so far, you probably get an idea about the kinds of benefits that you will get if you decide to sell your own private label products using Amazon FBA. But to give you a clearer view of the different benefits of Amazon FBA that can help you decide if it is something that you want to try, continue reading the next points.

1. Efficient logistics, cheaper shipping rates, and faster delivery time

If you are selling a few products, it is easier to handle everything on your own and in your own house. You do not really need to rent a place for storage or to hire people. But if you are thinking of starting an e-commerce business as a main source of income, and you are going to sell a lot of products, then you need a more efficient way to handle and ship all your items on time. And hiring professionals to do all these things for you may be expensive. With Amazon, you are taking advantage of their expertise and experience with shipping and logistics. After all, they are the biggest e-commerce website in the world right now, and being efficient goes with the territory.

Moreover, when shipping items, you have to consider different rules and regulations. Different factors affect shipping fees such as the weight and size of the product, the kind of product you are going to ship, and so on. You also need to research about international shipping (in case you decide to make your products available to international buyers), areas served by the courier, prohibited and restricted commodities, insurance, and so many things. If you use Amazon FBA, you do not have to worry because Amazon will take care of these things for you.

Third party sellers like yourself and online shoppers both benefit from this because the entire shipping process is a lot faster. After all, your items are already in their warehouses and they have partnerships with big courier companies because they ship thousands, if not millions, of items worldwide. Amazon also has fulfillment centers all over the world, which allows them to deliver customer orders within just a couple of days. This is because when a customer buys a product from you, they do not necessarily get the exact item that you sent to Amazon. Amazon sort like products together, so if a customer buys a specific item, say, a Mickey Mouse t-shirt, and you live in the United States and your buyer lives in Canada, they will search for a similar item in the fulfillment center closest to the buyer, which significantly shortens the delivery period and also makes shipping fee a lot cheaper.

Shipping is also generally cheaper if you let Amazon handle it for you because, as I mentioned previously, they have partnerships with big shipping companies and they can get discounts because they ship a lot of items (i.e. economy of scale). And to attract higher sales, Amazon passes on this incentive to the sellers and buyers. You, as a seller, can get reduced shipping costs when sending your products to one of their fulfillment centers. And FBA products are often eligible for free shipping, especially to buyers who are Amazon Prime members. It boosts Amazon's sales, attracts more buyers for you, and saves customers on shipping costs. It is a win-win-win type of situation for all parties involved.

2. More free time for you

Managing an e-commerce business can be time-consuming especially if you handle everything by yourself — from sourcing products to sell, taking pictures, storing, packaging, pricing, shipping, and handling customer service. If you leverage the Amazon FBA business model, you are freeing up a lot of your time that you can use to concentrate on more important things such as choosing products for your online store, sourcing the products, and taking great photos. And the more time you spend on these things, the higher quality of products and the better photos you will have in your online store. And besides, these are the fun parts of selling products online.

Shopping for things to resell or making them yourself is what makes people do online selling. A lot of sellers also enjoy photography so taking pictures of their products is just like a hobby for most of them. The boring parts of managing an e-commerce business are the shipping and logistics, and also handling returns and customer complaints. And thankfully, this can all be taken care of by Amazon through FBA. You can use your free time to research on what products to sell, how to improve your products, how to promote your products, the current prices of similar products on the market, and how to scale up your business. You can also focus on taking great pictures of your items for sale. Remember that in online selling, pictures paint a thousand words, and it is sometimes what makes or breaks a sale. If your picture does not look good, some people will question the quality of your product and will not buy them, no matter how great your product actually is.

Aside from spending your free time doing things to grow your business, you can also use it for doing personal stuff, such as travelling, spending time with your loved ones, learning a new hobby, and so on. It gives you the perfect balance between your business and your personal life. Some people even continue working their regular full-time job while managing their e-commerce business.

3. Huge storage space

You can live in a tiny house and still sell huge products without the need for a large storage space if you are using Amazon FBA because all of your stuff will be stored in their humongous fulfillment centers. Not having enough storage space at home sometimes stops a lot of people from selling big items or keeping a large inventory. Your house or even a rented commercial space can only hold a limited amount of stuff.

You do not have to worry about boxes and packages cluttered in your living room or bedroom because Amazon takes care of all this. Having boxes and packages that you need to step over inside your house can be hazardous and can cause accidents. You do not want this to happen at all. And renting your own warehouse can be costly, especially if you are just starting because apart from the monthly rent, you have to pay for utilities such as electricity, internet connection, and even water in some instances.

Another good thing about sending your stuff to Amazon is that there is no minimum inventory required. Heck, you can even send just one product if you really do not have any storage at all in your house. Amazon also gives an incentive to sellers whose products move fast, meaning they don't stay for a long time in the storage facility. You can get unlimited storage if your items sell like hotcakes, so to speak.

Moreover, Amazon fulfillment centers have the right kind of storage for certain products. For instance, if you are selling leather bags or shoes, you do not want to store them in your basement where the high humidity and temperature can cause damage to your products.

4. Amazon's good reputation

It is not hard to believe that Amazon is the leading online selling platform because it is reliable, and a lot of buyers and sellers trust its business platform. If you use Amazon FBA, you are also benefiting from Amazon's strong reputation. They have already established their brand name and collaborating with them will do your business a lot of good. For people who are just starting to sell online, selling products through Amazon will bring them higher sales than selling their products through their own website.

Although there is nothing wrong with having your own website, it poses a bigger risk for individual sellers than if they bring their business to a well-known selling platform that already has an established reputation, such as Amazon. And it is even better if you use Amazon FBA because buyers would know that a large company is handling certain aspects of your business for you.

As you establish your own brand and reputation, you can maybe then focus solely on selling on your very own website. But for now, Amazon is the easiest way to get higher sales. In fact, even established companies and sellers still use Amazon as an online selling platform because they know that they will get a higher reach since millions of people are now using Amazon.

5. Handles customer service and returns

This is another one of the less attractive features of having your own business—handling customer service and returns. Before buying a product, some customers already have a lot of question. And this is handled by people who work at Amazon. They have customer service centers that provide support 24/7 through phone calls, emails, and chat. If they have more questions or even complaints upon receiving the item, Amazon will also take care of it for you. This is a really great benefit, especially for people who love the whole mechanics of selling online, but not the part where you have to talk to the customer.

In fact, a lot of people prefer online selling over the traditional form of selling where you have to talk to the person face to face because they are not comfortable at this kind of set up. This is why having someone else do this for you is a great help. Moreover, Amazon customer service representatives are trained to handle different concerns and complaints. They can handle even the most irate customers because that's what they are trained to do.

Another thing that they handle for you is returns. Handling returns can be a hassle because you not only have to deal with upset customers but also the logistics and administrative aspect of having the product returned to you and the payment returned to the customer. They also have to do inspection to check if the item is really damaged before shipping it to the customer or not. All of this is handled by Amazon. Of course, there is a corresponding fee but it is worth the small amount that you have to pay for the work and trouble that they take off your plate.

6. Increase your sales

Ultimately, this is the main goal of all this, why you are selling online and why you are partnering with Amazon. You want to make sure that you have high sales even on a website like Amazon, where you will surely have a lot of competitors. All the benefits that you can enjoy using Amazon FBA boil down to this — attracting more buyers and boosting your sales. You may think that you are getting less because you have to pay Amazon different kinds of fees, but the efficiency and expertise allow you to sell more items at a quicker rate, which means higher sales for you in a shorter period of time. Besides, the fees are worth it because you are using their top-of-the-line facilities and expertise in online selling. You are even saving money because you do not have to pay for your own warehouse and hire staff or assistants who will help you with all of these once your business starts to grow.

What are the disadvantages of Amazon FBA?

Just like with all kinds of business models, Amazon FBA also has disadvantages, although it is already an incredible online selling platform. After all, no business model is perfect. You also need to understand the different disadvantages of Amazon FBA before you decide to use it in your e-commerce business.

1. Amazon FBA costs money

Not everything in life is free, and if you expect to get top notch service and expertise, then you should be willing to pay the price. This is also true if you decide to use Amazon FBA. You have to pay for the storage of your products. The longer your products stay in their fulfillment centers, the more you have to pay. This is why it is important to ensure that your products sell quickly. Do not let them stay in Amazon storage for more than six months.

Be prepared to pay sky-high storage fees if your inventory sits for a long time. Because of this, you have to take this into consideration. Will you still make a profit even after all the storage fees that you paid for that particular item? Although you can sell large items, you have to make sure that they will move fast because this can cost you a lot in terms of storage. It is also not ideal to store cheap items where you only get a small profit in Amazon fulfillment centers because you might end up paying more for the storage than the actual product itself.

2. Monitoring inventory can be challenging

Although you can always ask Amazon about your inventory, it is still more difficult to track your inventory if you do not see them in person. It is hard to determine what products you still have, what's been sitting in storage for months, what you need to re-order, when you need to buy more, and so on. If your inventory is in plain sight, you will be able to know right away which ones are selling and which ones are not. This makes it even more challenging during the holiday season, when people buy a lot of their gifts for their loved ones online and orders come in by the thousands.

3. Co-mingling can be tricky

Amazon sorts similar items together in their fulfillment centers for efficiency. For example, Amazon will group all Adidas Stan Smith sneakers from different sellers together. This means that a person who clicked your listing and purchased the item does not necessarily mean that he will be getting the sneakers that you sent, although he will still get his Stan Smiths. You have the option to take advantage of this feature if you want to.

However, this can be scary for some because not all sellers are reliable and trustworthy. Some even send damaged or counterfeit products, and if you are unlucky and the buyer got that damaged or counterfeit item that another seller has sent, then you will be the one getting the negative feedback. Some legitimate sellers were even banned from selling on Amazon because of this, although this is a rare case.

4. Amazon controls about half of your business

When partnering with Amazon via FBA, you are giving up a lot of control over your business. For example, you cannot choose the kind of packaging that you want for your items and you cannot also add a personal touch such a short thank you note or some customized stickers and freebies into the package because Amazon handles all the packaging and shipping. You cannot tell them to use a silvery packaging paper or use eco-friendly packaging. They do things their way, which is of course more efficient but does not have the personal touch that you would want your buyers to experience when they buy items from your online shop.

5. Product prep can be difficult

You need to follow certain guidelines when sending out your inventory to Amazon. It can be time consuming and tedious, especially for beginners but you will soon get the hang of it after doing it several times. For example, there are different rules to follow for sending multiples of the same products in one package, single products, single products with different parts, and so on. You also have to use the right kind of bag for your items. There are also special instructions for sending adult products, e.g. using a shrink wrap or a black, opaque poly bag. There are so many things to consider when prepping, packaging, and labeling your products to be sent out to Amazon that there is a separate chapter only for this topic, which you will see later on.

Private label business model and other ways of selling on Amazon

This book is all about selling private label products through Amazon FBA. There are different ways to sell on Amazon, and one of them is by selling private label items.

1. Private label

As the name implies, private label means you choose a specific product to sell under your own private label or brand via Amazon FBA. If you are a private label seller, you decide on which product you want to sell, for instance clothes. You source them from a supplier, usually from China, and make them your own private label or brand. A third-party supplier under a contract manufactures the items.

To find products that you can sell under your own private label, you need to do a lot of research and studying, especially involving the market and what sells profitably and what doesn't. You are also responsible for contacting the suppliers or manufacturers. This is something that you cannot delegate to Amazon. You even have the option to have all the products shipped directly to Amazon by the third-party supplier, which means that all you need to do is to sit behind your laptop and manage your whole business.

With private label, you are not hindered by not having enough resources or skills to create the product that you want to sell because you can find a supplier who will do all of these for you. For example, if you want to sell clothes under your own logo or label, you do not really need to be a seamstress or buy all the materials needed for making clothes because all you need to do is to find someone who can do this for you. You can order them in bulk and have the products shipped to Amazon either directly by the manufacturer or by you.

2. Retail arbitrage

This is another way to sell products on Amazon. You search for low-priced branded products online or in retail stores, and resell them on Amazon at a marked up price. Retail arbitrage sellers often go to the clearance racks of giant retail corporations such as Target, Walmart, and Home Depot for their inventory.

For example, there is a sale on school supplies in Target and you are able to purchase a pack of 12 ballpoint pens for a discounted price of $3. You buy them and resell them on Amazon for $8, which is a little lower than their regular price of $12. You still earn a profit even if you sell it at a significantly lower price compared to the regular price. You also have the choice to sell it at the regular price of $12 if you want, especially if you know that these pens are highly sought after.

Private label sellers, on the other hand, only source their products from one manufacturer. The products are also sold under their own brand name while retail arbitrage sellers keep the brand name of their products, unless they want to be sued for intellectual property theft. Retail arbitrage is what a lot of people do when they sell online, especially those who are just part-time sellers who do not have a huge budget to buy things in bulk and establish their own brand name.

3. Wholesale

Buying wholesale from manufacturers and selling them as is on Amazon at a higher price is another way of selling on Amazon. You cannot sell the products under your own name or add value to the products because you are selling products under an established brand name. For example, you can buy wholesale Sony mobile phone cases directly from Sony and sell them as Sony mobile phone cases. You cannot rename the brand and change it to your own private label or you will be sued.

It is a bit similar to private label because you buy in bulk. The main difference is that you go to a manufacturer with the intention of buying their products in bulk and reselling these products while keeping the manufacturer's own brand. With private label selling, you go to a manufacturer and you agree upon a contract that includes buying their products in bulk that suits your business requirements, adding value to these products, and selling them under your own brand.

Wholesale buying and reselling is also kind of similar to retail arbitrage because manufacturers get to keep their own brand name. The main difference is that in wholesale, you source bulk products from one manufacturer, and in retail arbitrage, you source them from many different retailers.

4. Used book sales

Selling used books via Amazon is one of the easiest ways to start an online business that does not require a lot of capital. Financial risk is much lower when you sell used books. After all, you can just sell whatever you already have at home and you can easily buy used books for just a few dollars. Moreover, selling used books will also not get you as much complaints or returns from consumers as compared to selling other types of products unless you mistakenly sent the wrong book. You can even use the money that you earn from selling used books to launch your own private label business.

Pros and cons of private label vs. other ways of selling on Amazon

Private label vs. retail arbitrage

The drawback of retail arbitrage is that you have to continuously search for items on sale at different places. With private label, you already have a contract with one supplier, unless you decide to change your supplier or add more products to sell, which makes sourcing a lot easier. Your shop will also have more variety in terms of type or brand if you do retail arbitrage whereas private label selling means fewer types of products and only one brand (your private brand) to sell.

The amount of products you can buy depends solely on your budget if you decide to do private label selling. On the other hand, the amount of products you can sell using retail arbitrage depends not only on your budget but also on the availability of the product. The pens that you were able to buy for $3 and resell for $8 may no longer be available next time there is another sale. Because of this unpredictability, it is difficult to get consistent sales with retail arbitrage. Your profit margins will be variable, depending on how much you were able to get the item for.

Going back to our pen example, you might be able to find them again the next time they are on sale, but the discounted price may not be the same. It may be higher ($5 for 12 pens) or lower ($1 for all 12!). Retail arbitrage depends a lot on chance (of stumbling upon great deals) while private label is all about careful planning. This is why selling private labeled products has a bigger potential to grow, but at the same time, the risks of losing a lot of money is also much higher, especially if you are selling a single type of product in your shop.

Private label vs. wholesale

Both methods of selling get their products in bulk from one supplier, which means that sourcing is easy for both. And since both buy products in bulk, profit margins can easily be determined because they already have an idea about the base price of the products, and how much they go for in the market.

The main difference between the two, as mentioned earlier, is the branding. When you buy wholesale from a manufacturer, you resell the products under the manufacturer's brand. When you do private label selling, you can add value to your product and sell them under your own brand. Private label selling gives you more control because you can do whatever you want with the products once you buy them from the manufacturer.

Another difference between wholesale and private label is that in wholesale, you have to find a manufacturer that is not already selling directly on Amazon. You see that a lot of these popular brands also have their own accounts on Amazon. And how can you compete with the manufacturer selling their products on the same online selling platform?

But if you really become successful in private label selling, you can turn your online business into a multimillion company. Your name will be associated with your brand, which you created all on your own. Multimillionaires did not become rich by reselling products that they buy from existing brands. They created their own brands, and source the products somewhere else. Or better yet, you can create your own product. But that is another topic for another day.

Private label vs. retail arbitrage and wholesale

Basically, you are building your own brand from scratch with private label selling, unlike wholesale and retail arbitrage. It involves a higher financial risk than the other two but the rewards are also much greater if your business becomes successful. With retail arbitrage and wholesale reselling, the products that you sell already have an established brand. You do not really need to launch or promote them because the manufacturers already have their own ads for their products on different media such as TV, radio, print, and online. All you need to do is to make sure that your shop is visible enough so that when the customers search for the products, they will see your online store on top. People already know the products and the brand that you are selling. With private selling, you have to do a launch to let people know about your brand and the kind of products that you sell. You also have to make sure that you promote your products by advertising and making your shop more visible online.

Who are the stakeholders in the private label business model?

The three main stakeholders in this kind of business model are the following: the business owner (you), the manufacturer, and Amazon. In between and under these categories, there are minor players that make up the whole business model and make things run more smoothly and efficiently. Let's discuss the major stakeholders first.

1. The business owner

This refers to you, the person who has the idea to start an online business selling niche products under his own brand. You are responsible for determining the kind of products that you can sell through Amazon or even other channels. This means that you have to spend time doing research. There are already thousands of sellers of clothes. You can still sell clothes, but you need to find a niche where no one or very few has gone before. For example, you can sell funny hats instead of normal looking hats.

Your products need to stand out from the rest if you want people to notice and buy them. As the business owner, you are also responsible for finding the right manufacturer that can provide you with your orders in bulk. Again, research is your most powerful tool. It is also necessary that you have enough funds to make a bulk order from the manufacturer, pay Amazon fees, and cover miscellaneous expenses.

Setting up an Amazon account and registering for their Amazon FBA service is also your sole responsibility. Creating your own brand (e.g. coming up with your brand name and logo), prepping the products, adding your listings, monitoring your inventory, tracking your shipment, filing your tax, and so on are just some additional responsibilities of the seller. You can also choose your own freight forwarder to have the products shipped out to Amazon.

2. The manufacturer

Once you have found the manufacturer that meets all your business requirements, you can now contact them and start doing business with them under a contract that both of you agreed upon. Your chosen supplier is responsible for manufacturing the items that you ordered—whether it is 1,000 units of funny hats or 500 pieces of planners. If you have your own design that you want to sell, you can contact a manufacturer who can make the products for you according to your own specifications. If you just have an idea but you have not created a design of your own, you can simply find a manufacturer through different channels such as Alibaba, which is basically like China's Amazon.

You pay for the finished products, which means that the manufacturer is responsible for finding the materials required for making the products and paying for the workers who are going to make the products. All of these are accounted for when they quote you a price. Once the products are finished, the manufacturer has to find a shipping company to have your orders delivered either to you or directly to Amazon. It's all up to you.

3. Amazon

The third key player in this whole business model is, of course, Amazon. Whether you decide to sell via FBA or FBM (stands for fulfilled by merchant, meaning you just use Amazon as an online selling platform but you take care of the fulfillment aspect), you still need to use Amazon's services. Amazon's involvement begins when you decide to sell your products through their website. After registering, you need to send your items to their fulfillment centers. You can choose to ship using Amazon's partner shippers. With the FBA business model, Amazon has added responsibilities, such as storage of your goods, sorting, shipping to customers, and handling customer complaints and returns.

4. Shippers

The shippers are responsible for moving the products from the manufacturer to you as the seller or to Amazon's fulfillment center. They are also responsible for shipping the orders to the customer, and reverse shipping in case the customer wants to return or exchange the product. Basically, shipping the products to one of Amazon's fulfillment centers can be done by the manufacturer or by the seller. It can be a little tricky if your manufacturer is located overseas, like in China, because shipping can be more expensive, especially if you decide to do air freight.

The better option for international shipping is sea freight, especially if the items are big and heavy. It is cheaper but it takes much longer for the items to reach their destination. If you have the products with you, you also have the option to use traditional courier services such as FedEx or UPS via Amazon Partnered Carrier Program.

And when a customer buys the product, Amazon will deliver the order using their partner courier, mainly UPS, or FedEx and DHL in places that are not serviced by UPS.

5. Inspectors and prep services

Prepping your products to be shipped to Amazon can be challenging because Amazon has strict requirements. To make your life easier, you can simply hire inspectors and prep companies to do these things for you. These companies are responsible for inspecting the items to ensure that they are not damaged or counterfeit and that they adhere to Amazon's strict standards, packing of products, labeling, sorting, photography of products, and forwarding of shipment to Amazon fulfillment centers.

This is especially useful if you are buying from a manufacturer which is located overseas or far from where you live. The prepping company and inspector will ensure that the goods are in good condition and they are packaged, labeled, and sorted according to Amazon's requirements. This saves you a lot of time and trouble because goods that do not pass the standards of Amazon's warehouses will be sent back to the manufacturer or the seller, depending on where it came from. Some examples of these companies are FBAinspection, FBAshipuk, and McKenzie services, to name a few. These companies ensure that your products are perfect before they are shipped to Amazon.

You have the option not to hire the services of inspectors and prep companies but if you want to make sure that the whole process will go smoothly, it is best to work with these professionals. This is especially helpful for sellers who have to prepare a high volume of orders. As a seller, it is your responsibility to communicate with the manufacturer and prepping companies the schedule and timings of pickup or delivery.

6. Others

Aside from these, you might also want to hire someone who will create your brand logo. This is an important step that a lot of private label sellers take for granted, thinking they can just use any logo that they come up with. Your brand is important, and it is best to hire a professional graphic designer who can make your brand logo. If you have the talent to do these kinds of things, then go ahead and make your own logo. If not, and all you can do is create random shapes in Paint, then the best thing for you to do is hire a professional. You can hire plenty of good professionals from Fiverr or Upwork. Searching the keyword *"Logo Design"* on Fiverr will bring up a list of freelancers, go through their portfolio and reviews and choose one that meets your taste and budget.

Once your company grows, you should also consider hiring a professional number cruncher a.k.a. an accountant. He will be responsible for balancing your business' books to check how much you are earning, and if you are earning in the first place. This is a must, especially if you are shelling out thousands of dollars to start this business. You also do not want to get in trouble by filing the wrong tax forms and returns. All of these can be done by your accountant.

Pretty soon, as your company continues to grow, you should also think about hiring your own lawyer, who can look over your contracts with manufacturers and suppliers, and also who can give you legal advice in case somebody decided to sue you for something. You might also need to hire your own staff or assistance who can do menial tasks for you so that you can focus on more important things. All of these are a must once your business becomes huge and you start earning hundreds of thousands of dollars.

Chapter 2

Getting Started

Now that you have an idea about how Amazon FBA works, you should now learn the step-by-step procedure for getting started on your e-commerce business. It is not as difficult as you think. Maybe as you are starting, you find it a bit challenging with all the people, tools, and processes involved. But as you progress, the entire process will become second nature to you. And the more you feel comfortable doing it, the more efficient your business will be.

Steps on how to start private label selling via Amazon FBA

This is assuming that you already have the money to start a business, because it's easier to progress when you have the financial wherewithal. If you haven't got the money, don't worry. The last chapter of the book, **Credit Card And Credit Repair Secrets** goes into detail with regards to different sources of funds you can explore for your business.

Later on, you will get a lot of information regarding the costs and fees involved in starting an Amazon FBA private label business. For now, here are the things that you need to do to get started. Although each of these will be discussed in length and depth in the next few chapters, you still need to have a clear idea of the step-by-step procedure that you need to do to start a private label business via Amazon FBA.

1. Determine the product that you want to sell

This requires a lot of brainstorming and research on your end. You cannot just simply start selling a product because that's what you like - although selling something that you like is also important because it adds passion to what you do. You should be selling products that the market demands for. Otherwise, no one will buy your goods.

You can research about the types of products that are selling online. Your first stop should be Amazon itself. Check the different categories and look for interesting products. There is one category called "Hot New Releases" and you might just be able to get ideas from here. You can also simply Google the top-selling products on Amazon. You can also look for unique products in different social media platforms. Check the pages of popular influencers and find out what they are currently using or wearing.

Sometimes, inspiration will strike when you are not looking for it, maybe when you are window-shopping in your favorite boutique or even when you are having a conversation with your friend. You will know and feel when your idea is worth pursuing because you will feel excited to start your business.

2. Look for a manufacturer or supplier

Now that you already have an idea about the kind of product that you want to sell, you should now start searching for a supplier who can manufacture the products for you. If you can find a manufacturer or a supplier in your area, lucky you because you can easily visit the company in person and check the products that they make. You can also talk to them in person, which makes it easier to communicate your needs. If not, you can always check overseas suppliers.

A lot of Amazon private label sellers get their products from manufacturers located in China. How do they find these Chinese suppliers? Through Alibaba, AliExpress etc. Alibaba is like the yellow pages of Chinese manufacturers. You can contact the manufacturer through the app. You will see the retail price per unit and the minimum number of orders that they accept. You can also ask for a sample if you want to see if the quality of their products is up to your standards. It is best to contact more than one supplier, maybe 3 to 5, just to give you more options and to get the best deal.

3. Finalize your brand

While you are waiting for your products, you can use your time creating your brand. That is, if you have not created it before you started searching for the product. You might already have a vague idea of what you want your brand to look like but you still need to finalize everything. Since you are selling private label products, you can put your brand name or logo on the packaging or on the product itself. In some cases, it is best to already have a finalized brand name and logo so that the manufacturer can already add it to your product, for example, if you are planning to sell clothes. If not, you can always use other ways to incorporate your brand to the product.

You can maybe add a sticker or a tag that carries your brand name and logo. You can also design your own packaging, although it will still be hidden inside the poly bags that Amazon requires you to use and the final layer of packaging for when the item is going to be shipped to the customer. You should try to include your shop's contact details on the packaging or tag, such as website URL, phone numbers, social media pages, and other useful information that will lead the customer to your shop.

4. Create your Amazon account

This may be complicated for some people, but you have to master the Amazon website because this will be your selling platform. All you need to do is to go to the website and sign up if you do not have an Amazon seller account yet. If you do, you still need to create your Amazon FBA account by simply going to the Amazon FBA home page. The step-by-step procedure for creating your Amazon FBA account will be discussed later on in this chapter.

5. List your items

After creating your Amazon seller account, you can now start adding your listings. You can do this even when the products haven't arrived yet as long as you already have the photos and the specifications of the products. Be sure to tick the box that says you want Amazon to ship your products and to provide customer service to take advantage of Amazon FBA.

6. Prepare your inventory

Once the manufacturer is done with your orders, you can now start preparing your inventory to be shipped to Amazon's fulfillment center. You can hire a prepping company to do this for you, as discussed previously. Or you can do it yourself if you think you can follow Amazon's policies regarding product prepping.

7. Ship your items

Your products are now ready to be shipped to Amazon. Once your products arrive at Amazon's fulfillment centers, your listing will become active.

Once your products reach Amazon's warehouse, the rest of the process is pretty much Amazon's responsibility. You can sit back and wait for the orders to come in, but it is also important to keep promoting and advertising your business so that your products and brand will become more visible.

How to create an Amazon seller central account

This is what will connect you to Amazon. You cannot do business with them without an account, especially if you are planning to sell via FBA. Assuming that you don't have an account with Amazon yet, here are the steps that you need to follow.

1. Go to Amazon website

Just go to this website URL and click the Start selling button. Since you do not have an account yet, just click the Create your Amazon account button and enter the following details: your name, your email address (it is better to use a business email address, which is different from your personal email), and password (should be at least 6 characters).

2. Professional vs. individual

You need to choose what type of account you want to have as a seller—professional or individual. You might say, of course the obvious choice is professional because this is your business. However, it is important to note the differences between the two so that you can choose which plan will work best for you.

For both plants, you will have the option to sell via FBA. The main difference between the two is the number of items that you can sell per month. If you are going to sell more than 40 items per month, then it is best to choose the professional account. If your inventory will only have less than 40 items per month, then choose individual account. A professional seller plan also has a monthly fee of $39.99 per month while an individual seller plan doesn't require you to pay an upfront fee. However, individual sellers are required to pay $0.99 every time they sell an item. This fee is waived for professional sellers. If you are confident that your items will sell like hotcakes, then go ahead and pay for the professional seller plan.

If you are not yet sure, you can always try the individual seller plan first, then later on upgrade to professional plan as you start getting the hang of selling on Amazon.

3. Seller information

The details that you need to provide after creating a username and password are your legal name (for taxation purposes), the name of your business (or your display name) and the website URL (if you are already selling online), and your contact number (mobile or telephone). You can choose whether you want to receive a phone call or an SMS for your PIN verification. Read the seller agreement and tick the box. If you are an international seller, meaning you don't reside in the US, you need to read additional important information, which is also on the same page.

When asked to provide your business display name, it is best to use your brand name because this is the one that buyers will see next to your items. It should represent the kind of products that you sell and it should also be easy to remember.

Click next.

4. Verification

You will receive a phone call or a text message to verify your phone number and your account.

5. Set up your billing method

You also need to provide your credit card details for billing and bank account details for deposits. Just give your bank account number and routing number that you can find in the package given to you when you first opened your bank account or if you already lost it, you can just contact your bank. You will also see here your selling plan (professional vs. individual) and the corresponding fees that you need to pay. This is also the part where you can choose Amazon FBA as a way of selling.

6. Provide your tax information

This is a mandatory step and basically, it is just like filling out your W-9 form. You will be asked different questions about your tax information such as the income beneficiary, if you are a U.S. citizen, your name as shown on your income tax return, and your federal tax classification. This will be validated by Amazon.

7. Product information

This is an optional step for account setup. You can do this later if you are pressed for time. The questions that you will be asked are if you have Universal Product Codes (UPC) for your items, if you manufacture and brand your products, and the number of different products that you want to sell.

Voila! Your Amazon seller account is now set up! The next step is exploring your seller central space, which is all about managing your inventory and orders. This is where you will add your listings. It has several tabs that include Inventory, Pricing, Orders, Advertising, Reports, and Performance.

What tools are required?

When it comes to selling online, you will have a lot of options with regards to different tools that you can use to help you boost your brand and sales. These tools also help you run your business more smoothly and efficiently. Some of the tools that you should know as an Amazon FBA seller are as follows:

For niche research

If you have a product in mind and you want to know if it has a good market, you can use certain software for niche research such as Viral Launch. It'll help you find the best ideas with regards to what products to sell, sales estimates for these products, competitor tracking, opportunity scores (products that are considered good opportunities will be given a high score), and many more. You cannot simply rely on your gut instinct when it comes to choosing the best products to sell, especially if a lot of money is involved.

For keyword research

In the world of online selling, keyword is KING. You may have the best products, but if you are not using the right keywords for them, people will still not see them. You need to familiarize yourself with SEO and how it works in online selling. Viral Launch also provides keyword research assistance. You can also try Merchant Words, Keyword Tool and Sonar-tool.

For URL shortener

You do not want to scare your customers away by giving them links that are too long, and include so many weird looking characters. You should shorten your URLs using software such as Bitly and Google Short URL.

For calculating profit margins, fees, etc.

There is a tool called FBA Calculator for Amazon (you can't get any more specific than that!) that helps you calculate your profit margins. Calculating your profit margins while selling via Amazon FBA is not as simple as calculating typical profit margins because there is a lot of fees involved. There is also a specific calculator for freight rate called Amazon FBA Freight Rate Calculator.

For managing feedbacks and reviews

This type of software helps boost your rating as a seller because it helps you send feedback request emails to customers. Sometimes, customers do not make an effort to write a review when they purchase a product because no one is urging them to do it. When they receive an email from you asking them to write a review, they will remember and will be more than willing to do it because you made a specific request. One example of this type of software is AMZFinder. It gives you 500 free auto-emails per month that will help you receive more positive reviews, which can in turn boost your sales and improve your ranking.

For managing reimbursements

Amazon may be a huge company that has topnotch facilities and efficient staff but just like all companies, they still make mistakes. Sometimes, these mistakes can cost sellers money. Maybe they mishandled a product and when the customer received it, it's already damaged. Or maybe they unknowingly received a counterfeit item from another seller, and they sent out this particular item to your buyer, and when the buyer received the item, he understandably returned the item and asked for a refund. Things like these can happen, and it is a normal part of running a business. But you can minimize your losses using software such as AMZ Refund and Refunds Manager that help manage eligible reimbursements.

For multi-channel selling and inventory management

If you are selling on other platforms and websites, or if you have a high volume of inventory, you should consider using a tool that will help you manage all your listings. They will let you know when you are running low on supplies so that you can restock. They can also help integrate multiple online selling platforms into one system to make it easier for you to track your sales, orders, and inventory. Some examples of these software are Brightpearl, RestockPro, and Forecastly.

For product content optimization

Sometimes, duplicate content makes it difficult for search engines to choose which version is more relevant. Search engines also penalize duplicate contents, which is why some pages do not get high rankings even though they have similar content to those that are on the first few pages. Maybe you have been penalized by Google, and you just don't know it. Certain tools can help you with these kinds of issues such as Content26, Geek Speak Commerce, and mobiReady.

For pricing solutions

In such a huge market platform like Amazon, you will surely have several competitors, no matter how unique your niche may be. And if there are multiple sellers selling the same product, where will the buyer take his business? To the seller which offers the lowest price. This is also what you will do if you are the buyer. This is why it is important to monitor and compare prices of the kinds of products that you sell. You can use certain tools designed for this such as Price Checker 2.0, Appeagle, and Feedvisor.

For product launch

You need to launch your product, especially since you are a private label seller. The main goal of doing a product launch is to let people know about your products and also about your brand. Certain tools can help you with this such as Viral Launch, SnagShout, and iLoveToReview.

For accessing online courses, mentors, and community of sellers

Beginners like you will benefit a lot if you have someone who can give you advice regarding selling on Amazon. If you have extra money, you can hire a mentor in consulting marketplaces such as Clarity, where you have to pay per amount of time spent with the mentor. For an online course, you can try Proven Amazon Course, which includes Proven Private Label. You can also search for online communities of Amazon sellers. Some forums that you should check out are Ecommerce Fuel, Amazon Seller Central, and Reddit's Fulfillment by Amazon Subreddit.

These are the basic tools that can help you with your journey as a beginning Amazon private label seller. You will find out what tools you *really* need as you start selling.

What are the costs involved in selling via Amazon FBA?

1. Sourcing the product

This is the initial cost that you need to cover because without products, you will not be able to start your business. The product cost depends on the number of units you want to order from the manufacturer. Since you are a beginner and you do not want to shell out tens of thousands of dollars right away, let's assume that you only want to order about 200 to 300 units of the product that you have in mind.

Wholesale orders usually run from $0.50 to $10 each unit. This is again dependent on the kind of product that you want to order. Let's say you want to order 300 units of canvas bags with fun prints and the price of each unit is $2 each. You have to pay $600 to the manufacturer. The cost of sourcing your product is less than $1000.

2. Shipping

You still need to do a little shipping even if you are selling via Amazon FBA. You need to ship the items to Amazon and you can use your own courier if you want to. Shipping fees depend on how you want the items to be shipped—by air or sea. Air cargo is more expensive than sea cargo, although air is much faster than sea. This is why people who want to expedite the delivery of something usually use air cargo. If your products have regular size and weight, the typical computation of the shipping fee is about 60% to 80% of the cost of the product. This percentage already includes the courier fees and the declared value of your items. Going back to the example in the previous point, if your manufactured products cost $600, your shipping cost would be around $360 to $480.

3. Branding and logo

This is an optional cost, but if you want your brand and logo to look professional, you might want to hire someone who can do it for you, unless of course you are good at doing such kinds of things. You can easily hire someone to work on your branding and logo on Fiverr. You just need to pay $5 (hence the name Fiverr). Aside from Fiverr, you can also search for freelancers on other sites (e.g. upwork). They can provide you with your logo and packaging design. Let's say you will spend around $50 for this.

4. Photography

Online selling requires great photos of your products because this is what your future customers will see. Although this is also an optional cost, having professionally done photos will make your products stand out among the rest. You will notice the difference when you browse through the different listings. It might be easier these days to take great photos even by just using your phone's camera but it is still a better idea to have professional-looking pictures.

These professionals know things than an amateur photographer might not know such as the right way to take pictures of certain items, lighting, and so on. Again, you can use the same website that you used for finding a freelance graphic designer. You might have 300 items but they are more or less the same so you do not really need to take a picture of each. Let's just say for all the photos that you need, maybe 10 different shots, you have to pay $100.

5. Online tools and software

These include product and keyword research tools, calculators, profit monitoring software, product tracking software, pricing tools, and so on. For beginners, you probably won't get all of these software tools at once. You will probably only get the one with the most features, say, Viral Launch. They offer different packages for beginners which cost $29, intermediate for $59, and pro for $99. If you decide to get the intermediate version like most sellers, you have to pay $59.

6. Inspection service

This is another optional cost because this depends on how much you trust your supplier. If your products are simple, like canvas bags, then hiring a company that provides inspection services is not necessary. But if your product is kind of complicated and the manufacturer is from abroad, you might want to have your products professionally inspected. This will cost you around $100 to $300.

7. UPC barcode

You can send a UPC barcode to the supplier so that you can have it printed on your products before they get sent out to Amazon. This will cost around $5.

8. Running ads

As a seller, you have the option to have your products sponsored. You can choose products and keywords that you want to appear for on Amazon's specific pages such as product detail pages and in search results. The cost of sponsored products and brands depends on how many times your ads get clicked. You can also set the budget that you want to spend for your ads. To give you an idea, the minimum daily budget for keyword targeted ads is $1.

9. Amazon costs

Amazon will not be doing all of these for free. There must be some fees involved. And you are right. In fact, Amazon sellers pay a lot of different fees for different purposes.

Product fees

There are three types of product fees that sellers pay to Amazon.
- Referral fee - 6% to 20%, average is 15%, based on category and selling price
- Minimum referral fee - $0-$2, if referral fee is smaller than minimum fee, based on category
- Variable closing fee- $1.80, for all media categories

To illustrate, let's say for instance you are selling 4 pieces of mugs for $5.99. The 15% referral fee would be $0.89 and the minimum fee for this category is $1. Since the referral fee of $0.89 is smaller than the minimum fee of $1, you will pay $1 to Amazon. Let's take another example. If you are selling a set of four fleece blankets for $24.99, your referral fee will be $3.75, which is bigger than the minimum fee of $1. In this example, you will pay the $3.75 referral fee.

Variable closing fee is a flat rate of $1.80 no matter how much the product costs. This will be added on top of the referral fee. Some examples of media categories where you have to pay variable closing fees are video games, video game consoles, software, music, DVD, and books.

Seller account fees

As discussed earlier, there are two types of seller accounts—individual and professional. Individual seller accounts have no monthly fees, but they have to pay a $0.99 listing fee when the item is sold. This account is ideal for occasional sellers. On the other hand, professional sellers, or those volume sellers and businesses, have to pay $39.99 per month, but they no longer need to pay $0.99 per listing.

Amazon FBA fees

The two major fees that you will pay if you decide to use FBA are:
- Fees for picking, packing, and shipping
- Monthly fees for storage (which means that the longer your products stay in the fulfillment centers, the higher your fees will be)

These fees are based on the size and weight of your products. They divide the product size into two categories—standard size and oversize. Any item with dimension less than 18"x14"x8" and weighs less than 20 pounds once packaged are considered standard-sized. Oversize products, on the other hand, are anything exceeding the dimension and weight mentioned above.

Amazon further divides each of these product size categories:

Standard-size:
- Small standard size that weighs 1 lb or less- $2.41

- Large standard size that weighs 1 lb or less- $3.19
- Large standard size that weighs 1 to 2 lbs- $4.71
- Large standard size that weighs over 2 lbs- $4.71 for first 2 lbs + $0.38 per additional lb

Oversize:
- Small oversize- $8.13 for first 2 lbs + $0.38 per additional lb
- Medium oversize- $9.44 for first 2 lbs + $0.38 per additional lb
- Large oversize- $73.18 for first 90 lbs + $0.79 per additional lb
- Special oversize- $137.32 for first 90 lbs + $0.91 per additional lb

The abovementioned fees include picking, packing, handling, shipping, customer service, and returns. Storage fees, on the other hand, are based on the volume of your inventory and the calendar months.

Standard size:
- Jan-Sept: $0.64 per cubic foot
- Oct-Dec: $2.35 per cubic foot

Oversize:
- Jan-Sept- $0.43 per cubic foot
- Oct-Dec- $1.15 per cubic foot

These are the basic fees that you need to know as an Amazon FBA seller.

Chapter 3

Product Research

Given that your product is the heart and soul of your business, it's very important you research what kind of products will sell well on Amazon. Here are some tips that you need to know when it comes to choosing the right product for your business.

Criteria for selecting a good product

1. Good demand

You have probably learned this in basic economics. For your business to flourish, there should be a good demand for the products you are selling. You have to understand that demand sells. One of the reasons why a product is not selling is because there is no demand for it, meaning people do not want or need it. Another is that you have overestimated its demand, which led you to overprice the product. Or maybe you are simply selling your products to the wrong market. Having a high demand for your products will surely lead to high sales. If you already bought your products and you realized later on that the demand for them is quite low, you can still do something about it by artificially creating a demand.

One way to create an artificial demand is through *exclusivity*. Ever wonder why Apple products are highly sought-after even if they are extremely expensive? One reason is exclusivity. For one, they are expensive, which means only people with that kind of money can afford them. Second, Apple does not release products left and right, unlike its competitors. Third, they have their own tech centers, app stores, and so on. This makes the owners of Apple products feel exclusive.

You cannot simply increase the price of your products, or sell them to certain groups of people. You can instead use other techniques, such as selling "limited edition" items. Or, you can sell certain items at a limited time only. This makes potential buyers think that your products are scarce, that if they don't buy one now, they might not have the chance to buy later. You can also offer incentives to first time buyers to increase demand.

2. Not too much competition

Finding a good product that has a high demand but does not have a lot of competitors is a dilemma that most sellers face. After all, if a product is in demand, a lot of business owners will surely want to sell them. Certain types of products such as clothing and shoes are already highly saturated by a lot of sellers.

You need to find a product that has a demand but does not have a lot of sellers that offer them. One such product is a niche product. There is probably a large group of people out there looking for certain types of products that typical businesses don't sell. For example, clothing is an in demand product, but there is too much competition. But, if you really want to sell clothes, you should find ways to tweak your product a bit to make it unique and original that will sell to a certain group of people. For example, you can sell vintage-style swimsuits instead of the regular swimsuits. You can also sell kinky outfits for couples who love to do role play sex.

These are under the clothing category, but you are targeting a niche. Another popular niche clothing product is vegan or sustainable clothes. You will still have competition, but it won't be too high as compared to mainstream types of clothes like what H & M or Forever21 sells.

3. Not too seasonal

Seasonal products are those that are in demand during a particular season such as Easter, Christmas, Fourth of July, Halloween, etc. Seasonal products are highly profitable if you are selling them at the right time. When they are no longer in season, these products will sit in the Amazon shelves for months, collecting dust and accumulating storage fees. This is why you should avoid buying a lot of seasonal products for reselling, such as decors, costumes, or treats. Do not spend thousands of dollars on these items because they will surely sit for a long time in storage. You can still buy seasonal products but only a limited amount and you should also know when you should start buying them – timing is critical.

If you really want to sell seasonal products, maybe you can sell something that will cover different seasons. For example, fairy lights can be a great Christmas décor, but they are also used by a lot of people as regular room décor. You can also sell generic gift baskets that can be given as gifts on Mother's Day, Christmas, graduation, and so on.

4. Affordable retail price

You might think selling high-priced items is the best way to go if you want to earn a high profit, but you are wrong because it is still best to choose products that you can sell at an affordable retail price. For example, if you decide to sell private labeled watches that have Swarovski crystals on them, this will cost you a lot of capital, which means that you have to sell them at an even higher price if you want to earn a profit.

People may not be willing to spend hundreds of dollars on a brand that they have not heard of. This is why you should sell affordable products as you are establishing your brand. Moreover, expensive items can sit for a long time in storage because people are generally more cautious when it comes to buying more expensive items. If you sell them products that will only cost them a few dollars, they will not even think twice, and just simply click the buy now button even if they don't really need it and without researching about it.

5. Fewer reviews

You might think that selling a product with a lot of reviews is a great idea because it means that a lot of people are buying them. Although this can be true, it also means that the market is highly saturated because there is already a lot of sellers selling the same product. A product with fewer reviews means that it does not have a lot of sellers yet. It is still an untapped market that has a lot of potential.

6. Room for improvement

Selling a perfect product may not be a great idea because it means that nothing else can be done with it. It is already the final and ultimate version of that product. No more improvement can be made, which means that the price remains the same. Although there is no such thing as a perfect product (after all, nothing is perfect in this world), there are still products that give you very little room for improvement.

The design or structure of the product is not something that you can tweak to modify. This is not a good kind of product to sell, especially for private label sellers because you cannot add any value to it to make it your own. You should choose a product that gives you a lot of wiggle room, a product that gives you enough space for creativity. In one of the examples given before, selling canvas bags is a good idea because it allows you to customize different designs and prints.

7. Not in gated categories

There are certain types of products that require sellers to get Amazon's permission before they can start selling them on the website. There is an approval process that sellers need to go through if they want to sell products under the gated category, which is why this is not a good product to sell on Amazon, especially for startups. Amazon has to "gate" certain items to protect their reputation, especially since the number of third-party sellers have increased dramatically over the last few years.

This is Amazon's way of protecting their reputation. They do not want to have counterfeit or low quality products being sold on their website. Some examples of gated categories are fine jewelry, DVDs, watches, grocery items and gourmet food, fine arts, collectibles, and automotive. During the holiday season, Amazon also gates toys and games.

8. Not likely to attract litigations

You should also choose products that are not likely to get you sued. First, you need to know the kinds of products that attract litigations. Some examples are food, vitamins, cosmetics, and anything that you put inside your body or apply on your skin or hair. If you want to avoid litigations, you better choose products that are not applied on the body, eaten, taken orally, or inserted inside the body.

Choose something easy and safe, such as canvas bags, pens, clothes, notebooks, blankets, and so on. There are thousands of products to choose from that are not likely to attract litigations. These types of products are for sellers or brands that are already established, such as Kylie Cosmetics or Hershey's. These are large corporations that have a team of lawyers handling these litigations. You, on the other hand, are a one-man team who is just starting and cannot afford (yet) to hire your own business lawyer.

9. Not too fragile

If you are a very patient person and money is not an issue, go ahead and sell products that easily break such as eyeglasses, ceramic mugs, plates, light bulbs, and so on. Selling these products can lead to a lot of returns because they get damaged easily, either during transit or while in storage. No matter how the product gets broken, you still have to process the return and refund or exchange and this is a lot to handle, especially if you are processing multiple return transactions. Just imagine if all of your products are easily breakable. You will probably spend more time and money processing returns than selling the product itself.

Five best selling categories on Amazon

Since you are planning to sell on Amazon, you should also know the best-selling categories on the website. This will give you an idea about the kinds of products that you can sell that will give you the highest sales volume and profits.

1. Books

It all started when Jeff Bezos, the founder of Amazon, started selling books online. This is why books are one of the top selling categories on Amazon. Books are Amazon's very first product category. We are not talking about digital books here. We are talking about the traditional kind made of paper and ink. You might think, are there still people reading physical books? Aren't there e-books that they can easily download on their Kindle and iPad? Yes, there are still a lot of readers who prefer paper books over e-books. This is why this is still a huge market. Moreover, books have a large profit margin.

You can buy books wholesale for just one dollar, give or take a few cents. And you know how much one paper book costs. You can mark up your book items at 1000% of the original price. Selling books on Amazon may not be something that you can consider as your major source of income, but it is definitely one of the most stable categories on Amazon that has a huge market, and will definitely give you a solid income regularly.

2. Workout clothes

These days, a lot of people enjoy doing physical activities — going to the gym, running, yoga, and so on. This makes exercise clothing one of the highest selling categories on Amazon. People want to be comfortable and at the same time look good while doing their favorite workout, especially since they take a picture of themselves wearing their exercise gear and post it on social media. In fact, the popularity of exercising and working out gave birth to a fashion trend called athleisure.

You will now see a lot of people wearing workout clothes not only in the gym or while exercising, but also when going to the grocery or even to parties. You see them wearing sports bra with leggings and running shoes everywhere. And despite the increasing number of people who buy second hand clothes, a lot of them still prefer brand new workout clothes. Nobody wants to wear a pair of used leggings or sports bra. It is a huge market right now, and you should definitely take advantage of that.

The only downside is that it is hard to find a manufacturer that can make high quality athleisure clothes. Low quality workout clothes are not comfortable to wear, and comfort is one of the things that you should look out for when it comes to buying workout clothes. You should also be aware of the characteristics of the workout clothes that you should be selling. There are clothes that absorb sweat or pull sweat away from the body. You also have to pick workout clothes for different physical activities and seasons.

3. Electronic items and accessories

For Amazon FBA sellers, electronic items might be difficult to sell because people would generally buy electronics from a well-established and known brand. What you can do instead is to just find electronic accessories to sell. You can sell a wide variety of accessories for different electronics—phone cases, laptop sleeves, laptop bags, phone pouches, power banks, memory cards, screen protectors, and so on. You can easily find a manufacturer for these. All you need to do is to find one that offers the best deal. There are a lot of different electronic devices that come out every few months and you can be sure that people will buy accessories for these.

However, having new devices come out every month is a double-edged sword. It is a positive thing for sellers because it means more things and varieties to sell for them. It is also a negative thing because devices get replaced fast, which means that you might still have some accessories for a device that is already obsolete. The key here is to monitor trends and do not buy too many items for one particular device.

4. Baby items

Baby items are always in demand because humans always procreate. And babies need a lot of stuff. In fact, they need more stuff than adults. Their stuff also get replaced fast because babies grow and develop fast, unlike an adult who can own and wear the same clothes for ten years. One advantage of selling baby items is that they are usually small and lightweight, unless of course you are selling baby furniture. They are also inexpensive, which can give you a huge profit margin. However, you should avoid selling baby items that can get you sued such as baby food or feeding supplies. Just stick with regular items like clothing, toys, blankets, and so on.

5. Clothing, shoes, and jewelry

These are always in demand anywhere you go. People always buy clothes, shoes, and jewelry. Workout clothes have a separate category because it has its own huge market. However, there is still a lot of people who buy regular clothes, and also shoes and jewelry. Please note that this does not include jewelry made of precious metals such as solid gold and expensive materials such as Swarovski. These are regulated products and might be difficult to sell.

Clothing, shoes, and jewelry have always had a huge market whether it is online or in physical stores. You can also buy them in bulk for dirt-cheap because there are already a lot of manufacturers to choose from. They are also easy to ship because of their small size. You can never go wrong selling them. The only drawback is that because they are a popular category, you will have a lot of competition. This is why you need to add something to your products that will make them stand out from the rest. Maybe you can focus on selling only one type of clothes, such as sleepwear or lingerie. For shoes, maybe you can sell foldable flat shoes that they can easily store in their bags. For jewelry pieces, you can sell vintage-inspired jewelry that are quite popular these days.

These are the things that you need to consider when it comes to selling products on Amazon FBA. Once you find the product that you want to sell after careful research, you can now proceed to finding a reliable manufacturer or supplier who can make these products for you or sell them to you wholesale.

Chapter 4

Sourcing the Product

You should now search for the manufacturer or supplier where you can get your products from. This can be intimidating for a lot of people, especially beginners because once you contact a supplier and order hundreds of units of an item, you can no longer back out or change your mind. You cannot simply say to the supplier that you do not want the items anymore after they started making them. You also cannot simply decide not to sell once you receive the products after spending hundreds or even thousands of dollars. What are you going to do with 100 pieces of baby clothes or 500 pieces of memo pads? Contacting a manufacturer signals the beginning of your business. You are already involving other groups of people, and you need to be professional about it.

Choosing a supplier may sound scary but it is not that difficult, especially today when everything is right at your fingertips. However, you should still be cautious because there are a lot of scammers out there, especially if you are ordering from abroad. To help you find and choose the right manufacturer or supplier for your business, here are some tips that you should know.

Where can you find suppliers?

These days, everything is made in China, and it is no wonder because there is a lot of manufacturers and suppliers of products in China. Although it is best to go to China and talk to the manufacturers in person, you can also simply contact them online. Here are some Chinese websites that you should check out.

https://www.alibaba.com/

This is probably the most popular website used by Amazon sellers. It is one of the biggest companies that do business with ecommerce sellers. Alibaba is based in China and has other websites—Tmall and Taobao. It is used by millions of people, including merchants, businesses, and individual sellers. Most of the people selling on Amazon get their products from Alibaba. Alibaba is like the yellow pages of manufacturers and suppliers. You will find here hundreds of companies that make products in bulk, usually by the hundreds. Their unit price is also dirt cheap, which gives you a chance to sell them at a higher mark up.

https://www.aliexpress.com/

Alibaba owns Aliexpress, and the two are not the same. The owner of Alibaba uses Aliexpress to compete against ecommerce giants such as Amazon and eBay. You can buy items per piece from Aliexpress, but not from Alibaba. However, you can still source your inventory from Alibaba because they offer their products at factory prices in smaller quantities.

https://www.made-in-china.com/

Founded in 1998, Made-In-China is also one of the leading B2B ecommerce websites in China. It works the same way as Alibaba, by bridging the gap between Chinese suppliers and international sellers. It makes it easier for people all over the world to contact Chinese manufacturers.

Aside from Chinese suppliers, you can also find manufacturers and suppliers in the US and Europe, although pricing can be a little more expensive.

Here are some websites that you should check out.

http://www.zentrada.eu/

This website is one of the largest sourcing platforms used by ecommerce sellers in Europe. Individual sellers are given new ideas for ordinary products that help them to succeed. Currently, they have around 400 thousand units of different products that come from different manufacturers, importers, and wholesalers worldwide.

http://www.koleimports.com/

If you live in Los Angeles, California, you can try contacting Kole Imports, a family-owned business in the US. It is one of the biggest general merchandisers and direct importers of different consumer goods. Established in 1985, Kole Imports gets their products directly from manufacturers abroad, and sell them in bulk to retailers and wholesalers. You can visit their website by clicking the link above or you can go to trade shows where they are participating.

http://www.closeoutfortune.dollardays.com/

Also based in the US, Closeoutfortune offers wholesale products at a low price. They have a wide assortment of products to choose from, and they also have a wide range of customers — non-profit groups, retailers, e-sellers, and even schools. They are a great source of items to sell, especially for small businesses and non-profit organizations.

How to evaluate reliability of suppliers

The knee-jerk reaction for most people searching for a supplier is to choose the one that offers the lowest price. This should not be the case because the most important thing is to find a supplier who can deliver what they promised. If you find a reliable supplier, you won't have to keep searching for new suppliers every time you need to replenish your inventory.

1. Main product

When choosing a manufacturer for your product, you need to make sure that the product you want them to make is their main product and not just something that they sell on the side. For example, if you are planning to sell bed sheets, you should go directly to a manufacturer that makes bed sheets, instead of going to a manufacturer that sells mainly mattresses but also makes bed sheets on the side.

2. Main markets for exports

Manufacturers whose main target markets are businesses in developed countries are generally more reliable than those whose target are businesses in developing countries. This is understandable because developed countries have stricter policies when it comes to product quality and safety standards. They closely monitor defects and compliance to regulations imposed by different government bodies.

3. Compliance to product safety

You also need to choose manufacturers that comply with product safety standards. As a seller, it is your responsibility to ensure that your products are safe to use by the general public. Some product safety regulations that you should know as a seller are electrical safety regulations, product packaging regulations, toys and children's products regulations, textile regulations, and so on. You need to know what regulations your intended product to sell should adhere to. And then, you need to find a manufacturer that makes products that will pass such regulations with flying colors.

Compliance to such standards is critical when it comes to importing from overseas, especially China because it can lead to product recalls, fines, seized cargos, and even litigations. This might even cause you millions of dollars, especially if the damage caused by your product is fatal and serious.

4. Quality management system

Monitoring the quality of the products that a manufacturer makes is a must in any manufacturing company. They have to closely monitor their products during and after production to minimize the number of units with defects. The higher the number of defective units, the lower the sales will be. This also has a negative impact on the manufacturer's reputation, which is why they try hard to keep their defects at a minimum. You need to find a supplier that follows QMS or quality management system. Unfortunately, only a small percentage, about 5% to 10% of manufacturers follows QMS. To find them, they should have an ISO certificate, usually ISO 9001.

5. Transparency

Manufacturers who are not willing to undergo factory audit or quality inspection probably have something to hide. You can eliminate unreliable manufacturers by telling them early on that you are going to do quality inspections and testing of samples. If they refuse, you should not do business with them because a reliable supplier will be more than willing to have these inspections.

Criteria to use when evaluating a supplier

Your business has its own specific needs, and you need to make sure that you choose a supplier that meets these needs. You need to create a list of criteria that will help you choose the one that will be able to provide you with the kind of products and service that you are looking for.

1. Cultural fit

The manufacturer should uphold the same cultural value that your business stands for. For instance, if you want to sell items made from bamboo because you want to promote the use of sustainable products and at the same time earn money through your business, you should find a manufacturer who adheres to the same principles.

2. Cost

The cost of everything—from the production of the goods to shipping—should be within your budget. You need to find a manufacturer that can offer you the lowest cost per unit but still maintains the quality of the products that you are looking for.

3. Order quantities

This depends on how many you want to order. Most manufacturers have a minimum order requirement. If you are just starting, you might want to choose a supplier that allows you to order by the hundreds, say, 300 units of the item.

4. Follows safety standards and quality control systems

The company should follow all the required regulations in terms of safety and quality standards imposed by the country where you live. You can ask for certifications, ISO numbers, and other permits to ensure that you are dealing with a legitimate supplier.

5. Turnaround time

How long can the manufacturer finish the product? The faster the products are finished, the faster you can launch your business. However, make sure that the short turnaround time will not negatively affect the quality of the products.

6. Flexibility

They should be willing to adjust if there are changes to be made to the orders and the product itself, of course with necessary pricing adjustments.

These are just some of the things that you should consider when choosing a manufacturer or supplier to do business with. These should be laid out before you decide to search for suppliers to ensure that you are choosing the right one for your business needs.

How To Spot Shady Suppliers

Hopefully, in your journey as an online seller, you will never come across a shady supplier or a scammer who only wants your money. These shady suppliers can be avoided by knowing the signs that you are dealing with one. Here are the things that you should look out for.

1. Too good to be true

You always hear the saying if it is too good to be true, it's probably not true. This also applies when choosing a manufacturer. If they promise to move heaven and earth just to finish your product within a very short period of time, and they are working on low capital because the quote that they gave you is too low, then this is probably not legit. Low price does not always mean a great deal. You might be dealing with a scammer who just wants to attract people to scam by giving them unbelievable deals.

2. Too much self-promotion but no substance

When you contact the supplier because you are attracted by their rates, and you notice that the supplier talks too much about all the great things that they can give you but you do not really see a lot of positive reviews from previous customers, chances are they are just building themselves up to make you sign that deal. A legit supplier will ask questions about the work that you want them to do and will show you proof of successes from previous clients.

3. Quote is too generic

When you ask for a quote, they should be able to give you the breakdown of everything and how they arrived at that amount for you to understand what you are paying for. A shady supplier will probably give you a cookie-cutter quote that he got from Google.

4. Hidden fees

If the pricing that they give you is vague, which gives them an opportunity to change the price in the future, you should be wary because you are probably dealing with a shady supplier. If they say something like "you need to pay us around 600 dollars, but we're not sure yet about the kind of materials you want and we can only find out once we start to make the products after you make the payment", you should back off because this is not how it should be done. A legitimate seller will give you an exact amount to be paid. After all, they are supposed to have been doing this for years, so they should know by now how much they should be charging their clients.

5. Delays in communication

Delays in responding to your calls or messages can mean that the supplier does not have a designated department for handling questions of potential clients or is simply too busy or disorganized. Either way, you wouldn't want to communicate with such a seller because it shows unreliability. This might cause problems in the future when you need to talk to them urgently and no one is responding.

Ordering samples

One way to ensure that you are getting products that meet your standards is to ask for samples from the manufacturer.

Why order samples?

To test the quality.

Pictures are sometimes not enough because they can be misleading. If you have the sample in your hand, you will be able to see, smell, and feel the actual product that you are going to buy and later on sell to your future customers.

To test the supplier.

This is also a great way to test the supplier. You will know if they are willing to send a sample and you will also find out how they communicate and work with their clients. You will also see their packaging and how fast they process and ship their orders.

To let them know that you are serious.

This is a subtle way to let them know that you are serious about your orders. Suppliers also weed out hundreds of "buyers" that don't actually order anything. This will let them know that you are willing to go further if you are satisfied with the sample.

How many samples should you order?

Ideally, you should order one sample per product that you will be ordering. However, you have to consider your budget and shipping fees because if you have a lot of different products, you might want to limit your order to a few samples. Maybe if you are ordering everything from one manufacturer, you can order a couple of samples just to see if their real products are the same as the ones in their picture. Some manufacturers will also not buy materials and spend time and money on labor just to make one item. You have to consider different aspects and make sure that you ask your supplier how you should go about ordering samples.

Why hire an inspector to check the products before shipment?

Although you might need to pay extra if you hire a professional inspector, you will at least get professional inspection of the products that you are going to sell. This is also cost effective in the long run because you don't have to go to the supplier's factory in person just to check your orders. This also means lower return rates because products meet the quality standards. Hiring an inspector is also beneficial because they would know what to look out for. After all, it is their job and they are trained to spot defects and subpar quality products that an ordinary person might miss. And inspectors like these are usually located in the same country as the manufacturer, which means easier communication among the supplier, the inspector, and you because the inspector can act as an intermediary.

Searching for the right supplier is not difficult as long as you know where to look and what to look for and look out for. The next chapter will teach you how to ship the products once the manufacturers are done with your orders.

Chapter 5

Shipping the Products

Once the manufacturer has completed your orders, the next step is to have them all shipped to Amazon FBA warehouses. You need to research this part before you place an order, especially if you decide to source your product from Chinese manufacturers because there is a lot of processes involved when it comes to importing items from abroad.

For illustration purposes, let's assume that your manufacturer is from China, where most Amazon FBA sellers get their inventory.

Shipping from China to Amazon Warehouse

There are three ways to ship form China to Amazon Warehouse:
- The items will be sent directly to Amazon Warehouse from China.
- The items will be sent to your home first and then to Amazon Warehouse.
- The items will be sent to a third-party company and then to Amazon Warehouse. This company will also check and prep the products for you.

Chinese supplier - Amazon Warehouse

A lot of people use this first method because it is the fastest and cheapest way among the three options for obvious reasons. This is especially true if you decide to use air or express cargo. You have to pay for the shipping fee twice if the products have to go through your home or a third-party company.

Chinese supplier - You - Amazon Warehouse

Some sellers prefer that they see the products that they ordered first hand before selling them online. This is especially helpful when it comes to ensuring that the items meet Amazon's quality requirements. This is also ideal if you live near the US main ports, like Los Angeles. It will add more to your shipping expenses if you live far from major ports because of the additional transportation costs from the port to your home. However, if you do decide to have the items shipped to your home first, you will be responsible for prepping your products, which can be a tedious process, especially for beginners like you.

Chinese supplier - Third-party – Amazon Warehouse

If you want your products to be inspected, prepped, and monitored professionally, and you have extra money to spare, you can hire a third-party company that can do all these things for you. You need to find a third-party company that is also located in the same state as the Amazon FBA warehouse if you want to have low shipping costs. If it is located in a different state, the shipping costs will be a lot more expensive.

Shipping by sea or air

1. Sea freight

This is a complicated method of shipping items for export and import because it involves a lot of steps. It may be complicated but it is still one of the major ways to transport products from one country to another because it can accommodate a large shipment at a much lower cost. The main disadvantage is the length of time. Shipping by sea has several stages:
- From the Chinese supplier to Chinese port (domestic)
- From the Chinese port to the US port (international, export and import)
- From the US port to your home, to the third-party company, or directly to Amazon FBA warehouse (domestic)

Two forwarders are involved in the entire process — the Chinese and US forwarders. They have to coordinate with each other and handle all the processes involving importing and exporting these goods to and from their respective countries.

You can either find your own freight forwarder or you can let your supplier find one for you. You need to understand that Amazon is not responsible for anything related to customs clearance and does not provide any delivery support. They also do not act as a contact for overseas customs clearance. These are all the responsibilities of the freight forwarder and also the seller. If your goods do not meet the requirements of the customs, they will be detained and the freight forwarder should know how to handle such scenarios.

Finding your own freight forwarder vs. letting your supplier find one for you

If you think you will continue having this business for many years to come, you might want to find a freight forwarder that you can rely on. Sounds cheesy, but that's how it should be. Moreover, finding your own forwarder is beneficial because you can find someone who speaks the same language as you do. And you are satisfied with what you have researched about them. You can choose someone who meets all your business needs. You can choose either a freight forwarder who is located in China or in the US, although the former is preferred by many. The main reason is the ease of communication, as stated previously, and there will also be no time difference that can affect communication because you live in the same state.

If you find your own freight forwarder, your Chinese supplier should deduct the cost from the total amount that you have to pay. The amount depends on whether the forwarder will ship from the supplier's warehouse or from a seaport in China.

Most beginners usually resort to the second option of letting their supplier find a freight forwarder for them because they do not have a lot of contacts yet. But as they continue doing their business, they will get recommendations from fellow sellers on where to find the best freight forwarder. But you can still choose to let your supplier handle the shipment process. This is especially a great idea if your supplier has done business with an Amazon seller before because they already know how it works. You do not have to explain about Amazon fulfillment centers, and the right way to prep the products. Just make sure to ask about the shipping costs because sometimes, they do not include the cost of shipping from the US port to Amazon.

The benefit of letting your supplier find a freight forwarder for you is that you do not need to search for it. And searching for freight forwarders and knowing what questions to ask can be challenging. With the expertise and connections of your supplier, you can be sure that you will have a reliable freight forwarder who can handle your shipment for you. The only downside is that you are not learning the nitty gritty of processing shipments and searching for your own contacts because you let your supplier do it for you.

Cost of sea freight

As mentioned earlier, there are a lot of steps involved when it comes to shipping goods by sea. However, it is still the cheapest way to ship because it can accommodate a large volume of shipment, unlike air freight, which has a limit. The cost of sea freight depends on *where the shipment is coming from, where it is going and what month you are going to ship*. But for reference, you can use $300/CBM which includes all shipping costs from a seaport in China to one of Amazon's warehouses located in the south of the USA. This will at least give you a rough estimate of how much you will be paying. The United States is a large country, and the shipping costs also depend on where you are located in the US. If the Amazon warehouse is in the west coast, the shipping fee will be much lower than if it is located in the east coast.

There is also a minimum shipping capacity when using sea freight, which is 2-3 CBM per shipment. Keep in mind that when using sea cargo, most of the fees and charges that the freight forwarders need to pay in the entire process of importing and exporting the goods are fixed no matter how much CBM shipment you have. The minimum is 2-3 CBM which is not difficult to reach since you are shipping goods in bulk.

Shipping time

So how long does it take for your cargo to reach Amazon's warehouse from China if you use sea freight? There are so many factors involved that it usually takes at least 30 days for a shipment to reach Amazon's warehouse located in the west coast coming from a Chinese seaport. If the Amazon warehouse is located in the east coast, it will take an additional 10 days, so 40 days in total. This is the minimum timeframe, but it could take longer than that. For example, if you ship during the holiday season in the US or during a festival in China, your cargo might take a longer time. There are also times when the customs clearance takes a longer time to complete because they are processing a higher volume of cargos than usual. Other factors that can affect the delivery time are the weather, labor issues at seaports, seasonal behaviors, and so on.

Christmas is the best time to sell online because a lot of people are buying gifts for their loved ones. So if you are planning to sell stuff for Christmas, you have to make sure that your shipment leaves China by the last week of October. If not, you will suffer delays and your shipment that you intend to sell on Christmas will arrive late, probably after Christmas. During this time, there is a much higher volume of shipment, which is why things get stuck at the customs.

2. Air freight

The second method of shipping is via air freight, and this is ideal if your shipment exceeds 1000 lbs. If it is below 1000 lbs, you can try express cargo, which involves a courier company such as DHL, FedEx, and UPS. However, most sellers on Amazon use either sea cargo or air freight because they usually have a lot of stuff to ship. Just like with sea freight, goods shipped via air freight also have to go through customs clearance. And just like sea freight, you also need to find a freight forwarder who will handle the entire process, including clearing customs. You have to make it clear to your freight forwarder that you want to pay for the total cost of shipping the products. You do not want to pay fees again when the shipment reaches your home or for import and export fees. This should be clarified by the freight forwarder before you decide to use their service.

Cost of air freight

When it comes to air freight shipping, the cost depends largely on the weight and volume of your shipment. Typically, air freight shippers charge per dimensional weight or actual weight, depending on which one is higher. To calculate the dimensional weight, you need to multiply the shipment's volume in CBM by 167. For example, if your shipment has a dimension of width-60 cm x height- 60 cm x length-60 cm, you will get 216,000. Divide this by one million and you will get 0.216. To get the volumetric weight, multiply this by 167. Your shipment's volumetric weight is 36.072 kgs. If this is bigger than the shipment's actual weight, you will be charged based on the volumetric weight, or vice versa.

Compared to sea freight, air freight is a lot more expensive, especially if you are shipping heavy items. Imagine if you are shipping items that weigh a total of 2000 lbs in a medium sized box by sea from Shenzhen, China to New York, USA, you only have to pay $1200. But if you ship the same item via air freight to and from the same destination, you have to pay a whopping $4000.

Shipping time

Obviously, shipping via air freight takes a much shorter time than sea freight because airplanes are 30 times faster than ships. It will only take your shipment 3 days to one week, again depending on different factors such as speed of getting cleared at the customs, holiday season, and so on. This is why air freight is a lot more expensive than sea freight.

If you are pressed for time, you should consider choosing air freight. Maybe you are planning to sell before the holiday rush and you want your items to reach on time. Or maybe you are selling goods that have expiry dates or items that are seasonal. Electronics and other expensive items are also usually shipped via air because they will have a lower chance of getting lost or damaged because of the shorter shipping time. They are also more protected in planes than in ships in terms of storage conditions.

CO2 emissions

You already know that airplanes emit a large amount of C02 in the air. And if your business values sustainability, you might want to consider shipping via sea freight. According to a research conducted by the UK government, an ocean liner carrying 2 tonnes of shipment for 5000 km will only have 150 kgs of CO2 emissions. Compare this to 6605 kgs CO2 emissions of an airplane carrying the same load and traveling the same distance, choosing sea freight over air freight will seem like a no-brainer for people who are pro-environment and sustainability.

Import duty of products and other taxes

You also need to know the different fees involved in shipping your items. It is not just the cost of the service provided by the freight forwarder. They also have to pay different fees and taxes throughout the whole process. Import duty and taxes are calculated based on customs value and category of goods or HS code.

Customs value

Ideally, the customs value is calculated as: cost of product + cost of transportation to the Chinese port + export clearance in China. However, freight forwarders just estimate the amount at 20% to 30% of the value of the product in the United States, and this is what they declare at the customs clearance. To estimate the tariff of the product, you just multiply this amount to the current tariff rate.

HS code

Customs also assigns a standardized classification system to determine customs duty. HS Code means Harmonized Commodity Description and Coding System or simple Harmonized System. This consists of classification names and numbers to sort out traded goods that come in and go out of the country. You have to ensure that you assigned the correct HS code to your goods. Otherwise, you may be charged the incorrect customs duty.

Since you are not shipping the goods yourself, you do not really have to worry about these things because the freight forwarder or the courier company handles the entire process from start to finish. All you have to do is to be aware of these details so that you at least have an idea how much you need to pay when shipping your products. Once your products are shipped, or even before they reach their destination, you can now start preparing the products for sale by creating and building your brand.

Chapter 6

Preparing the Product for Sale by Branding

After receiving your items or even before receiving them, you need to prepare your products for sale by creating and building a brand. Your brand is a lot more than the name and logo of your business. It is the complete package—your products, business model, methods of advertising, values, and customer experience. This is why building a good brand is just as important as having a good product to sell.

Building a brand that is sustainable

These days, the more popular meaning of sustainability is being green and eco-friendly. And this is something that a lot of companies should strive for because more and more consumers are becoming more aware of the impact of their consumption to the environment. Another meaning of sustainability in terms of branding is lasting for a long time and remaining relevant for many years. This is also something that your business branding should aim for. You have to make sure that your branding is not just a fad or a trend. It should be sustainable and last for a long time to ensure that you have continuous business.

Choose a product that allows you to add other related products

When it comes to choosing a product to sell, you have to make sure that it allows you to add other related products as time progresses. And choose a brand that does not only focus on your specific product. For example, if you are selling quirky notebooks and your branding is something like All Quirky Notebooks, people will automatically assume that you are only selling fun notebooks with quirky designs. Sure, maybe you can add other related products like memo pads or pens and pencils, but that's about it.

What you can do is to change your branding into something more inclusive, like All Things Quirky so that you can add other related products later on as long as they have a quirky design. Another great example of this is selling electronic devices. Mobile phones, for instance, have different kinds of accessories such as cases, screen protectors, chargers, power banks, and so on. By selling complementary products, you will retain regular customers because they will not go somewhere else to look for accessories or other related products and you will also attract new customers who want to buy your other items.

Continuously create a need for your products

To keep your products' relevance in the market, you should continuously create a need for your products that will make people want to buy them. One way to do this is by promoting exclusivity of your products. For example, you can offer your products as limited editions that will make people think that they will not be sold after a particular time. You can also make your products or your promotion available only to a specific group of people. For instance, you can offer your discount or a specific product only to your Amazon customers and not to people who buy them from your physical store or other online selling platforms. This will create a need for your products that can make your business more sustainable.

What you need to know about trademarks

You always hear the word trademark but what does the word really mean? It is sometimes used interchangeably with branding which is the representation of the company. It could be a symbol, logo, phrase, or word that a company uses. Basically, a business needs a trademark to protect its intellectual property. To make your business qualified for trademark, you have to make sure that you use the brand for commercial purposes and the brand must be unique to your business.

There are certain things in your company that you can trademark such as unique names of your products and business, the words or phrases that you use for your products or marketing campaigns, symbols and logos that your company uses, and so on. You can even trademark scents, colors, and sounds that are unique to your brand and you do not want other people to use without your consent.

Types of marks

When it comes to name branding, there are four types of marks that you should know
- Descriptive,
- Suggestive,
- Arbitrary, and fanciful.

Descriptive mark is anything that has acquired a secondary meaning. For example, if you want to name your business after your last name which is McDonald's, say, McDonald's Cakes and Pastries, you will not be allowed to do so because McDonald's already acquired a secondary meaning as an American fast food chain. The most commonly used trademark is the suggestive mark. It does not entirely describe the company or the product but it gives consumers a hint of the kind of products that the company sells.

Some examples of suggestive brands are Netflix, Airbus, and Citibank. The third kind of mark is the arbitrary marking, which is a word, or phrase that has nothing to do with the company or products that they sell. One example is Apple. Apple does not sell the fruit apples but mobile phones, laptops, and computers. Windows is another great example of arbitrary trademark. Finally, fanciful marks are any original terms created for your specific business or product, such as Kodak, Aveeno, Exxon, Pepsi, and Polaroid.

Why do you need trademarks?

As mentioned before, trademarks protect your business from intellectual property theft. It also allows you to set your company and your products apart from other similar businesses to prevent confusion. Trademarks also prevent unfair competition such as imitation, trademark infringement, and use of other company's confidential information or trade secrets. Having a trademark also allows consumers to buy with confidence, knowing that the brand they are buying from is known for selling quality products.

Trademarks also allow consumers to know where the products come from in terms of the sponsor, the manufacturer, and the seller. When you apply a trademark for your business, you have to renew it after 10 years. And if you continuously use your products for five years, you can apply for incontestable status, which will give your business better rights to ownership and better protection against infringement.

Having your own trademark gives you exclusive rights to use the branding in your business. If you find other businesses using your trademark, you can pursue legal action against them because you were given the right to use that branding exclusively for your business.

Should startups register a trademark?

Some people think that trademarks are only used by large corporations such as Coca Cola or Microsoft and startups/small businesses do not really need them. This kind of thinking is the reason why some people end up losing their business. They do not anticipate these kinds of things, thinking that their business will not become as big as these corporation giants. You need to think ahead if you want your business to succeed.

It is best to protect your business from the start, especially if you have a unique branding and if your products are one-of-a-kind. This will allow you to take legal actions if your business' intellectual property rights are violated in the future. The bottom line is that you also need to trademark your brand if you want to protect your business from potential intellectual property theft in the future.

To illustrate the importance of acquiring a trademark for your brand, let's take a look at this made-up scenario. Emily started selling clothes that she designed herself in her neighborhood that she calls New Threads. She didn't bother to get a trademark for her business because she thought it was just a small business and nothing would really come out of it on a larger scale.

After some time, she noticed that a competitor in a different neighborhood who is also selling clothes also uses the same name. This case is still easy to handle because it's in a small area. As long as Emily can prove that she started using the name before her competitor, she can continue using the brand for her business.

The problem will be much more complicated if there is another competitor in a neighboring state that uses the same name and who already filed an application for a federal trademark for the name New Threads. Emily might still have the right to use the name in the area where she loves, but she can't really sell interstate because another company has already trademarked the name, which means that Emily has to change her business name if she wants to expand her business outside her town.

This could have been avoided if she filed a trademark from when she started the business. She could have chosen a different name for her business because another company is already using it. Or if she is the first one to use the name, she will have all the rights to the brand and the competitor will not be allowed to use that name in the first place. And if Emily is going to change her name to be able to sell to other states, she might lose customers because some of them might not know that it is the same company.

This is why it is best to trademark anything related to your business that could potentially cause intellectual property lawsuits and claims in the future. However, you have to make sure that you have finalized your branding before you consider filing for a trademark. Maybe in the beginning, you are still unsure about the name and logo of your business and you might still want to do some small changes to them. The most important thing to remember is to file as early as you can once you are sure about the kind of branding that you want your business to carry.

Perform a trademark search

Once you have decided to have your name or logo trademarked, the first thing that you need to do is to conduct a trademark search. You need to understand that just because your trademark application was approved, that does not mean that no other company is using it. As a business owner, it is your responsibility to find out if someone else has already used the name you chose for your business. This means that a company who owns the trademark to the name that you are both using has all the right to take a legal action against you. If the other company wins the case, you need to stop operating your business under that name.

You can do a personal search online, which is relatively easy and inexpensive. This will not be your final search but is just a preliminary search that will filter out a lot of names that have already been trademarked. You can conduct your own trademark search by going to the following websites:
- http://www.wipo.int/branddb/en/
- https://www.tmdn.org/tmview/welcome
- http://tsdr.uspto.gov/
- https://igerent.com/trademarkstudy

Aside from conducting your own trademark search, you can also seek the help of a professional. Be sure that the searches that these companies perform include not only state registered marks but also federal. And you shouldn't just be searching for registered trademarks. You also have to make sure that you also search unregistered trademarks. Although you will have a bigger chance at winning a case against a company who hasn't registered their name, you still wouldn't want to experience the hassle of proving that you own the rights to your brand.

How much does it cost to register a trademark?

You can go about this in two different ways. The first one is to file the application yourself either online or on paper. You can submit your trademark application via an online service or using TEAS or Trademark Electronic Application System. The fees for applying online can range from $225 to $400 per class of services or goods. If you decide to go via the paper route, you need to pay $600 per class of services or goods. The more types of products or services you are planning to sell under that name, the more trademark fees you have to pay. Keep in mind that the fees are non-refundable even if your application to register the trademark was rejected.

The second way to register a trademark is by hiring a lawyer. Depending on the lawyer, you may need to pay around $125 per hour or more, or a flat fee decided by the lawyer.

As stated previously, you need to renew your trademark application every ten years, which will cost you $300 if you do it online, or $400 if you submit a paper application.

Now that your products are ready, you now need to launch your products to the public. You can check out the next chapter that will talk about the step-by-step process on how to do a product launch.

Chapter 7

Product Launch

Conducting a product launch is important if you want to let people know about your products and business. A product release is different from a product launch. A product release is just a company releasing a new product and announcing it to the public. A product launch is more fun and exciting, and usually creates buzz and stirs interests among the general public. A product launch is not just something internet marketers do. Everyone who has target customers or audience can do a product launch and will benefit from it, especially startups like your business.

Reasons for doing a product launch

Create a cash windfall

For those who do not know, a cash windfall is a sudden increase of income due to a single event, such as a product launch. One popular example is Apple's product launch of their latest iPhone. Their product launch was extremely successful because people lined up to different stores all over the world to be one of the very first ones to own the new iPhone. Apple experienced a spike in sales several days after the launch of the product because they were able to create hype around their latest gadget for sale, and people participated in the hype and bought iPhones within a few days after its initial release. If your product launch is successful, you will also experience a cash windfall.

Leave a lasting impact

Although the main objective of starting a business is to earn money, you should also want to leave a lasting impact on others, especially the people who patronize your product. You can achieve this if you do a product launch. If you conduct a product launch for your goods made of bamboo, you will be known as that startup company that sells sustainable and eco-friendly products made of bamboo.

Achieve strategic positioning

Conducting a product launch also helps you properly position your business and your products in the market. There is already a lot of businesses selling things made of bamboo, so how can you position your business in such a way that you are not just another business selling bamboo products? You need to make sure that in your product launch, you position your products using the superlative—the "most affordable", the "most sustainable", etc.

Gain more customers

If you don't have a product launch for your business, only a few people will know about your business—your family, your friends, your family's friends, your friends' friends, etc. But if you have a product launch, more people will hear and know about you, even those people whom you are not connected with in any way will know about your product. And the more people know about your business and products, the higher your sales potential will be.

Establish your authority

Businesses that have product launches are most often considered the authority in the industry. This is because they are more visible to the general public. Anything that is more visible to the eyes of the public is more likely to have a bigger influence over them. And you can achieve visibility for your business by doing a product launch.

Open doors

Product launches are not only done for your intended customers. Other people who may help you with your business such as other owners of startups, influencers, manufacturers, and so on will also hear about your products. This can also help you build your network or connections that can help you get ahead in your chosen industry.

How to do a successful product launch?

Run Facebook Ads

Many successful Amazon sellers use Facebook Ads to boost their rankings on Amazon and also to increase sales, while at the same time creating a network of audience that consists of fans who cannot get enough of your products. Running Facebook Ads is one of the most cost-efficient sources of traffic outside your online selling platform, in this case, Amazon. It is no wonder because there are over 2 billion people who actively use Facebook every month. Facebook Ads are shown to people who are interested in your product or anything related to it. And these same people will most likely be converted as your buyers.

One important thing that you should do is to create a landing page. Do not make the mistake of most sellers who lead traffic directly to their Amazon products. Remember that people who are browsing on Facebook are not looking to buy anything. Besides, there is no way for you to collect your potential customers' contact information if you direct them to your Amazon listing right away. A landing page can do this for you. If you can't capture their email address and they don't buy from you, you will no longer have any way to contact them in the future to make them interested again in buying your product.

Basically, the route of a customer that comes from Facebook should look like this:

> Facebook → Landing Page (capture email, send promo code) → Amazon (sale).

Split testing is also a must when it comes to running ads on Facebook. It is creating different versions of your ad based on your target audience. If you are selling clothes and you have two kinds of audience, one is a mother and the other is an unmarried female, you should use two different pictures or copy according to their different needs. A mother will most likely click on wholesome and practical pictures while a single female will be more interested in something fun and flirty. I go into a lot more details in my book <u>Facebook Marketing For Beginners – Learn The Basics Of Facebook Advertising And Strategies In 5 Days And Learn It Well</u>

Create a Facebook fan group

This one is quite popular. If you are an active user of Facebook, you are most likely a member of at least one Facebook group. If you live under a rock and you have no idea what a Facebook group is, it is a page on Facebook regarding a certain topic or interest where a group of people join and interact with each other. There are Facebook groups for people who love to crochet, for people who love Ariana Grande, and so on. You can also create a Facebook group for your business. This allows you to network, recruit brand ambassadors, establish relationships with customers, support customers who need assistance, and create a community for your business.

Run Amazon ads

The first step that you need to do to run Amazon ads is to create a campaign. Just select a product that you want to advertise, set a budget, and decide on the length of your campaign. For instance, you can set a $10 budget per day and not set any end date for your campaign so that Amazon users can see your ad anytime. You can either choose automatic or manual targeting that allows you to pick keywords for your products. Automatic targeting is best for beginners. Once you have completed the setup, your sponsored products will be launched immediately. Your ads will then be shown to customers who are searching for your products or related items. When they click on your sponsored product ad, they will be directed to your product listing where they can read the product details and information.

Build an email list

This is one of the key elements of modern marketing. An email list is a collection of your visitors' and customers' email addresses that you can use for marketing. You can send promotions, news, and updates about your business via email to your existing and potential customers. You cannot just randomly ask people for their email address because that will look a little scam-y. You need to use effective and subtle strategies that will make people give you their email address. One way to do this is to create a personalized CTA or call-to-action for your landing page, blogs, or any write up about your business.

A CTA is something that a visitor of the page has to do, such as "Click on this link to answer a free quiz" or something like that, and then they will be asked to enter their email address to see the results. Product launches are also a great way to get email addresses. You can ask all participants to leave their contact information to register. You can also ask them to register on your website if they want to learn more about your products. Conducting contests, raffles, and giveaways on different social media platforms or during your product launch is also a great way to build your email list.

Do giveaways

There are different ways to do a giveaway. One way to do this is by posting your giveaway event on your Facebook page or group and asking your members or followers to join by simply typing in their email address, tagging their friends, and sharing your page. This is also a way to build your email list.

You can also do it by sending out details of your giveaways to your email list. There is also a lot of websites that you can use to promote your contests and giveaways for free such as the ones below:
- http://www.giveawaymonkey.com/submit-giveaway/
- https://www.theprizefinder.com/upload-competitions
- http://juliesfreebies.com/giveaway-submission-form/
- http://giveawayfrenzy.com/giveaway-submit/
- http://www.totallyfreestuff.com/submit.asp?m=13

All you need to do is to provide the details of your giveaway or contest and once they are live on these sites, you can share them on your Facebook page and group, Instagram page, blogs, and other online platforms.

Get reviews

One reason why you want to conduct a product launch is to let people know about your product and get reviews from them. Having reviews, especially positive ones, is beneficial because people are more confident to buy a product that has a lot of positive reviews. Selling great products is already a given if you want to get positive feedbacks from your customers. But to get them to review your product in the first place is the challenging part. What you can do is to send an email requesting reviews or feedbacks to your email list.

You can also ask your Facebook community to write reviews and leave a rating after using your product. Amazon also offers the Early Reviewer Program for new sellers because they know how difficult it is to obtain a review from your first time buyers. For a fee of $60 per SKU, Amazon will send an email to those who have already bought your product, offering them an incentive of up to $3 for writing a review. To be eligible, you have to be a registered seller in the U.S. and your product should cost at least $15 and up and has less than five reviews at the moment.

Choosing the right photographer for your product

For your product launch or your business in general to be successful, you need to have high quality pictures that will encourage people to buy your products. The picture should not only be clear but also accurate and honest. You may have a good DSLR camera, but if you are not a professional photographer, the pictures may still not look quite as good as what you see online. This is why it is better to hire someone who can take professional pictures of your products. You may need to pay extra but at least, your pictures will look amazing.

To choose a photographer, here are the things that you need to consider.

1. Portfolio.

Professional photographers should have a portfolio where you can see their past works and projects with different clients. You will know if their photography style suits your needs. It is best to choose a photographer who has already worked with online sellers previously because they know what needs to be done.

2. Experience.

Ideally, you should hire a photographer that has at least three years of experience taking pictures professionally. Hiring a newbie may be the cheapest option, but it can be risky because you have no idea how they work and what kind of photos they can create.

3. References.

Asking for references is a good way to know more about the photographer from a past client's perspective. You can ask about the photographer's work ethics, honesty, professionalism, and quality of output.

4. Pricing.

Be sure to ask about the pricing before you make any commitment. The pricing should be clarified in advance so that there will be no misunderstanding or surprise expenses in the future. You can either pay per image or per package deal, depending on how many pictures you need.

5. Communication.

The photographer should also be easy to contact. You might have some specific styles in mind and details that you want to highlight about the product, and these are things that you should tell the photographer. You should have the photographer's email address and phone number in case you need to ask or tell them something.

6. Free trial.

You can also ask for a free trial before you decide to hire the photographer's services. This is a great way to learn more about the photographer's creative style and work ethics.

Optimizing product listings to boost sales

If you want to improve the ranking of your Amazon listing that will make your product more visible to Amazon users, which in turn will increase your sales, you need to know how to optimize your product listing. Amazon product optimization is one of the best things that you can do for your business. There are different ways to do this.

Optimizing keywords

You already know how this works. The use of good keywords is the key to the success of your online business. Put yourself in the shoes of your target customer. If you are planning to buy, say, Disney bed sheets, you will definitely type Disney bed sheets in the search field. As a seller, you should use Disney bed sheets as your keywords. But you can also use additional keywords such as Aladdin bed sheets (or whichever Disney character you have), Disney bedding, Disney bed linen, and so on. These are the relevant keywords for the product that you are selling. If you just put bed sheet in your product listing without the word Disney, your item will not appear when a customer looking for Disney bed sheets searches for the product specifically. Here are some things that you should know when creating your listing:

- Your product title should include the top five keywords.

- You should add generic keywords (or backend keywords) aside from your most relevant keywords that do not exceed 249 bytes.
- You can use keywords in your product description and bullet lists, but make sure that the sentences still flow naturally.
- You can also add keywords (men/women) to make sure that you reach your target buyers.

Optimizing the content

Keyword optimization ensures that your product appears in the search results when the customer types relevant and related keywords. Optimizing your content, on the other hand, will make your target customer click on your listing. To improve your content, you need to focus on these three important points:
- Product information,
- Product texts and
- Images.

Product text and information overlap because they are both about the write up or description of the product. Product information is about the details that a buyer needs to know about the product such as the dimension, weight, material used, features, and so on. The advantages or benefits should also be included. The product text, on the other hand, is the way you present it to the customer. All these details and information should be presented in such a way that they are easy to read and understand. You can present some of the information in bullet points and be sure to be as straightforward and concise as possible.

The images that you use for your product listing should also be optimized. After all, this is the first thing that the customers see in the search results. You need to post one main image and additional images. The main image should show the core product as clearly as possible. It should have a white background and occupy 85% of the image frame. You can add more pictures for the accessories, packaging, demonstrative graphics, important features, environments, and so on.

Avoid duplicate content

One common mistake that online sellers make is using the same content in all their online selling platforms. Duplicate content is a big no-no because search engines will see this and think that you are copying content when both are just written by the same person—you. You should use a different write up for your Amazon listings, a different one for your own website, and so on.

Anatomy of a product listing

a) Product title

Amazon gives you a 250-character limit or about 50 words to write your product title. You need to use it wisely by making sure that all the words are important. When writing the product title, you have to keep in mind that you are writing for humans, not robots. Amazon may be using algorithms but these algorithms are still based on the search patterns and behaviors of humans. *You should also consider adding at least one key element or a benefit that sets your product apart from the products sold by your competitors.* For example, you can add keywords like biodegradable or eco-friendly. And remember that the keywords that you put in the title are more important than the words in the description because this is what the algorithm is looking into, so choose your words carefully. Make sure the keywords in your title are relevant to your product.

b) Product photos
Amazon allows you to upload up to 9 photos and you should definitely use all of them. When people scroll through the results of their searches, the first thing that they look at is the image, then the title. They will only click on the listing if they find the image and the title interesting. This is why you have to make sure that your image catches the attention of your target buyers. Your main image should have a white background and should be 85% of the entire frame. In the remaining pictures, you can show different angles of the product, zoomed parts, the packaging, and so on.

c) Important features
The character limit of this part of your listing is around 240 words or 1000 characters. It is best to write a bulleted list because no one likes reading a text heavy paragraph. You should have at least five bullets and *the most important features should be at the very top of the list.*

d) Description
This is where you can write in sentences but you should still make sure that your paragraphs are not too long. You can elaborate on the features that you already have in your bulleted list and add more important details about the product. The limit is 2000 characters including spaces, which is about 300 words.

Amazon Advertising (AA)
Amazon Advertising (formally called Amazon Marketing Services, AMS) is a system or a set of online tools that help sellers drive traffic to their listings. This was touched briefly while discussing how to run ads on Amazon and you already know that there are two types—automatic and manual. Basically, manual targeting depends a lot on you as the seller. You have to do some research and define your target keywords yourself. Automatic AA, on the other hand, is much simpler and easier because you leave everything to Amazon. All you have to do is to set it up.
Whether you are using manual or automatic, you can still get the same kinds of benefits. The first one is that you improve your visibility to potential customers by improving your ranking using relevant keywords. It also helps increase your sales at a faster rate, which makes Amazon more willing to promote your products. After all, Amazon will be more than happy to help sellers who have fast moving items.

Using AA ads search report to your advantage
Did you know that you can check how well your keywords performed in the actual searches? All you need to do is to download the data that will give you valuable insight about your keywords.

You can pull out account-level data and also choose dates that you want to study in the past 90 days. This way, you will see what makes your campaigns successful or not. For example, if you see a significant increase in sales in the past two weeks, you can pull out the data from that time frame and check out how customers reached your listings in terms of the keywords that they used. You can also determine which keywords do not work. This way, you can use the effective keywords and discard the ineffective ones in your future listings.

Testing different price points

Pricing is not as easy as adding a few dollars to the original cost to earn a profit. There are so many other factors that affect pricing and have nothing to do with how much has been spent making the product. The demand, for instance, hikes up the price. Just look at hotel rates and airfare. The price of your product also will dictate its perceived value. For instance, if you are selling a pen for a dollar, people will think it is just an ordinary pen. But if you are selling it for $100, people will think that there must be something special about that pen. And of course it should have something special about it. Maybe it is gold-plated or it was a designer pen. You cannot simply increase the price without a valid reason to do so. The price of your product gives people an idea about the quality. So be sure that your product meets their expectation.

To decide on your products' pricing point, you need to conduct a competition analysis. This means that you have to research on your competitors' prices. How much are they selling the same product? Are people buying them? This is important, especially if there is a lot of other vendors selling the same thing. It is difficult to increase your price because buyers will surely pick the cheaper option if the items are just identical.

You can either sell something unique which no one has ever sold before so that you can dictate the pricing of the product in the market. Or you can add value to your product and make it stand out. You can also do some simple manipulations such as using a different picture or name. If you find in your research that the same product that you are selling range from $5 to $10, you might want to price yours at $7. People will not go to the cheapest one because they will think there is a catch or maybe the quality is too low. They will also not buy the expensive one because they can find cheaper options. They will surely go for the mid-priced item because it meets all their needs.

You can also try split testing on Amazon. You can do this by tweaking certain parts of your listing to know which ones give you the highest sales. You can change the product title, the bullet points in your product description, the images, and of course, the price. For example, on the first couple of months, you can set the price of your pen at $1 each. The next couple of months, you can change the price at $1.50 each. After conducting your split testing, check which period gives you the highest number of sales.

When doing split testing, you should be patient because it may not tell you anything right away, especially if you are not making a lot of sales. If you only have one or two sales, you do not have enough data to work with. You should also avoid running too many tests at once because it will be hard to know what's working and what's not.

Remember that the price of the product is one of the major factors that help consumers decide what product to buy. This is why you have to choose the right pricing point for your goods.

Chapter 8

What Comes Next?

Having a successful launch does not ensure a successful business. It is just the beginning because you still have a lot of things to do. As they say, your product launch is just the beginning of your marketing journey. It's not the end goal. Pat yourself and your team (if you have one) on the back for a successful launch. Go home and enjoy your success. But afterwards, you still need to do something to maintain the success that you achieved on your product launch.

A successful product launch should touch on the first three levels of the marketing funnel.

- **Reach** - Getting your business message across to your target audience.
- **Attract** - Getting your target audience to check out your website, which will turn them into leads.
- **Convert** - Turn these leads into customers and getting them to sign up to your website and receive news and updates.
- **Educate** - Teach customers everything they need to know about your product and business to make them love your product even more.

Product launches significantly increase the volume of traffic to your website, which means that you achieve the "reach" and "attract" part of the marketing funnel. But for your launch to be considered successful, you should also have a high conversion rate, which means that people who receive your message and visit your website also sign up and buy something.

But to have consistently high sales, you need to reach the fourth stage, and that is to continuously educate your existing customers about your product to make them love your product and not buy anywhere else. You can do this by sending them news and updates about your products and ongoing promotions through email. You can also make them feel appreciated by giving them discounts and freebies.

Analyze post-launch feedbacks

A successful product launch results in people buying your products. But what about those who don't? What keeps them from buying your product? To know the answer to these questions, you need to analyze the feedbacks you receive after the launch. You probably have expectations as regards your target audience and the reasons why they are going to buy your product. These are just assumptions, which will only become clearer once you get their unfiltered feedbacks. Listen to the different feedbacks of people who buy your products and people who don't, and analyze the reasons behind their actions.

You need to analyze both quantitative and qualitative data. Quantitative data could include the number of people who give you a feedback, the number of people who participate in your launch, the number of people who give you a positive or negative feedback, the number of converted leads, and so on. Qualitative data, on the other hand, involves the content of their feedbacks. Analyze the words and phrases that they use. If the words "expensive" always comes up, it could mean that they find your products expensive which keeps them from making a purchase.

Improve the product

The act of selling a better version of a product is called upselling. To continuously satisfy your existing customers and to attract new ones, you need to make sure that your products continuously evolve for the better. To do this, you need to understand the product you are selling. What makes customers buy your products? What are the key selling features of your products? On the other hand, what are the weak spots of your product? You can find out the answers to these questions by reading customer feedbacks. To make product improvements, you can either add new features or improve existing features.

If you decide to add a new feature, be sure that it is something that will add value to your product and the customers will be happy about. Adding a new feature often creates a big marketing splash because people are excited to hear about changes to something that they already know. Outsiders will also hear about the new feature and will become curious, and might end up buying the product just out of curiosity. Adding new features may be risky, but it can also be highly rewarding if done correctly.

Improving on an existing product feature is a safer route to take, and you can do it in three different ways. The first one is deliberate improvement in which you improve on a feature so that the product works much better. The second one is frequency improvement wherein you improve a product feature so that the consumer will use it more often. And the third one is adoption improvement where the change leads to an increase in the number of people who are using the product.

Making changes on a product is a great way to maintain sales, but make sure that you are not adding unnecessary features or making unnecessary changes. Remember the saying "if it ain't broke, don't fix it"? This also applies to product improvement. This is especially true if you already have a large group of customers who have been using your product and are satisfied with it. What you can do is to create new products, which leads us to the next point.

Create new products

This is also a great way to attract more customers and make existing customers buy more. By adding new products to your already existing ones, you are reaching out to a larger group of people while at the same time not losing your loyal customers. If you simply add or improve a feature, there is a bigger chance of losing existing customers who are not happy about the change. If you simply create a new product and add it to your store, you will only attract new customers and also give more options to your existing customers. For example, if you are selling unscented shampoo bars, you can create new products with different scents and continue selling your unscented ones because these already have a loyal following. There is no reason to stop selling something that a lot of people buy.

Add complementary products

Selling new products that complement your existing products is called cross-selling. This does not mean that you are going to offer anything that you can think of. If you are selling coffee, selling teaspoons or saucers might work but it is not the perfect complement for coffee. Instead, you can sell creamer, French presses, mugs, and so on. Maybe you can sell teaspoons and saucers but only when you already have these other complementary products.

Again, put yourself in the shoes of your customer. If you buy coffee, what's the next thing that you need to buy? Teaspoons? Of course not. Creamer or sugar, maybe? Definitely. By selling complementary products, you are increasing the checkout price that the customer is going to pay even though he or she was only planning to buy coffee. With that being said, one advantage of cross-selling is increasing your sales because they buy more products from you.

Selling complementary products also improves customer loyalty. This is because your customers will feel satisfied whenever they buy from your shop because they have everything they need. It improves customer experience, which results in loyalty to your brand. Selling complementary products is also easy to manage because it is like buying a bundle. And you know that it is more cost-effective and easier to manage if one person buys two complementary products than if two people buy one same product each. This is also a great way to introduce less popular products. If you really want to sell your teaspoons and saucers, you should first sell your mugs and teacups. This way, people would want to buy the complete set. It would be weird if you're just selling teaspoons and saucers.

There are two terms that you need to know to understand the main objective of cross-selling—skimming and consumer surplus. Skimming is trying to sell a product at the highest price possible at the beginning. Later on, the price of these same products is lowered so that people who are not willing to spend the initial price can also buy the product. Skimming is basically trying to get as much money from your customer as possible. Doesn't sound too ethical, but selling products and starting a business is all about earning profits, right? Not so.

Consumer surplus, on the other hand, is the difference between the amount that a customer is able and willing to pay (depends on the demand) and the amount that they actually spent (depends on the current market price). As the demand for your product decreases, maybe it is no longer trendy or it is almost the end of the season for selling it, the price of your product will decrease. And you can no longer implement skimming because your product is no longer in demand.

Cross-selling helps minimize consumer surplus by offering them a complementary product. Let's say, a customer is willing to spend $50 on a pair of shoes which was trendy months ago, but because of the decrease in demand, you are just selling it for $30, which gives you a $20 consumer surplus. To make the customer spend this amount on your shop, you should try offering complementary products such as socks, insoles, shoelaces, running shorts and t-shirts, and so on. This way, the customer is still spending the entire $50 on your shop. You still make him spend all the money that he is willing and able to spend on your shop.

This is the reason why a lot of businesses bundle things together. Just look at fast food chains like McDonalds, which sells burgers with fries and drinks. Or gaming consoles like Nintendo, which also includes a couple of games and a controller in their bundle. They also upsell by asking you if you want to upsize your drinks and fries or by offering you a higher version of the gaming console.

The key to a successful cross-selling is anticipating your customers' needs. Again, you shouldn't just offer complementary products just for the sake of making an offer because that's just annoying. You need to know if the customer *actually* needs it.

Different ways to cross-sell

a) Sending a follow-up email

You can manually cross-sell by sending an email to your customer. For example, if a customer recently bought a laptop from your shop, you can send a follow up email after a few days offering him accessories such as a laptop bag, mouse, laptop sleeve, and so on.

b) Using a customer's browsing history

There is also automatic cross-selling which Amazon is extremely good at. If a customer visits Amazon and searches for baking sheets, even without actually buying one, your browsing history will be saved. When you visit the website again, you will see suggested products for baking such as baking molds, pans, spatula, rolling pin, and so on.

c) Social proofing

You will also see what other people bought or searched for while you are looking at a particular item. When you see that a lot of people are also buying the same items, you feel more confident about buying the same thing. It's just how humans work. We are social beings, after all, and we value our peer's approval. You will feel that your decision to buy a certain product is validated. Moreover, you will become curious when you see that certain products are bought together by some people. And you will end up buying the bundle yourself because other people are doing it, so there must be a reason.

d) Using a customer's wish list

If you have a wish list saved in your account, they will also customize the suggested products that you see based on the items that you have on your wish list. Your buying history also plays an important role on how the algorithm decides which products you may be interested in.

e) Offering minor yet essential products

You can also sell essential yet minor products to make your main product work. One great example is batteries. If you are selling battery-operated toys, you can be sure that people will also want to buy batteries for these toys. And of course they'd rather buy the batteries from the same store where they bought the toys than to search for them somewhere else. It's not much but it is still a sale.

f) Selling an entire look

Another great example of cross-selling is selling an entire outfit, for those who are selling clothes. You can make suggestions based on what goes well with a particular clothing item. It is just like having a mannequin in your online store. The mannequin gives ideas to potential buyers on how the clothes can be styled and worn. You can do the same thing by creating outfits from your products.

Believe it or not, people who are clueless when it comes to putting together an outfit always appreciate it when there is a complete outfit that they can buy without thinking too much about it. IKEA is also good at this. They showcase room designs using IKEA products and people go crazy over them. They give people ideas on how to decorate their own space using mostly IKEA furniture and décor, of course. This creates a desire among the consumers that they should get the whole look because they can see how great it looks.

When is the best time to cross-sell?

There is not one perfect time to cross-sell because it depends on the customers buying behaviors. However, you might still want to look at the different moments when customers are more willing to buy complementary products.

- You can make offers while the customer is still looking to buy the first product. This is where Amazon comes in. They customize what a buyer can see when they start browsing and shopping by suggesting products that other people bought or products that complement what the customer is planning to buy.
- You can also cross-sell in the shopping cart, just before the customer completes the transaction. This way, they can add the extra before they check out, which will instantly boost your sale for that day.
- There are people who do not want to be distracted during the entire buying process. In this case, it is best to offer them complementary products after completing the transaction, on the thank you page. Some sellers think that the thank you page is not really useful aside from telling the customer that you appreciate their business but it is actually a great page to offer more. They are in a great mood because their transaction was successfully completed and you have their trust and confidence. Plus, they still have their credit card with them so be sure to take advantage of the thank you page.
- You can also send them emails a few days after making a purchase.
- Retargeting, or indirect cross-selling through advertisements, is another great way to offer complementary products. You can use Facebook ads and ads from other platforms to make customers buy complementary products.

You do not have to choose only one method. Just choose which one to use. For instance, if you notice customers are always abandoning their carts, you should not cross-sell before they complete the transaction to prevent distractions. You can also combine two or more methods and test out different strategies at different times to see which ones work best for your business.

Explore opportunities for cross-selling

If you have no idea what to cross-sell, you might want to do a little research for you to get an idea what other products will complement the ones that you are already selling.

- The first thing to do is to check your competitors' listings and see what kind of complementary products they are offering. If you are selling shoes, check out other vendors that sell shoes and see what they offer as add-ons.
- You can also conduct a survey by sending it to your email list or by posting it in your Facebook group. Ask them what they would like to see in your store or what kinds of products would go well with your main products.
- Asking your manufacturer what complementary products they can make is also a great idea. Some people often overlook this step because they think it's all about the customers (it really is most of the time) but you should also look at the kinds of products that your manufacturer makes. This is even more helpful if they are also making products for other Amazon sellers.

Chapter 9

Scaling $10,000 a Month and Beyond

This chapter is the culmination of everything that you have learned in this e-book. Every vendor's end goal is to earn as much income as possible by selling via Amazon FBA. If you just want to help people, maybe you should just donate to charity? This is real life and in real life, you need money to pay the bills and take care of your family & loved ones. And you can earn good money by selling on Amazon. It would be even better if you can earn at least $10,000 or even more by selling on Amazon.

This is achievable because a lot of people are earning five to six figures on Amazon. How can you do that? Here are some of the important steps that have been discussed in the previous chapters and additional information that can turn your business into a money-making machine.

1. Continue evolving as a business

Coca-Cola and Apple did not reach this level of success because they have remained the same. Times change and the needs of the people and their buying behavior change as well. If your business cannot keep up with the changing times, you will surely be left behind.

A lot of people change their branding to make them look more modern. One popular example is the logo of Lord and Taylor or Instagram. They used to have logos that look old school and traditional but they changed them to make them more suitable for the modern consumers.

Another thing that you should do is to add new products, improve existing products, and add complementary products. You already know that doing these things can only lead to a significant increase in sales. Cross-selling was discussed in depth in the previous chapter, and how selling one product can lead to sales of another related product. This is why selling complementary products can improve your business.

However, keep in mind that it is best to approach this method slowly because adding too many products at the onset can be detrimental to your business. Startups should not use all their money buying different kinds of stuff to sell. It is hard to take action if your money is tied up to your inventory. It is also harder to keep track of the items that sell and the items that don't because you have way too many to track. It is also more difficult to build a core community because your customers have different interests. You can release more products once you know how your initial products did in the market.

Aside from changing your branding and adding and changing products, you should also consider adding value to your brand. For example, consumers these days are more conscious about buying things. A lot of people prefer sustainable brands which are generally lesser known than mainstream brands. This is because they promote sustainability, they are cruelty-free, they are ethical, and they are vegan. They are sometimes even more expensive than mainstream brands, but people still buy them because of this advocacy. You should also consider doing this to your brand. Make it sustainable, if you can. However, you shouldn't just do it for the sake of earning more profits. You need to do it for the right reasons for it to be successful.

2. Build an online community

These days, it is important to have an online community of people who love your products. You should never underestimate the power of social media in terms of influencing others to make decisions. These online communities such as Facebook groups and fan pages can be great support hubs for people who need help with your products. They serve as a place for updating and educating others about your business. If a new customer has a question about the product that he just bought, the community can help him by sharing their own experiences or information that they gathered from other resources. One perfect example is Amazon's Seller Central where you can discuss certain topics and issues with other sellers.

The fact that there is a community of people that joined together because of your product says a lot about your business. It means that a lot of people patronize your business and love your products, and are willing to meet others who share the same interests. These loyal customers will keep buying from you. This is why you should take care of them and make them feel appreciated. Maybe you can conduct raffles and contests for those people who are a part of your online community. Maybe you can give promo codes to those who are members of your Facebook group. Do these things and they will love you even more.

3. Continue doing product launches

If you think a product launch is only done at the start of your business, you are wrong because you can continue doing product launches as long as you have new or improved products to sell. This is why your products have to keep on evolving. You already know that doing product launches can lead to a high volume of traffic that can then be converted to sales. If you have product launches every time you have a new product or an improved feature of an existing product, just imagine how much income you will earn.

Just like what you did in your very first launch, you should also send out emails to your email list and invite people in your Facebook community to participate. The difference between your very first launch and your subsequent launches is that you now have more people in your email list and in your community. You already have loyal customers. Before, everyone was new to your product and they didn't know much about your business. You may have had achieved high traffic during your product launch, but a lot of them probably didn't end up buying. This will change when you do your succeeding launches because you now have a bigger following who know about your product and your business.

Releasing teasers leading up to the launch can also build up the hype and interest in your new product. You can maybe post a riddle about your new product days in advance. You can also conduct a countdown. Doing things like this will make the launch more exciting, and people will surely anticipate what you have in store for them. Just make sure that your product will live up to the expectation of your customers, especially since you are responsible for building up the excitement over your product.

4. Continue optimizing your product listing

Optimizing your product listing is something that you should not overlook because how your customers see your product can make or break a sale. Your product listing is the first thing that Amazon users see when they search for certain keywords in the search field. It is important that they find your listing easy to understand by presenting all the important details and information about the product as straightforwardly as possible.

If they are satisfied with the image and description, and they think that your product is what they are looking for, they will surely buy it and who knows? Maybe they will come back and buy more next time. To ensure that your product is presented as accurately as possible and that it is visible whenever an Amazon user searched for that kind of product, you need to optimize your product listing. It increases traffic to your shop, boosts sales conversion, and therefore improves profits.

The anatomy of a highly profitable product listing consists of a title, images, key product features, description, product reviews, and rating. The first four parts are the seller's responsibility and the last two come from the customers. It is not their responsibility to write a review or leave a rating, which is why you need to encourage them to do so. This will be discussed next.

5. Increase social proof

Social proof is a psychological phenomenon wherein people are more likely to do certain actions because other people are doing it as well. Knowing that someone else has already bought the product and is using it will make a consumer more confident and at ease in buying the same product for the first time. It's like people are looking for validation for their actions. In fact, study shows that product reviews are 12 times more trusted than the product description itself. You want to hear what people who have used the product have to say.

You always witness and experience social proof in your day to day life. You are more likely to eat in a restaurant filled with diners than an empty one. You have seen online clothing stores posting pictures of celebrities wearing the same clothes they are selling. People line up to buy milk tea, the latest iPhone, and so on. You think these products are worth your money because others are also buying them. Social proof is everywhere and you can also use this to your advantage.

The most important social proofing technique that you can do is to gather reviews from your customers. You can send follow up emails to customers asking them to write a review and rate the product. You can also ask your most loyal customers to create a video testimonial and post it on Amazon. Products that have more reviews are more likely to attract buyers because of social proof.

Your target should be to get 4 to 5 stars. If you have mostly 4 or 5 stars, you are on the right track. If not, you should understand why people are giving you a rating lower than 4. You need to read your bad reviews as well and do something about it. Maybe it is something that can be fixed. And gathering as much positive reviews and rating as you can will balance out a few negative reviews. As long as you only have a couple of negative reviews, you will be fine. Potential buyers will just think that the customer who gave you a bad review is difficult to please if the rest gave you positive reviews.

6. Gain more visibility using AMS

Amazon Marketing Services or AMS can help improve your product rank and your listing gain more visibility. As discussed earlier, AMS is a tool used by sellers to run ads. The ads are pay-per-click, which means that you only have to pay when an Amazon user clicks the ad. This is a great way to make your listings more visible. It is easy to set up AMS. Just login to your Amazon advertising console account and just follow the steps. When customers see your products all the time, you can be sure that your income will increase dramatically.

7. Explore creating a YouTube channel

If you want to maximize all the social media platforms, you should not forget YouTube. YouTube is a great platform for influencers and sellers because they attract huge traffic to their online stores like Amazon. For instance, a lot of resellers on online selling platforms such as eBay, Poshmark, and Depop have YouTube accounts and have hundreds of thousands of subscribers and viewers. These people may not know about their online store but after watching their YouTube videos, they will visit the store and end up buying what they have seen in the video.

Creating a YouTube channel does not only drive traffic to your online store. It can also be another source of income in itself. It is definitely a win-win situation for you because not only are you boosting your Amazon sales, you are also earning money from your YouTube videos. For instance, if you are selling clothes on Amazon, you can do a haul or a look book video using all your products for sale. People who love watching YouTube videos may see your video and love one particular outfit. They may not have bought anything from Amazon before, but they might just start now after seeing your video. If you are selling software, you can create YouTube tutorial videos. You do not really need to be in front of the camera if you are a shy person. You can ask someone to model the clothes for you or you can just simply do a voiceover and just record your tutorial on your computer.

These are the things that you can do to earn $10,000 or even more via Amazon FBA. It is definitely hard work, but everything is worth it once you start seeing the money rolling in.

Conclusion

I'd like to congratulate you for completing this book from start to finish.

I hope this book was able to help you to learn everything you need to know about selling via Amazon FBA.

The next step is to take action and do everything you have learned in this book. Come up with a product that you can sell if you haven't thought of anything yet or contact a manufacturer.

I wish you the best of luck!

The End

Thank you very much for taking the time to read this book. I tried my best to cover as much as I could. If you found it useful please let me know by leaving a review on Amazon! Your support really does make a difference and I read all the reviews personally so I can get your feedback and make this book even better.

I also pride myself on giving my readers the best information out there, being super responsive to them and providing the best customer service. If you feel I have fallen short of this standard in any way, please kindly email me at **michael@michaelezeanaka.com** so I can get a chance to make it right to you. I wish you all the best with your journey towards financial freedom!

Appendix A

Solution to Chapter 1 Quiz

Question Number	Answer
1	B
2	C
3	A
4	A
5	B
6	B
7	B
8	D
9	A
10	A

Appendix B

Solution to Chapter 2 Quiz

Question Number	Answer
1	A
2	C
3	D
4	A
5	A
6	A
7	D

8	A
9	A
10	A

Appendix C

Solution to Chapter 3 Quiz

Question Number	Answer
1	A
2	D
3	A
4	D
5	A
6	A
7	B
8	A
9	B
10	D

Appendix D

Solution to Chapter 4 Quiz

Question Number	Answer
1	A
2	B
3	A
4	B

5	B
6	A
7	B
8	C
9	A
10	D

Appendix E

Solution to Chapter 5 Quiz

Question Number	Answer
1	A
2	B
3	A
4	C
5	B
6	C
7	C
8	A
9	A
10	C

Appendix F

Solution to Chapter 6 Quiz

Question Number	Answer

1	C
2	A
3	A
4	B
5	D
6	C
7	B
8	C
9	B
10	D

Appendix G

Solution to Chapter 7 Quiz

Question Number	Answer
1	D
2	C
3	A
4	A
5	D
6	A
7	D
8	C
9	A
10	D

Appendix H

Solution to Chapter 8 Quiz

Question Number	Answer
1	D
2	B
3	D
4	C
5	C
6	D
7	C
8	A
9	C
10	C

Appendix I

Solution to Chapter 9 Quiz

Question Number	Answer
1	C
2	A
3	B
4	C
5	B
6	B
7	B
8	D

9	C
10	A

Appendix J

Solution to Chapter 10 Quiz

Question Number	Answer
1	B
2	C
3	B
4	A
5	B
6	B
7	C
8	B
9	A
10	A

Appendix K

Solution to Chapter 11 Quiz

Question Number	Answer
1	C
2	C
3	A
4	B

5	A
6	A
7	A
8	A
9	D
10	A

Appendix L

Solution to Chapter 12 Quiz

Question Number	Answer
1	C
2	B
3	D
4	A
5	C
6	A
7	D
8	C
9	D
10	A

Appendix M

Solution to Chapter 13 Quiz

Question Number	Answer

1	A
2	C
3	A
4	C
5	A
6	A
7	A
8	D
9	A
10	D

Printed in Great Britain
by Amazon